First Edition
First Printing, 2019

Book format by Samantha Penn
Cover design by Kevin R. Brown
Cover illustration by Ryan Pancoast
Editing by Laura Kurtz
Interior art by the Llewellyn Art Department except for The Lunar Keys: A Teaching Song

Llewellyn Publications is a registered trademark of Llewellyn Worldwide Ltd.

Library of Congress Cataloging-in-Publication Data
Names: Telyndru, Jhenah, author.
Title: The Mythic Moons of Avalon : Lunar & Herbal wisdom from the Isle of
    Healing / Jhenah Telyndru.
Description: First edition. | Woodbury, Minnesota : Llewellyn Publications,
    2019. | Includes bibliographical references and index.
Identifiers: LCCN 2019001048 (print) | LCCN 2019005149 (ebook) | ISBN
    9780738757193 (ebook) | ISBN 9780738756851 (alk. paper)
Subjects: LCSH: Sisterhood of Avalon. | Moon—Mythology. | Medicine, Magic,
    mystic, and spagiric.
Classification: LCC BL325.M56 (ebook) | LCC BL325.M56 T45 2019 (print) | DDC
    299/.94—dc23
LC record available at https://lccn.loc.gov/2019001048

Llewellyn Worldwide Ltd. does not participate in, endorse, or have any authority or responsibility concerning private business transactions between our authors and the public.
    All mail addressed to the author is forwarded but the publisher cannot, unless specifically instructed by the author, give out an address or phone number.
    Any Internet references contained in this work are current at publication time, but the publisher cannot guarantee that a specific location will continue to be maintained. Please refer to the publisher's website for links to authors' websites and other sources.

Llewellyn Publications
A Division of Llewellyn Worldwide Ltd.
2143 Wooddale Drive
Woodbury, MN 55125-2989
www.llewellyn.com

Printed in the United States of America

To my beloved children, Ariana and Gareth:
May your lives always be filled with love and with joy,
just as you have filled my life with love and with joy.
I believe in you.
I am here for you.
I love you.
Always, and in all ways.

CONTENTS

Part Three: Cultivation

Conclusion: The Great Work 373

ACKNOWLEDGMENTS

The work presented in this book is the result of almost two decades' worth of research, experimentation, and esoteric exploration. Because the system of the Lunar Keys which make up the Avalonian Cycle of Revealing is not traditional, much time and effort has been put into identifying native British plants having energetic resonance with each moon as well as spiritual affinity with the goddesses and the stories with which these herbal allies have become associated. It is because of this that I am grateful for the women of Rhosyn Du Hearth, the original "beta testers" of this work, most especially Debbie S.; her herbal expertise and dedication to the work of Avalon made her an invaluable resource in the finalization of this herbal system in the late nineties.

I am also deeply grateful for the Sisterhood of Avalon and for all of my beautiful sisters. It has been my life's honor to walk this path beside each and every one of you. I am especially grateful for the loving support and encouragement given me by the women of the Council of Nine and the SOA Board of Trustees, past and present. Your deep wisdom, insight, and dedication to our Sisters and to the Ladies of Avalon both humble and inspire me each and every day. Special thanks go out to Lori Feldmann for her brilliance and her cheerfully rendered editorial assistance. I less than three you very much! I am also deeply grateful to gender and sexuality expert Christy Croft, for her suggestions and insights around embracing a language of inclusivity.

I could not ask for a more incredible publishing team than the wonderful folks at Llewellyn Worldwide. Their support and expertise along every step of this publishing journey has helped me to grow as an author and I know that my work is better for it. I do not have the words to adequately thank my amazing editor Elysia Gallo for all of her patient support, good humor, and ability to hold a strong vision of the big picture, even as we address the minutiae. Thank you a thousandfold for believing in this work and in me.

I am grateful as well for the incredible circle of friends who have blessed my life in so many ways—who support and uplift me, who encourage and hear me, who understand and are patient with me, who arrange sleepovers with our children so that I can meet deadlines, who make sure that I eat and sleep, and who are truly reflections of the divine in the world. To Lori, Tiffany, Elisa, Judi, Gaia, Aria, and Shelly: thank you my dear, incredible, brilliant, and talented heart-sisters!

To my most beloved James—thank you for inspiring me with your gifts, challenging me with your mind, embracing me with your arms, and understanding me with your heart. I love you very much and am so grateful to have you in my life.

And last, but not least, to my dearest children—my heart and my center—thank you for the privilege of being your mother. You fill me with great joy, pride, admiration, wonder, and hope for the future. Thank you for the side-splitting laughter, the deep conversations, the challenges and triumphs, the never-ending hugs, and for all that you both teach me every day. I love, love, love you both, and I love our lives together. I know it's probably not easy having such a strange momma, but I hope you know that I love you fiercely and unconditionally, and I want nothing more for you than for you to be who you are meant to be, to know and do your will in the world, and for you to know only love and happiness all the days of your lives.

Introduction

THE WAY OF AVALON

WHAT WOULD YOU RISK TO become the person you were born to be? Where would you journey? How far would you walk to re-claim the priestess path that leads you through the depths of the soul's shadow and reveals to you the height of your inner illumination? What tools would you pack to help you along your pilgrim's trackway? Who would you choose as your companions on this ever-unfolding journey?

Imagine with me, then, a place of women's healing. An island of women defined by their wisdom, praised for their knowledge, and sought after for their skills. A sisterhood bound in the spirit of service to the Feminine Divine—a service which manifested not only in the maintenance and per-petuation of the college temple Avalon may have been, as well as in care and respect for the self. Visualize what life may have been like living in community with like-minded and empowered women. Imagine the ways their lives unfolded as they embraced the cyclic harmonies of nature as the template they emulated in both their communal and inner spiritual lives.

Reflect upon the lessons we can glean from meditating upon the Holy Isle of Avalon as many believed it to be. Was it a historical place? An element of a lost Celtic myth about a blessed Otherworldly island which produced everything it needed of its own accord? Perhaps it was a British reflex of the enclaves of shapeshifting oracular women healers we see in the lore and legend found in other Celtic lands? And what if Avalon never existed at all outside of literary tradition and artistic imagination? Perhaps none of this is as important as what the essence of Avalon represents in the soul process of today's seeker who resonates with the Holy Isle and feels called to her shores, be they literal or metaphorical.

What if we each, like the island of Avalon, were a complete and whole entity unto ourselves? What if we could provide for our every physical, emotional, and spiritual need? What if we could harness the gifts of our inner resources and achieve our life's greatest potential to the fullest? What if we honored our deepest wisdom, embraced our ability to transform our lives and our circumstances, acknowledged our power to heal ourselves and, by extension, our communities and even the planet? How would our world be different if we embraced other women as our sisters, instead of comparing ourselves to them and competing with them? How differently would we see ourselves if we truly valued all that which makes us women, and entered into aware and honoring relationships with our family, friends, and lovers? What would we reflect out into the world if we placed the goddesses at the center of our lives and consciously adapted a lifelong practice that aligned us with the great natural cycles turning around and within us?

What if we lived our lives as if Avalon existed in the here and now, dwelling nowhere but within us, as steady as our heartbeat and as close as our next breath?

The practices presented here build upon the work shared in my book *Avalon Within*. They are part of a system of spiritual discipline that aims to guide the journeyer on a path of self-discovery, to build a strong and lasting connection with the Holy Isle, and to foster a true and meaningful relationship with the Celtic British goddesses honored in the Avalonian Tradition and beyond. Although inspired by Celtic legend and Welsh folklore, these tools are not ancient, nor have they come out of traditional practice. While we seek to honor Brythonic culture and the deities worshiped by our spiritual ancestors, it is important to acknowledge that little is known about the beliefs and practices of the ancient Celtic Britons, and because the stories of the figures we honor as divinities were written down in the medieval period when Britain was no longer Pagan, they are nowhere identified as gods. And so by necessity, although inspired by what lore we do have, the methods and framework is presented in these pages is of modern origin. I can only hope that there is some small spark of Awen that informs and dwells within the work. For while the practices and systems of correspondences are new, they are intended to be vehicles to help us touch what lies deeper within us. These are tools to help us move through layers of time and bridge cultural differences so that we may better connect with the ancient divinities, spiritual guardians, and innate wisdoms which, taken together, comprise the fabric of Ynys Afallon—the Holy Island of Healing.

So let us begin the next phase of our journey, and explore the mysteries of the Otherworldly Cauldron of Healing that dwells within Avalon's keeping. We will begin by looking to the past in order to examine the literary traditions of Avalon as a place of healing and rebirth. We will be introduced to the Avalonian Cycle of Revealing, a modern lunar system which is keyed into the prominent energies of the thirteen moons of the year, and, using the language of the modern Avalonian Tradition and its relevance to the priestess path of the contemporary seeker, we will explore the corresponding energies of the goddesses of Avalon. We will do so by delving into their myths and legends from a psycho-spiritual perspective so that we may better understand the lessons they hold for us and the examples they have set for our own spiritual revelations. Along the way, we will explore ways to come into relationship with our herbal allies in order to solidify our partnerships with them as they act as companions on our deepening journey, and we will seek out the wisdom of coming into alignment with lunar rhythms as they cycle both around and within us.

HOW TO USE THIS BOOK

Part one of this work sets the foundation for the work ahead.

- It explores the power of the moon through the filters of traditional Celtic lore, magical energetic correspondences, scientific insight, and modern psycho-spiritual perspectives and applications.
- It discusses the influence of the moon on the plant kingdom and presents tools to help us establish connections and build relationships with our Green Allies.
- It introduces the seeker to the Avalonian Cycle of Revealing, a system of personal growth and spiritual evolution comprised of fourteen Lunar Keys, each of which represents a monthly synergy of moon energy, herbal action, and goddess mythos. The goal of this annual immersion is to follow the mythic map lain by the stories of the Welsh goddesses honored in the Avalonian Tradition and to reflect the lessons of these tales onto our own lives.

Part two of this book is a month-by-month guide on how to engage with the Avalonian Cycle of Revealing as a tool for immersion into the myths of the goddesses of Avalon and the ways in which these are reflections of the story of our own lives.

- Each Lunar Key is presented with its corresponding mythic portion, which is accompanied by an analysis of the myth that both places the story in its original cultural context as well as offers a perspective on the psycho-spiritual application for the present-day seeker.

- Each month is accompanied by a supportive resource that provides a weekly focus for the suggested work of each moon in order to assist us in staying on track with our work, as well as to provide a jumping in place so that anyone can begin engagement with this work at any time in the cycle. It is not necessary to begin with Moon One. Start where you are.

- Each chapter concludes with guided inner journeys to facilitate connections with the goddess of that time in her sacred site within the mythic Otherworld. We will journey to Ceridwen at Llyn Tegid, Blodeuwedd at Llyn Morwynion, Rhiannon at Gorsedd Arberth, Branwen at Bedd Branwen, and Arianrhod at Dinas Dinlle, near Caer Arianrhod.

Part three presents information to assist in the cultivation of the sovereign discernment these practices can serve to develop, while deepening our relationship with the available traditional and cultural streams of information.

- It explores medieval Welsh herbal practices of the Physicians of Myddfai, traditionally said to have their origins in the fairy realms.

- It recounts the legend of the Otherworldy ancestress of the Physicians of Myddfai, the Lady of the Lake connected to Llyn y Fan Fach, while also delving into Welsh fairy lore and providing both cultural and symbolic analysis of this and other Lake Maiden tales.

- It presents an Avalonian *materia medica*, a compilation of the medicinal, magical, and folkloric uses of the fourteen herbs associated with the Lunar Keys of the Avalonian Cycle of Revealing. This information is intended as a starting point for the seeker's herbal explorations in support of their energetic and intuitive work with these herbal allies.

- PLEASE NOTE: In order to safeguard the integrity of the system of engagement espoused by the Avalonian Tradition in support of the development of personal discernment and coming to trust in one's inner wisdom, it is highly recommended that the seeker not consult any of the herbal information in the final chapter of this book until they have first undertaken the herbal energy immersion exercises and worked with the lunar elixirs. The underpinnings of this philosophy of magic is discussed further in part one of this book.

Part One

FOUNDATION

Chapter 1

THE ISLAND OF HEALING

Thither after the battle of Camlan we took the wounded Ar-thur ... and Morgen received us with fitting honor, and in her chamber she placed the king on a golden bed and with her own hand she uncovered his honorable wound and gazed at it for a long time. At length she said that health could be restored to him if he stayed with her for a long time and made use of her healing art.

—VITA MERLINI, GEOFFREY OF MONMOUTH

AVALON HAS BEEN KNOWN BY many names, has been accorded many attributes, and has inspired many ages on its journey down the stream of tradition to the present day. It is the Island of Apples, the Fortunate Isle, the Shining Isle, and the Island of the Blessed. It is an Island of Women, an Island of the Otherworld, and the Isle of the Dead. But above these all, Avalon is known best as the Island of Heal-ing, perhaps a reflection of its attachment to the Arthurian mythos, that current of lore which has been fed by many tributaries of legend and tradition. Perhaps it is Avalon's role as the place where Arthur awaits Britain's need which has secured it to memory, acting as that sa-cred container where the hope of many Britons has been poured: that the folk hero, Arthur, held and healed in Avalon's embrace, would one day keep his promise and return to save his people from the bondage of foreign invaders. That the legendary king (who some believe may be of divine origin) would return and claim his sovereign right to rule over the land, uniting its people under the banner of the dragon.

It is thought that the belief in the return of Arthur is what kept the light of hope in the hearts of the Britons—the Welsh, the Cornish, and those of the Old North—as they faced wave after wave of invasion and war after Rome withdrew from its shores. It is this hope in Arthur, some scholars believe, that led to the discovery of his grave at Glastonbury Abbey in 1191, and which forever married the legend of Avalon with the real-world place of Glastonbury; if you find Arthur's resting place, you have found the island of Avalon. The monks of the abbey were said to have discovered a hollowed-out oak tree containing two skeletons; interred with them was a lead cross with the following inscription: *Hic jacet sepultus inclitus rex Arthurus in insula Avalonia*: "Here lies interred the famous King Arthur on the Isle of Avalon." One of the skeletons was said to still have strands of long blond hair and was believed to be the remains of Arthur's queen, Guinevere.

On the one hand, as this discovery came a few years after the abbey had experienced major damage from a fire in 1184, some historians believe that this discovery, and the subsequent pomp and circumstance—and visits from pilgrims—that came with the establishment of a cult to Arthur at Glastonbury, was a cynical ploy to attract funds to the abbey to assist in their rebuilding project. However, another motivation to perpetuate what most scholars believe was an elaborate fraud may have been even worse.

The period of time from the initial exhumation of the remains—apparently witnessed by well-regarded historian Gerald of Wales (also known as Giraldus Cambrensis) seven years after the fire at the abbey—through to the eventual creation of a marble tomb in front of the high altar in which the remains were re-entombed by Edward I in 1278, the English were fighting fierce wars against the Welsh. It is believed that the discovery of Arthur's grave was intended to function as part of a propaganda war against the Welsh—to destroy any sense of hope that Arthur, as messianic folk hero, could grant to them. If the famous king was proven to be dead, there would be little reason to believe he would be coming to save them from the English.[1]

Gerald of Wales gives his accounting of the exhumation of Arthur's remains in two of his works, and there is no reason to doubt that he was present at the event. A twelfth-century clergyman who was the author of seventeen books, Gerald was a staunch supporter of England, himself three-quarters Norman, and a quarter Welsh (the great-grandson, in fact, of Rhys ap Tewdwr, the Prince of South Wales). In 1216, he wrote about the deeper meaning of the discovery of Arthur's grave:

> *Many tales are told and many legends have been invented about King Arthur and his mysterious ending. In their stupidity the British people maintain that he is still alive. Now that the truth is known, I have taken the trouble to add a few more details in this present chapter. The fairy-tales have been snuffed out, and the true and indubitable facts are made known, so that what really happened must be made crystal clear to all and separated from the myths which have accumulated on the subject.*
>
> —*Speculum Ecclesiae*, Gerald of Wales

Gerald of Wales was also the first to write about the connection of Avalon to Glastonbury, in 1193:

> *What is now known as Glastonbury was, in ancient times, called the Isle of Avalon. It is virtually an island, for it is completely surrounded by marshlands. In Welsh it is called Ynys*

---

1. Philip Rahtz and Lorna Watts, *Glastonbury: Myth and Archaeology* (Stroud, UK: Tempus Publishing, 2003), 56.

Afallach, which means the Island of Apples and this fruit once grew in great abundance. After the Battle of Camlann, a noblewoman called Morgan, later the ruler and patroness of these parts as well as being a close blood-relation of King Arthur, carried him off to the island, now known as Glastonbury, so that his wounds could be cared for.

—Liber de Principis instructione, Gerald of Wales

The stories of Avalon became attached to the lore of Arthur but are inspired by a tradition far older. The earliest tales say nothing of Arthur's role as a savior; in the earliest historical mentions, he is a chieftain and a war duke. In Geoffrey of Monmouth's pseudo-history, *Historia Regum Britannia* (*The History of the Kings of Britain*), Arthur is the recipient of assistance from the enigmatic Lady of the Lake, who is his ally and benefactress. She gifts him with the sword of Sovereignty as a validation of his right to rule, a sword said to have been forged on the Holy Island of Avalon and used only to confer kingship upon a worthy man. Through this act, she reveals the underlying truth of her nature, identifying herself and the women of Avalon with the goddesses and holy women empowered to grant sovereignty on behalf of the land, as well as holding a resonance with the traditions of the Ninefold Sisterhoods know to us from the lore of many Celtic lands. In Britain, they are the keepers of the Cauldron of Annwn, muses and prophetesses, shape-shifters and weather witches, initiators and healers.

Although famed for its healing arts, Avalon is much more than this. It is a threshold place, a portal between this world and the Otherworld, between history and legend, between consciousness and the unconscious, between shadow and Sovereignty, and between Self and Source. And what is the way to pass over this threshold? How can we bridge the space between that which is known and that which can only be learned by delving into the deeper mystery? How can we part the mists that guard the space between and obscure the opening in the gateway through which we can reach the inner Avalon?

We can do so by way of the Island of Healing.

It is this outermost avatar of the Holy Island that is easiest for us to reach, and with good reason. Like the pilgrims in Arthurian legend, who must spend the night in vigil and prayer at the shrine of Beckery before being able to step foot on the Holy Island, we too must take the time to connect with our intention, and consciously engage in a practice of inner preparation—a practice that leads to self-knowledge and integration. This process of self-healing guides us in the use of our inner vessel—the cauldron or the grail—to catalyze the alchemy of the soul, bringing us to a place of greater understanding and unconditional acceptance of both the shadow and the sovereign aspects of the authentic self.

When we come to Avalon in this way, we can be relieved of our wounds. Like Arthur, we can take up the mantle of Sovereignty, and drink deeply of the vessel of regeneration that will heal the landscape—both within us and around us.

Sovereignty and the Land

In its most basic form, the concept of Sovereignty from an ancestral perspective is about acknowledgment of the interdependency of the people and the land. This may have developed as a consequence of the shift from a nomadic, hunter-gatherer economy to that of a more stationary, agrarian economy. Able now to set down roots in one place, people become connected to the land in a way they hadn't been when they moved from place to place, following the migration of herd animals and knowing where and when to harvest plant foods. Our hunter-gatherer ancestors' intimate connection with the cycles of sun, moon, and stars helped them survive by moving to the places where the resources, terrain, and weather would best support their needs.

The shift to full-time settlements taught our ancestors how to be in balanced partnership with the land they lived upon. Respecting the land and the resources it offered, rather than engaging in exploitative practices—such as exhausting the soil, befouling the waters, deforestation, and over-hunting—would support the continuing bounty of the land. Being out of balance with the land could lead to desperate times, desperate people, and desperate actions—bringing war and the Wasteland: famine, disease, and the suffering of people.

Tutelary goddesses—divinities connected specifically to a place—can be considered a resonance of animism, the idea of an indwelling divinity that permeates all things. A sacred marriage between a chief or king and the goddess of the land is a pact connecting the fate of the king with that of the land, making him responsible for the care and defense of the realm. This sacred bond is a sign of trust from energies of the land itself, investing the tested leader with its blessings and permission to serve as the husband (protector, lover, leader) and administrator of the land and all who dwell within its boundaries. What we may imagine as having begun as a true energetic bond and connection between the king and the land appears to have shifted over time to become more symbolic and metaphorical, likely due in no small part to the cultural shifts which accompany changes in technology, economy, and social structure.

Beliefs shift, and today the land is overwhelmingly looked at as a commodity to be exploited, not as a living and vital partner in need of consideration, respect, and honor. The place of women in society has also degraded, and ecofeminist theories have linked the status of women in society with environmental awareness and the nature of our cultural relationship with the Earth. When the planet is honored and respected, women are similarly treated; when the land is seen simply as a resource from which to profit, women's lives and bodies experience the same treatment.

Whether literal or metaphorical, there is a connection between women and the land, and the degree to which culture at large is in balance with one is mirrored by its relationship with the other. It makes sense that we who are seeking Sovereignty do so by taking an accounting both of our inner and outer landscapes—the realms over which we preside.

Shadow Work

It is no simple task to begin the intentional exploration the shadow aspects of the unconscious Self; by its very nature it is a road that is paved with pain, on a pathway lain by fear, and which is typically marked by obstructions built to protect us from any further hurt or horror. Our shadow is not something we can cut off, ignore, or throw away; it is a part of who we are—a part in need of love, gentleness, and understanding. Our task instead is to learn to love ourselves completely; to be able to celebrate our achievements and also be compassionate with ourselves when we falter.

The nature of shadow is that it arises as an adaptation to help us survive traumatic experiences such as abusive childhoods, sexual assault, chronic bullying, frightening accidents, and the painful loss of loved ones. When we experience these life challenges, especially (but not exclusively) when we are young, our psyche unconsciously creates a kind of mental and emotional subroutine to help us remain as intact as possible throughout the trauma. If we look at the shadow as the survival mechanism it truly is—an internal support system we should bless, not a disability we should disavow—it truly changes how we can engage in shadow work.

The issue with shadow tendencies is not that they exist within us at all, for in our times of greatest need they served a critically important role and could be seen as, perhaps, our greatest ally in those times of intense vulnerability. Problems arise when the compensatory behaviors and perspectives the shadow gifted us with have outlived the situations which birthed them; this causes us to react to situations in our lives which feel similar to the old traumas as if they *are* the old traumas. This prevents us from seeing the truth of the present situation with clarity because the shadow subroutine has been triggered and we unconsciously react to the old wound rather than the present moment. And that is the key: when we are anchored in past traumas that prevent us from seeing the present with clarity, we react rather than respond.

Effective shadow work therefore has several essential components:

THE ROOT: Identifying, where we can, the original cause of our woundings. This is the "why" of our shadow.

THE FILTERS: Seeking the ways in which these wounds have tainted how we view ourselves, others, and the world. This is the "what" of our shadow.

THE REACTION: Acknowledging both the situations which trigger us as well as the ways in which we act out when we are triggered. This is the "how" of our shadow.

The more conscious we are of these aspects of our shadow tendencies, the more we are able to see ourselves, others, and the situations of our lives for what they are, rather than interpreting these things through the filters of our past hurts and fears. Recognizing the patterns of behavior that arise from outmoded ways of being allows us to take responsibility for them, and this in turn empowers us to make choices when we are triggered. We can learn to respond consciously to the truth of the situation at hand, rather than to react unconsciously as if this were a past situation that caused us pain. However, before we can make this choice, we must first develop the discernment necessary to recognize our triggers for what they are.

It is the degree to which we are in relationship with our shadow that determines whether we react unconsciously to these challenges or we respond to them with clarity. This relationship is founded on how well we know ourselves, a skill that requires us to understand not only the nature of our shadow but also the extent of our Sovereignty.

Sovereignty and the Self

The overall focus of the Avalonian Tradition is to provide a paradigm of spiritual transformation through which we can come more fully into our personal Sovereignty; it is the loom upon which we can weave—and reweave—the whole and holy tapestry of our lives. We define Sovereignty as "fully conscious self-determination" that is, it is the state of loving, respecting, and knowing one's self so well that the choices we make about who we are and how we choose to be in the world is informed only by our true will, and not by our fears, wounds, perceived limitations, and the expectations of others.

To be sovereign does not mean that we have achieved complete empowerment or spiritual enlightenment, nor that we have utterly conquered our shadow and dwell in some kind of balanced bliss of light and love. It means that we understand our flaws, recognize our self-destructive patterns, are conscious of our fears, have accepted the pain of our experiences, and honor where we are in our process of growth. Yet, even with all these shadow tendencies still present, we nonetheless elect to make choices that reflect our greatest good, are in support of achieving our highest potential, and fortify our deepest connection to Source. When we are sovereign, we act *in* the world rather than react *to* the world.

So where do we begin? How do we cease to perpetuate behaviors which are outdated adaptations to old wounds? How can we work to shift our consciousness and sharpen our Sight so that we are able make different choices? How can we work to create a life for ourselves which is in greater alignment with our Sovereignty?

Revisiting the Avalonian Cycle of Healing

The Avalonian Cycle of Healing is a foundational paradigm of practice in the modern Avalonian Tradition as practiced by the Sisterhood of Avalon; an in-depth immersion into this work is the focus of my book, *Avalon Within*. At its core, the cycle was inspired by a tale of one of the powerful cauldrons of transformation known to us from Celtic myth, the Cauldron of Wisdom and Inspiration owned by the goddess Ceridwen.

In her tale, which we will examine in great detail in chapter 6, the goddess brews an herbal elixir which, when complete, will bring the gifts of wisdom and prophecy to whomever receives the three drops which emerge from the brew. Although intended for Ceridwen's son Morfran, it is the servant-boy Gwion who steals the cauldron's yield for himself. Ceridwen pursues him, and the pair embark upon a shape-shifting chase through the five elements, which sees the boy destroyed and reborn as one possessing great wisdom. It is this five-fold chase, long been believed to encode a Druidic initiation rite, as well as the five seeds of the star revealed in the cleaved apple of wisdom that gives Avalon her name, which inspired the Avalonian Cycle of Healing as a pathway of inner understanding and a vehicle for affecting deep and lasting change in our lives.

The fundamental premise of the Avalonian Cycle of Healing is to embrace our connection to the energies of cycle that are the prime mover of the universe in a quest to match our personal nature with Nature. Once we acknowledge that we are a part of the Universe and not apart from it, we can consciously come into alignment with the energies of the great cycle, whose repetitions are seen in the tiniest subatomic particles through to the great whirling galaxies that make up the known Universe and beyond. This expression of the Hermetic principle of correspondence—as above, so below; as within, so without—allows us to harness the macrocosmic/microcosmic paradigm of the universe and use it to empower our changes as we ally ourselves with the turning of the great wheel in all of its iterations.

The Avalonian Cycle of Healing teaches us to look at the progression of changes in the world around us in a practical way, giving us the tools we need to tap into the greater movement of the cycle and channel it so that it is the battery that powers our inner work. The work of the cycle, simply put, follows this general pattern: we enter into the depths of the unconscious to seek out negative life patterns at the Station of Descent; look into the mirror of our soul's shadow at the Station of Confrontation to find the root of these energies; we bring the reclaimed energies from our hidden selves up into the light of consciousness at the Station of Emergence and redirect these energies to cultivate a harvest of self-actualization at the apex of the cycle that is the Station of Resolution. This spiritual harvest provides us with the resources needed to bolster our resolve from a place of increased clarity as the cycle turns down into the Station of Descent once more. The Station of Integration is the heart around which this perpetual cycle turns, while also existing in-between each of the other stations; indeed it is the totality of the cycle itself. Integration holds the energies of wholeness and unity and assists us in seeing the big picture of our soul growth and spiritual unfolding.

The Cycle of Healing informs our understanding and engagement with the holy days of the Celtic wheel of the year in the Avalonian Tradition. It mirrors what we know of the socioeconomic practices and religious traditions that our spiritual forebears engaged in as a result of their relationship to their land. While instead of a physical harvest we seek a psycho-spiritual harvest, the seasonal map we follow is roughly the same, as are the allies we seek to engage with along our journey.

Lunar Correspondences of the Cycle of Healing

Reflecting our transformational journey through the wheel of the year, the Cycle of Healing also reveals itself to us monthly through the silver wheel of the lunar dance. In much the same way we ride the wheel of the year, the cycle reveals itself to us monthly through the phases of the moon. Harnessing this energy every month is where the core of our inner work originates. We see the echoes of the greater cycle reverberating in the smaller one, pushing us through our day to day revelations, building up to the greater insights that come with the yearly cycle, culminating in the cycle of our lives when our time here is through. Indeed, even as we cycle around the incarnational wheel, the same energies move over and through us until we finally attain that ultimate wholeness—union with the Divine.

Station of Cycle	Element	Holy Day (Solar Cycle)	Moon Phase (Lunar Cycle)
Descent	Water	Calan Gaeaf	Third Quarter
Confrontation	Earth	Gwyl Mair	Dark Moon
Emergence	Air	Calan Mai	First Quarter
Resolution	Fire	Gwyl Awst	Full Moon
Integration	Spirit	The Cycle	Sovereign Moon

The cycle of the year, the cycle of the moon, and the cycle of our lives all weave the same pattern of progression described by the Cycle of Healing and its Stations of Descent, Confrontation, Emergence, Resolution, and Integration. As we align ourselves to these natural rhythms, we will find that our work parallels the point of cycle we are in. As we begin the process at the third quarter moon or the Station of Descent, we enter into the dark half of the cycle, focusing upon what hinders us and prevents us from being all that we are. The work continues as we come to the dark moon, the Station of Confrontation. Here, the shadow is revealed at this darkest point of the cycle.

We take this hard-earned understanding of our pain, our unconscious motivation, back up into the light with us, to the Station of Emergence into the light half of the cycle, at the first quarter moon. Here, we now plant the seeds of Sovereignty, laying down a new pathway through which the energies reclaimed from the shadow can flow, in support of the vision of ourselves which better reflects the authentic truth of who we are. The Station of Resolution at the full moon sees the seeds come into fruition. Transformation has taken place, and the results of our spiritual alchemy brings us to a place where we are in better alignment with our sovereign selves. With these accomplishments in place, we peel the next layer off the onion, and our energies wane down toward the Station of Descent once more but with new insights and new tools at our disposal. Although the cycle repeats itself, and we move through its stations and phases again and again, we are not treading the same ground. For even as we turn, we are spiraling ever-upward, ever moving to a greater connection to our sovereign self, and to Source.

Chapter 2

THE MIRROR OF THE MOON

LIKE MOST JOURNEYS OF A spiritual nature, we begin with the hero's quest. The Old Welsh poem *Preiddeu Annwn* or *The Spoils of Annwn*, believed to date back to somewhere between the ninth and twelfth century CE, tells the story of King Arthur's raid of the Otherworld in search of a magical cauldron. Although the earliest known versions of *Preiddeu Annwn* appeared in writing during the thirteenth or fourteenth century CE in the *Llyfr Taliesin* (*The Book of Taliesin*), the poem is filled with powerful imagery and evocative language which seems to place it in an even more ancient time.

Annwn (also written as Annwyn or Annwfyn), is the name of the British Celtic Otherworld, and it translates to mean the "un-world" or the "very-deep."[2] Arthur and his band of warriors move through Annwn and encounter many wondrous and enigmatic fortresses (or, alternatively, one Otherworldly fortress, which is given several epithets in the poem) in search of their great prize, a cauldron which is described thus:

> *My poetry, from the cauldron it was uttered.*
> *From the breath of nine maidens it was kindled*

---

2. Sarah Higley, trans. *Preiddeu Annwn: The Spoils of Annwn*, (Rochester: University of Rochester: The Camelot Project, 2007), accessed at: http://d.lib .rochester.edu/camelot/text/preiddeu-annwn.

The cauldron of the chief of Annwn: what is its fashion?
A dark ridge around its border and pearls.
It does not boil the food of coward; it has not been destined.[3]

It is believed that the mythic forerunners of the Arthurian Grail quest can be found in Celtic British legends like *Preiddeu Annwn* wherein kings and warriors seek cauldrons of wisdom and regeneration on quests over water to fantastic islands of the Otherworld. This journey over water is a motif seen time and time again in Celtic legend; the Otherworld is often associated with islands in the west or underwater fortresses. Votive deposits rich in material goods have been excavated from lakes and rivers throughout Celtic lands, perhaps reflecting a belief that bodies of water were a medium through which gods and spirits could be contacted and supplicated. Symbolically, water is a representative of the unconscious, and if we use ancient stories as a road map to the Otherworld—which in turn could be said to represent the spiritual self—the modern seeker can learn to gain access to the inner realms by journeying down the pathway that lies within.

Legends aside, the voyage to claim the Cauldron of the Otherworld is not necessarily an easy one. Arthur and his men staged a military campaign to claim their prize, yet only seven of them "rise up" from Annwn to return home, the poet Taliesin among them. Although there are many who seek the Pearl-rimmed Cauldron, even daring to enter the realms of the Unknown, only few ever obtain it—and those who do, often do so a at great cost. The journey is fraught with pain and can result in the death of outmoded shadow aspects of the Self, but it also serves to bring the quester into a place of greater actualization, for as the stories teach us, only heroes and poets and healers reemerge from the Otherworldly journey. In the same way, the spiritual seeker must dare to tread the inner realms of the unconscious in hopes of recovering the vessel of Sov-

---

3. Ibid., lines 13–17.

ereignty that has lain within us for so long, being quietly tended by the guardians of inspiration who feed our inner fire—that spark which inspires us to undertake the quest for wholeness.

The poem's description of the cauldron of the chief of Annwn is quite evocative. The vessel's edge is round like the cycle's circuitous path. Dark as the night sky, it is rimmed with pearls, and whether the poem refers to the round gems of the ocean or is describing the cauldron as being inlaid with mother of pearl, they both reflect the energies of the moon. It is not difficult to see how pearl's watery origin, rounded shape, and luminescent sheen could evoke the mystery of the moon, called *lleuad* in Welsh.

In the modern Avalonian Tradition, we look at the Pearl-rimmed Cauldron of the Otherworld as an allegory of the cyclic path that takes us through our soul's rebirth and transformation, with each of the lunar pearls holding an energy that contributes to this process of inner unfolding. If each pearl can be seen to represent a lunar month, then the entire circuit of pearls around the opening of the vessel of Sovereignty can be used collectively to symbolize to be the lunar mysteries which both define and crown that which lies within. As we travel around the cycle we also spiral down into ourselves and back up again, measuring both the diameter and the depth of our inner cauldron. As we undertake this inner exploration, we are able increase our understanding of the contents of our soul that lay shrouded in the shadow realms of the unconscious and are able to better evaluate the extent of our connection to Source—she who holds the womb/tomb portal of this Otherworldly vessel.

The Celts and the Moon

We believe that the Celts, like most ancient peoples, used the moon to mark and measure time. The fragmentary remains of a Gaulish lunisolar peg calendar inscribed on a sheet of bronze, known as the Coligny calendar, was discovered in France in 1897. Created in the second century CE (well after the Roman annexation of continental Celtic lands), scholars believe its purpose was to rectify the conquerors' solar calendar with the Gaulish lunar model. Precious little is known about the way the peoples of the British Isles rendered time, but it is significant to note that the pre-Celtic megalithic monuments acknowledged the moon by marking lunar events such as the lunar standstill and the metonic cycle of little over eighteen years, a value that can be reduced numerologically to nine, a number associated vibrationally with the moon.

Although the idea of the moon universally associated with a goddess is pervasive in modern Neo-Paganism, in several Indo-European-derived cultures, the deity associated with the moon is male, like the Norse god Máni. Similarly, while the gender of the word for "moon" in both Irish and Welsh is masculine, we cannot name Celtic deities that are directly related to the moon with any certainty. However, mythic symbols and name etymology seem to suggest that several figures from Welsh lore may indeed have lunar associations. The name Arianrhod, for example, means "Silver Wheel," which could be a reference to the full moon, while a potential meaning for Ceridwen's name as "White Crooked One" is evocative of a crescent moon.

Celtic lore provides some examples of women engaging in what could be interpreted as lunar rites. One of the oldest known Breton poems, "Ar Rannou" ("The Series"), is a teaching song containing what appear to be mnemonic references to a body of Celtic wisdom presented as a dialog between a druid and a child. In it, the child questions the druid about number associations. For the number nine, the druid replies:

> *Nine small white hands on the table in the area, near the tower Lezarmeur and nine mothers groan much. Nine Korrigan dancing with flowers in the chewant and robes of white wool, around the fountain, the clarity of the full moon. The sow and*

her nine piglets at the door of their lair, growling and burrow-
ing, burrowing and grunting, small! small! small! hasten the
apple! The old boar is going to to lecture.[4]

The korrigan are alternatively said to be a type of water fairy or a group of Breton priestesses who lived either cloistered on an island or deep in a sacred grove. There is a process in mythology called *euhem-erism* that describes the transformation over time of real people into legendary creatures or even divinities; it is therefore possible that the legends of the korrigan as water fairies is an example of this process and serves as a mythological memory of what had been an ancient priestess-hood. If this is the case, the korrigan may be an example of the isolated communities of sacred women found in myth, legend, and even in the historical record from all around the Celtic world. The above passage not only associates one of these Ninefold Sisterhoods (another example of which are the nine Morgens associated with Avalon) with the wor-ship of the moon, but also links the moon with the number nine. We see this connection frequently in Western tradition; in the Qabalah for example, the ninth sephira on the Tree of Life is Yesod, foundation, the realm of the moon.

It is not hard to see why the ancients would have associated the number nine with the lunar mysteries; they knew that the moon was associated with fertility, and would have connected the lunar month with the length of the average menstrual cycle, as well as noticed that women who lived together tended to bleed and conceive around the same time and in accordance with the waning and waxing of the moon. The nine-month gestation period for human babies would have further underscored the connection between women, the moon, and the num-ber nine. It is interesting to also note that in addition to "Ar Rannou" associating the number nine with the korrigan and birthing mothers,

4. Theodore Herbert La Villemarqué, "Ar Rannou" in *Barzaz-Breiz* (Paris: Franck, 1846), 10.

it also includes the apple—that quintessential symbol of women's wisdom for which Avalon itself was named—and the sow, the totem animal of the goddess Ceridwen, and a creature associated very strongly with the Otherworld in Welsh legends.

The Lunar Cycle

In modern practice, there are two ways to approach working with the moon. The first is to consider the greater cycle of the year and its dance of the thirteen moons that comprise the lunar months; this approach is what informs the majority of the lunar workings in this book. The second is to connect with the ebb and flow of the moon's energies within the cycle of the month itself, which manifest visually as the phases of the moon. There are a few key facts to keep in mind about the moon as we enter into a discussion of her phases:

1. As the moon revolves around the Earth, it is also rotating around its own axis.

2. Due to a phenomenon known as tidal locking, the rotation of the moon has slowed to the point where the time it takes for our moon make a complete revolution around Earth is about the same it takes to complete one full rotation on its axis. Not only does this make a lunar day appropriately equal to an Earth month, it is the reason why we only ever see one hemisphere of the moon; the so-called dark side of the moon (more accurately, it would be the "far side of the moon") is the one that faces away from us.

3. Lunar phases are caused by the position of the moon as it orbits the Earth and the angles it makes with the sun relative to our perspective from the Earth. As the angle between the moon and the sun increases, more of the illuminated side of the moon is visible from Earth; as the angle decreases, less of the illuminated side is visible.

4. Moon phases are not shadows cast upon the moon's surface by the Earth occluding light of the sun; this dynamic is, however, the mechanism of how eclipses occur, a matter discussed in great detail in chapter 9.

For now, let's take a closer look at these phases and the energies they hold.

Dark Moon

DURATION: From the day of the dark moon until three days after. (In this account, the new moon refers to the first sliver of a crescent visible in the sky).

SUN-MOON ANGLE RELATIVE TO EARTH: 0°

VISUAL: The moon's non-illuminated side is fully facing the Earth, so it is not visible. The only exception to this occurs during a solar eclipse, when the moon passes between the Earth and the sun.

MOONRISE AND MOONSET: The moon rises and sets with the sun.[*]

TIME OF APEX: The moon is at its highest point at noon.[**]

ENERGY: Turning within; confronting the shadow; banishing negativity; letting go of what no longer serves our greatest good.

Waxing Crescent

DURATION: From the third through the seventh day after the dark moon.

SUN-MOON ANGLE RELATIVE TO EARTH: 45°

VISUAL: The moon is partly, but less than one-half, illuminated by the sun.

---

[*] *These times represent a general guideline; the actual times of local moonrise and moonset is dependent on the time of year and the location of the observer on the globe.*

[**] *The time when the moon is at its highest point in the sky corresponds with high tide; the second high tide in a day occurs twelve hours later with low tides occurring six hours after each high tide.*

Moonrise and Moonset: The moon rises two hours after sunrise, and sets two hours after sunset.

Time of Apex: The moon is at its highest point in the sky four hours before sunset.

Energy: Cleansing of body, mind, and spirit; inner renewal; new beginnings; integration of the lessons derived from shadow work.

First Quarter

Duration: From the seventh through the tenth day after the dark moon.

Sun-Moon Angle Relative to Earth: 90°

Visual: The right half of the moon appears to be illuminated by the sun.

Moonrise and Moonset: The moon rises at noon and sets at midnight.

Time of Apex: The moon is at its highest point in the sky at sunset.

Energy: Emerging into the light; planting seeds for manifestation; seeking outer balance.

Waxing Gibbous

Duration: From the tenth day through the thirteenth day after the dark moon.

Sun-Moon Angle Relative to Earth: 135°

Visual: The moon is more than one half (but not fully) illuminated by the sun.

Moonrise and Moonset: The moon rises two hours before sunset, and sets two hours before sunrise.

Time of Apex: The moon is at its highest point in the sky four hours after sunset.

Energy: Cultivating growth; nurturing the Self; acknowledging potential and considering possibilities.

Full Moon

DURATION: Fourteen days after the dark moon.

SUN-MOON ANGLE RELATIVE TO EARTH: 180°

VISUAL: The moon's illuminated side completely faces Earth, allowing us to see the entirety of its sun-facing surface.

MOONRISE AND MOONSET: The moon rises at sunset and sets at sunrise; each night after the full moon sees the moon rise an additional fifty minutes to an hour later than sunset.

TIME OF APEX: The moon is at its highest point in the sky at midnight.

ENERGY: Revelation of the Higher Self; abundant manifestation; clarity of sight.

Waning Gibbous

DURATION: From the third day through the seventh day after the full moon.

SUN-MOON ANGLE RELATIVE TO EARTH: 135°

VISUAL: The moon is more than one-half (but not fully) illuminated by the sun.

MOONRISE AND MOONSET: The moon rises two hours after sunset, and sets two hours after sunrise.

TIME OF APEX: The moon is at its highest point in the sky four hours before sunrise.

ENERGY: First fruits; inner harvest; acknowledgment of bounty.

Third Quarter

DURATION: From the seventh day through the tenth day after the full moon.

VISUAL: The left half of the moon appears to be illuminated by the sun.

SUN-MOON ANGLE RELATIVE TO EARTH: 90°

MOONRISE AND MOONSET: The moon rises at midnight and sets at noon.

TIME OF APEX: The moon is at its highest point in the sky at sunrise.

ENERGY: Descending into the darkness; taking stock; seeking inner balance.

Waning Crescent

DURATION: From the tenth day after the full moon until the night of the dark moon.

VISUAL: The moon appears to be partly (but less than one half) illuminated by the sun.

SUN-MOON ANGLE RELATIVE TO EARTH: 45°

MOONRISE AND MOONSET: The moon rises two hours before sunrise, and sets two hours before sunset.

TIME OF APEX: The moon is at its highest point in the sky four hours after sunrise.

ENERGY: Identifying obstacles to growth; seeking the root of inner wounds; forgiving self and others.

The Ninth Phase: The Sovereign Moon

These are the eight main phases of the moon, but underscoring them all is a ninth consideration: the energies of the moon as she is without the illusory interplay of light and darkness—that is, without the influence of the angles she makes with the sun from the perspective of Earth which gives her phases. This is the authentic moon as she exists in space, the core underlying all of her apparent changes.

I call this ninth phase of the moon the *sovereign moon*. This moon coexists with each of the other lunar phases, providing the canvas upon which are projected both light and darkness. Yet, regardless of what it is we can see from our vantage point here on Earth, the moon herself does not change; the projections upon her are meaningless and she remains fundamentally the same no matter how we view her. This is the moon from her own perspective, relative to nothing but what she truly is.

We can take this principle and apply it to our own lives. The sovereign moon teaches us to acknowledge the whole and authentic Self that always dwells below the surface of our changes. She waits for us to see past the ebb and flow of our personal power and to see beneath the illusion of the limitations we have come to accept about ourselves. When we can do so, we are better able to know that truth of who we are is always present and always a perfect reflection of the Divine.

With this in mind, let us engage more fully with the energies of the sovereign moon.

Working: Visualizing the Sovereign Moon

Note: As with all of the meditations presented in this book, you can memorize these workings, or it can be helpful to record yourself reading these passage out loud so you can play them back to accompany you on your journey. Professional recordings of these workings are also available from the author's website.

Become aware of your breath and sit for a few moments with the rhythm of its natural ebb and flow. When you are ready, and with intention, use your inhalation to gather up all of the energies within you that are preventing you from being fully present. Use your exhalation to release these energies into the ground below your feet. Engage in several repetitions of the cleansing cycle of breath until you find yourself in a place of centered and receptive clarity.

When you are ready, envision the silver-white orb of the full moon as clearly as you are able. She is round and shining, a gleaming pearl set against the black velvet darkness of space. Her face is pocked with dark and ancient seas; lunar maria that hold no water, only the memory of what has come before while creating patterns that have inspired humanity throughout time and in every culture. Just as we see images in the crystalline vapor of clouds or illuminated symbols in the living embers of a fire, the areas of darkness on the surface of the moon have been seen as a rabbit and a toad, the face of a man, and the body of a goddess.

See the moon as large and as round, as bright and as shining as you can, and when you see her clearly on the canvas of your inner eye, feel her grow larger and larger until she has transcended that small inner screen and the totality of her now encompasses the whole of your being. Feel what it is like to have the fullness of the bright moon surrounding your body, superimposing itself over your own energy. Breathe into this image and feel yourself become an embodiment of the moon herself. You are vast and round—a sphere, not a disc, spinning slowly in synchronous orbit with the Earth below you. Feel every ridge, every crater. Experience the scars of impacts past, ancient seas of extinct volcanic flows, and the hints of frozen water like secret caches of crystal awaiting full discovery.

Bring your attention to the side of you that faces the sun, a star so distant and yet so strong that even the small portion of its light you are able to reflect renders you a welcome and trusted nighttime companion to all who dwell upon your sister, Earth. Indeed, even when the side of you that faces the sun has its back to the Earth, you are able to reflect the planetary light, the earthshine, back to the planet as well.

Experience this for a moment…what it is like for you to collect these solar emanations? How does it feel to be the moon in her fullness? What does it mean to be the bright and shining orb that lights the way of the traveler, rules the ebb and flow of the tides, influences the growth of plants, the fertility of animals, and helps count out the rhythm of time for those who mark the cycle of your changes? What energy does the full moon hold? What does she have to teach you in the light of the revelation of her fullness, the disc of her surface fully illuminated, standing across the void of space to make a direct alignment with the sun from the perspective of the Earth? What image do you experience on the face of the moon as you embody it? What does it mean to you and your inner process?

Feel yourself shift now, as the moon does, moving further along in your orbit around the Earth. As the angle between you and the sun grows smaller by degrees, so too does the phase you embody as observed from the planet below. The amount of light that you are seen to reflect grows less and less. You are waning now, your brightness receding, your darkness becoming more concentrated as you breathe into this moment... into this shift... into this change. And you find yourself holding space in this moment, embodying the energies of the third quarter moon, seen half in darkness and half in light from the vantage point of those looking up at you from the planet below. How does it feel to be the waning half-moon, holding a point of equilibrium yet moving ever more increasingly into the darkness? What energy does the third quarter moon hold? What does she have to teach you about embodying balance in the face of what is unknown? About being centered even while embracing the wisdom of caution?

When you are ready, you take up the celestial circle dance once more, and as the moon does, you continue in your familiar orbit around Earth. As the angle between you and the sun grows smaller and smaller, you wane darker and darker from the perspective of the planet below. The amount of light that you are seen to reflect grows less and less, until at last you find yourself pausing in the space where the sun is in front of you, illuminating your face as it always does; but the Earth is behind you, seeing nothing of your comforting light... only the stars as you sink into the depths of this mysterious and magnetic energy. Breathe into this moment and find yourself embodying the energies of the dark moon. What energy does the dark moon hold? How does it feel to be the dark moon, enrobed in night's great mystery? What does she have to teach you about embracing the shadow as a part of the path to holy wholeness and healing? What do you need most to see here in the most hidden places of your soul?

You shift once again. When you are ready, move forward once more away from the darkness, growing round and into the light. The amount of illumination you share with Earth below increases as the angle between you and the sun grows larger and larger, and you wax brighter and brighter, until you pause once again at a place of balance…shifting into the first quarter moon…holding space in that place half in light and half in darkness from the vantage point of those looking up at you from Earth below. How does it feel to be the waxing half-moon, breathing into a place of equilibrium, yet moving ever more increasingly into the light? What energy does the first quarter moon hold? What does she have to teach you about embodying balance in the face of increasing potential, and about being centered even when embracing the courage to change?

And when you are ready, move forward once more, tracing the well-worn pathway back to where you began, increasing your reflected light and angle to the sun until you return to the bright and majestic shining of the moon at her fullness. Breathe into this place at the height of lunar power, coming full circle to pause in the greatest extent of your alignment with the sun.

And then, in this moment, feel that light fall away.

It is not because you have fallen into shadow.

It is because there is no longer a sun, whose light you can reflect. There is no longer an earth to witness your changes as you cycle around her.

It is just you, the moon. Exactly as you are—no projections, no illusions.

Extracted from the matrix of your environmental context, you are no longer subject to spending your existence trapped in someone else's orbit, nor are you fixed in place by the requirements of another's gravitational pull.

Experience what it feels like to no longer be defined by your relationship to others. To have the truth of who you are be your only point of reference.

Without the reflection of external light or the filter of positional darkness, who are you truly? Taken out of your present context of relational and community systems that keep all of us structured and locked in an orbital path, what could you be? What is the nature of the projections and expectations of others? What are the consequences of the projections and expectations of the Self?

How is it that our moon, that heavenly body which has been present in our skies for millions of years before the dawn of humanity and will certainly still be shining after we are long gone, is able to hide a great secret from us in plain sight? There is no so-called dark side of the moon; there is no one face that stares forever out into the abyss of space while the other beams benevolently down upon earth month after month. The truth is that just as the Earth rotates on its axis as it orbits the sun, the moon rotates on *its* axis as it orbits the Earth. But because it takes an entire Earth month for the moon to complete one full rotation—and coupled with its month-long orbit around our planet—we only ever see the same face from the perspective of Earth. How does this change your perception of the moon? How does this illuminate the meaning of the sovereign self?

Likewise, who are you when you are seen as you are? What does it feel like to be seen and heard and acknowledged exactly as you are? What about you is hidden in plain sight from others? From yourself? Without limitation, without projection, without illusion, without expectation: who are you? What have you become? What do you like about the unvarnished truth of yourself? What would you like to change?

How can you bring greater awareness of the sovereign moon to your life? How can you bring in more of this sovereign essence to fortify your work and illuminate your path to wholeness?

Spend as much time as you need in this place of reflective Sovereignty. When you are ready, connect to a space of gratitude for your experience, and resolve to bring back with you all of the insights and information you received during this working. Take three deep, centering breaths … and return to the here and the now.

Cycles of Healing

There are two main iterations of cycle which are focused on by practitioners of the Avalonian Tradition: The Avalonian Cycle of Healing (outlined in chapter 1) and the Avalonian Cycle of Revealing. Both of these cycles provide an evolutionary paradigm of spiritual growth and personal transformation through the alignment of the Self with the cycles of nature both within and around us. The Cycle of Healing reflects a five-fold division of cycle that connects seasonal shifts, the major lunar phases, and the Celtic holy days to the stages of our inner process of unfolding. The Cycle of Revealing looks at the lunar mysteries of the yearly cycle and envisions each of the thirteen moons of the year as one of the pearls that rim the cauldron of the chief of Annwn. It is the Cycle of Revealing which forms the bulk of the focus for this book and will be explored in great depth.

Chapter 3

THE AVALONIAN CYCLE
OF REVEALING

THE SOVEREIGNTY OF SELF-KNOWLEDGE CAN be achieved in many ways, on many paths; in the Avalonian Tradition, this work begins by aligning oneself with the cycles of nature. The five-fold path of the Avalonian Cycle of Healing facilitates our exploration of the nature of the sacred landscape within us as a reflection of the sacred landscape around us. The Lunar Keys of the Avalonian Cycle of Revealing assists us in learning the mythic language of the Celtic Britons through the exploration of the lunar mysteries and their corresponding herbal energetics. Taken together, these are powerful tools to help us establish meaningful relationships with the goddesses revered in the Avalonian Tradition in a way that also results in spiritual insight and self-understanding.

The more we manifest our authentic selves and become the person we were born to be, the more the work we do and energy we hold reflect our innate divinity, that part of us that is and has always been connected to Source. Our gifts, our goals, and our dreams have purpose. When we live authentically and use our inner and outer resources in service to others, we not only co-create the world in accordance with the greater sacred vision, but we teach others that their gifts, goals, and dreams are not just important but vital.

Perhaps all this inward focus may seem overly self-involved, but the truth is that we can change the world by changing ourselves; indeed, we are the only person we can truly change. When we are content rather than resigned, when we come from a place of power rather than fear, when we make choices that are constructive rather than destructive, and when we give ourselves the reserves we need to act effectively in the world, we participate in the co-creation of the new reality coming into being every moment. When we are more authentically ourselves, we can put our gifts to work in service to our community. We empower others to do the same through the example of our lives and through encouraging others to pursue their dreams, take responsibility for their actions, and work to change their inner lives so they can transform what is around them. The more we are who we are meant to be, by using our skills and sharing our gifts, the more we become a clear vessel for the Divine. When we are sovereign and actively reclaiming our priestess selves, the goddesses are able to work in the world through us. What a humbling thought … and a huge responsibility!

There are similarities between the Cauldron of Annwn and the Cauldron of Ceridwen. Both are concerned with prophecy and wisdom, both require great feats of courage and soul challenges to obtain, and both are held in the keeping of women. If the fivefold paradigm of transformation in the Cauldron of Ceridwen informs the Avalonian Cycle of Healing, what can we learn from the Cauldron of Annwn? It is the description of this cauldron being rimmed with pearls that has inspired the Avalonian Cycle of Revealing, a lunar system of inner questing and personal transformation that nests within the overall Cycle of Healing. The Pearl-rimmed Cauldron, then, can be interpreted as symbolic of the annual cycle of moons which provides us with a monthly path of personal practice. This devotional discipline helps us harmonize with the universal tides, brings us closer to actualizing our sovereign and authentic selves, and draws us into an increased relationship with Source—the goddesses as they have revealed themselves to us.

The interplay between the Avalonian Cycle of Healing—which breaks the great cycle into five composite parts—and the Avalonian Cycle of Revealing, which harnesses the cyclic energy from a thirteen-fold lunar perspective, is one of mutual exaltation. The lunar cycle creates a monthly support system which assists in channeling the energies and focusing the intentions of the great inner work accomplished by the Avalonian Cycle of Healing. In this system, each moon has an overall lesson, a corresponding herbal energetic, and reveals an aspect of one of the goddesses of the Avalonian Tradition, all of which work in symphony with the five stations of the Avalonian Cycle of Healing. Aligning with both the solar and lunar energetics, as the wheel of the year turns and the moon does her cyclic dance each month, will ensure that there will always be a guiding energy present to assist in the work of personal transformation.

This very Avalonian philosophy of seeking the ways the greater patterns of the universe can be reflected within us informs this healing system and empowers its effects on all aspects of being—addressing energetic imbalances of the body, mind, and spirit. It does so because it operates on multiple levels at once, crafting a tapestry that builds upon the art of ancient herbal traditions, weaving in the weft of symbolic language transmitted to us through Celtic myth and language, and combining to create a pattern that reinvigorates the deep lunar mysteries at the heart of women's magic and connection to the Divine Feminine.

The moons of the Avalonian Cycle of Revealing are:

1—MOON OF INITIATION: First full moon when sun is in Scorpio; full moon in Taurus

2—MOON OF DISTILLATION: First full moon when sun is in Sagittarius; full moon in Gemini

3—MOON OF TRANSFORMATION: First full moon when sun is in Capricorn; full moon in Cancer

4—MOON OF GERMINATION: First full moon when sun is in Aquarius; full moon in Leo

5—Moon of Evocation: First full moon when sun is in Pisces; full moon in Virgo

6—Moon of Activation: First full moon when sun is in Aries; full moon in Libra

7—Moon of Revelation: First full moon when sun is in Taurus; full moon in Scorpio

8—Moon of Liberation: First full moon when sun is in Gemini; full moon in Sagittarius

9—Moon of Dedication: First full moon when sun is in Cancer; full moon in Capricorn

10—Moon of Consummation: First full moon when sun is in Leo; full moon in Aquarius

11—Moon of Purification: First full moon when sun is in Virgo; full moon in Pisces

12—Moon of Reconciliation: First full moon when sun is in Libra; full moon in Aries

13—Moon of Reflection: Blue Moon: Second full moon in any sun sign

To these thirteen moons we add the Moon of Cycle, a fourteenth lunar energetic occurring during a total lunar eclipse. This total eclipse of the moon provides us with a rare opportunity to experience the moon moving through all of her phases in one night, creating a powerful lunar mirror into which we may look, seeking the meaning of the greater patterns that influence our lives.

The Avalonian Herbal Moons

Each of the thirteen moons plus the Moon of Cycle corresponds with an herbal energy. This herbal energy represents the vibrational tone of the Lunar Key while also serving as an ally on that cycle's path to transformation. These plant allies match each moon's energetic quality while working medicinally on the physical body and vibrationally on the etheric body. The result is a potent combination that assists in affecting change on all levels of being.

It is important to stress that this lunar herbal system is not traditional; it draws upon no historical or literary precedent. Instead, it has been developed over the course of twenty years as part of the modern Avalonian Tradition. All the herbs in this system are native to Britain and boast medicinal, energetic, and folkloric properties in alignment both with the energies of the time of year and the aspect of the goddess tale with which they have become associated.

The Lunar Keys of the Avalonian Cycle of Revealing

Moon	Herb	Botanical Name	Welsh Name	Astrological Reckoning
1. Moon of Initiation	Mugwort	*Artemisia vulgaris*	Y Ganwraidd Lwydd	First full moon when sun is in Scorpio
2. Moon of Distillation	Yarrow	*Achillea millefolium*	Milddail, Llysiau Gwaedlif	First full moon when sun is in Sagittarius
3. Moon of Transformation	Wormwood	*Artemisia absinthium*	Wermwd Lwyd	First full moon when sun is in Capricorn
4. Moon of Germination	Vervain	*Verbena officinalis*	Cas Gangythraul, Llysiau'r Hudol, Y Dderwen Fendigaid	First full moon when sun is in Aquarius
5. Moon of Evocation	Broom	*Cytisus scoparius*	Banadle (N. Wales); Banadlen (S. Wales)	First full moon when sun is in Pisces
6. Moon of Activation	Meadowsweet	*Filpendula ulmaria*	Llys y Forwyn	First full moon when sun is in Aries
7. Moon of Revelation	Nettle	*Urtica dioica*	Ddynhaden	First full moon when sun is in Taurus

Moon	Herb	Botanical Name	Welsh Name	Astrological Reckoning
8. Moon of Liberation	Red Clover	*Trifolium pratense*	Marchfeillionen	First full moon when sun is in Gemini
9. Moon of Dedication	Burdock	*Arctium lappa*	Y Cyngaw	First full moon when sun is in Cancer
10. Moon of Consummation	Dandelion	*Taraxacum officinale*	Dant y Llew	First full moon when sun is in Leo
11. Moon of Purification	Wild Thyme	*Thymus serpyllum*	Grywlys Gwyllt	First full moon when sun is in Virgo
12. Moon of Reconciliation	Motherwort	*Leonurus cardiaca*	Llys y Fam	First full moon when sun is in Libra
13. Moon of Reflection	Woad	*Isatis tinctoria*	Glasddu, Glaslys, Gweddlys	True Blue Moon: Second full moon in any sun sign
14. Moon of Cycle	Queen Anne's Lace	*Daucus carota*	Moronwyn, Nyth yr Aderyn	Total lunar eclipse

Over time, working with these herbs each month aids in creating connections with the Ladies of Avalon, assists in gaining insights from the lessons found in each of their stories, and helps to serve as doorways into the aspects of the Self upon which the mirror of the moon shines during each lunar cycle.

Honoring the Goddesses of Wales

Each of the five Welsh goddesses honored in the Avalonian Tradition have particular times associated with them during the cycle of the sun and the cycle of the moon; these are times when their energies are the most accessible. The herbal moons of the Cycle of Revealing are in energetic alignment with these goddess times, and following the monthly discipline outlined in this book will not only facilitate building connections with the ladies of Avalon, it can also serve as a guide for directing one's personal inner work throughout the year.

In the Avalonian Tradition, the five goddesses we work with are divided into two energetic groups. The Cycle Goddesses—Ceridwen, Blodeuwedd, and Rhiannon—make up the bulk of the external wheel of the year, and each hold four moons in their care. The Polarity Goddesses, Arianrhod and Branwen, represent the active and passive energetics of the cycle respectively. Branwen is the still, quiet center, and hers is the thirteenth or true Blue Moon (here defined as the second full moon occurring while the sun is in the same sign), while Arianrhod is the spark which turns the whole of the cycle itself, and holds Sovereignty over the figurative fourteenth moon, the total lunar eclipse, called the Moon of Cycle in this system.

While the times of the Cycle Goddesses are more or less fixed in the cycle, those of the Polarity Goddesses are quite mutable; indeed, there may be years when they are not represented in the cycle of the moons at all. For example, the true Blue Moon only occurs once every two and a half or three years, while on the opposite extreme, a total lunar eclipse may occur multiple times in a year, or, like the Blue Moon, not at all.

Here, then, is a list of the moons of the Avalonian Cycle of Revealing, with their herbal correspondences and their relationship to the myths of the Welsh goddesses honored in the Avalonian Tradition. An image of the cycle in its entirety appears on page 53.

Time of Ceridwen
Mythic Source—"The Tale of Gwion Bach," from *Ystoria Taliesin*

1—MOON OF INITIATION
HERB: Mugwort (*Artemisia vulgaris*)

MOON: First full moon when sun is in Scorpio; full moon in
Taurus

MYTHIC PORTION: Ceridwen gathers components to create
brew of wisdom for her son, Morfran.

2—MOON OF DISTILLATION

HERB: Yarrow (*Achillea millefolium*)

MOON: First full moon when sun is in Sagittarius; full moon in
Gemini

MYTHIC PORTION: Ceridwen sets Gwion Bach to tending
the cauldron for a year and a day. He takes the three drops
meant for Morfran for himself.

3—MOON OF TRANSFORMATION

HERB: Wormwood (*Artemisia absinthium*)

MOON: First full moon when sun is in Capricorn; full moon in
Cancer

MYTHIC PORTION: Ceridwen discovers what has happened
and chases Gwion through elemental animal transformations until she consumes him in the form of a piece of grain.

4—MOON OF GERMINATION

HERB: Vervain (*Verbena officinalis*)

MOON: First full moon when sun is in Aquarius; full moon in
Leo

MYTHIC PORTION: After spending nine moons in Ceridwen's
womb, Gwion is reborn as Taliesin—the fully realized Shining
Brow. She places him in a coracle and casts him out into the
waters. He is later found in a salmon weir by a Welsh prince.

Time of Blodeuwedd

Mythic Source—"Math, Son of Mathonwy," the Fourth Branch of *Y
Mabinogi*

5—Moon of Evocation

Herb: Broom (*Cytisus scoparius*)

Moon: First full moon when sun is in Pisces; full moon in Virgo

Mythic Portion: When Arianrhod prohibits her son, Lleu, from marrying a woman of any race on the Earth, Blodeuwedd is "created" from nine flowers by Math and Gwydion.

6—Moon of Activation

Herb: Meadowsweet (*Filpendula ulmaria*)

Moon: First full moon when sun is in Aries; full moon in Libra

Mythic Portion: Blodeuwedd is wed to Lleu, and he comes into his own, ruling over lands granted by Math.

7—Moon of Revelation

Herb: Nettle (*Urtica dioica*)

Moon: First full moon when sun is in Taurus; full moon in Scorpio

Mythic Portion: Blodeuwedd falls in love with Gronw Pebyr and chooses him over Lleu.

8—Moon of Liberation

Herb: Red Clover (*Trifolium pretense*)

Moon: First full moon when sun is in Gemini; full moon in Sagittarius

Mythic Portion: Blodeuwedd is pursued by Gwydion as Lleu retakes his kingdom, and she is transformed into an owl.

Time of Rhiannon

Mythic Sources—"Pwyll, Prince of Dyfed," First Branch of *Y Mabinogi*; "Manawyddan, son of Llyr," Third Branch of *Y Mabinogi*.

9—Moon of Dedication

Herb: Burdock (*Arctium lappa*)

Moon: First full moon when sun is in Cancer; full moon in Capricorn

Mythic Portion: Rhiannon appears from the Otherworld on her white mare and is pursued by Pwyll, who is unable to catch up with her until he asks her to stop.

10—Moon of Consummation

Herb: Dandelion (*Taraxacum officinale*)

Moon: First full moon when sun is in Leo; full moon in Aquarius

Mythic Portion: After several challenges overcome by her cleverness and quick wit, Rhiannon marries Pwyll, her choice of husband.

11—Moon of Purification

Herb: Wild Thyme (*Thymus serpyllum*)

Moon: First full moon when sun is in Virgo; full moon in Pisces

Mythic Portion: Rhiannon's newborn son disappears; she is betrayed by her women and punished unjustly.

12—Moon of Reconciliation

Herb: Motherwort (*Leonurus cardiaca*)

Moon: First full moon when sun is in Libra; full moon in Aries

Mythic Portion: Rhiannon is reunited with her lost son, rejoins her husband, and is restored to her queenship.

Time of Branwen

Mythic Source—"Branwen, Daughter of Llyr," Second Branch of *Y Mabinogi*

13—Moon of Reflection

Herb: Woad (*Isatis tinctorial*)

Moon: True Blue Moon—second full moon in any sun sign

Mythic Portion: The whole of the tale of Branwen, sister of the king of Britain, whose mistreatment at the hands of her husband, the king of Ireland, catalyzes a devastating war between the two nations.

Time of Arianrhod

Mythic Source—"Math, Son of Mathonwy," Fourth Branch of *Y Mabinogi*

14—Moon of Cycle

Herb: Queen Anne's lace (*Daucus carota*)

Moon: Total lunar eclipse

Mythic Portion: The whole of the tale of Arianrhod, lady of her own island. Publicly humiliated by being made to undergo a virginity test that results in her giving birth to two sons, Arianrhod refuses to have anything to do with motherhood. She lays three destinies upon her second son, which her brother Gwydion helps him overcome with his magic.

––––––––––

It is important to note that when we speak of these moons we are talking about an entire lunar month, from the moment the moon enters into the full moon phase, to the moment before the next full moon phase. Similarly, the goddess times run from the moment the moon is full in the first month of her four moons (or her single moon as in the case of Branwen and Arianrhod) until the moment just before the moon of the next goddess comes into fullness. There is never, therefore, a time when there is no goddess in ascendance or when an herbal energetic is not active; one energy flows seamlessly into the next.

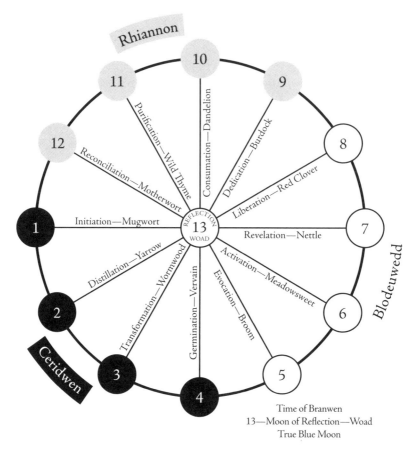

Figure 1

Time of Branwen
13—Moon of Reflection—Woad
True Blue Moon

Time of Arianrhod
14—Moon of Cycle—Queen Anne's Lace
(Overlays any Moon that is a Total Lunar Eclipse)

The Cycle Within the Cycle

A transformational way to work with the interlocking processes of the Cycle of Healing and the Cycle of Revealing is to consider the ways in which each cycle contains the seeds of the other within itself. The Cycle of Revealing breaks the year up into either twelve or thirteen lunar months depending upon the presence of a Blue Moon in that year. The Cycle of Healing takes that same year and breaks it up into a five-fold system of stations which correspond to the four Celtic fire festivals and are centered around the energies of Integration which are the whole of the cycle, not fixed to any given time. Overlaying these two systems upon each other results in an overlap of energies as each of the five stations of the Cycle of Healing also corresponds with one of the moons of the Cycle of Revealing:

Station	Holy Day	Moon
Station of Descent	Calan Gaeaf	Moon 1—Moon of Initiation
Station of Confrontation	Gwyl Mair	Moon 4—Moon of Germination
Station of Emergence	Calan Haf	Moon 7—Moon of Revelation
Station of Resolution	Gwyl Awst	Moon 10—Moon of Consummation
Station of Integration	No Set Holy Day	Moon 13—Moon of Reflection

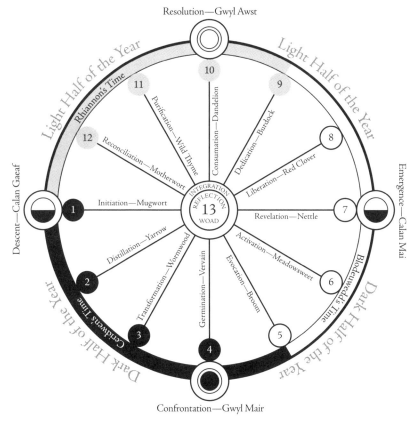

Figure 2

There is no redundancy or conflict in this correspondence; the work of the Station aligns perfectly with the Lunar Key associated with it, as illustrated in the glyph below. Navigating these compound energies will be discussed at length in chapter 4.

This compound cycle glyph above also illustrates several other ways to divide the wheel of the year. If we divide the year horizontally into halves, we can see the dark and light halves of the year; while if we divide the year vertically, the waning and waxing halves become evident. (Figures 3 and 4.)

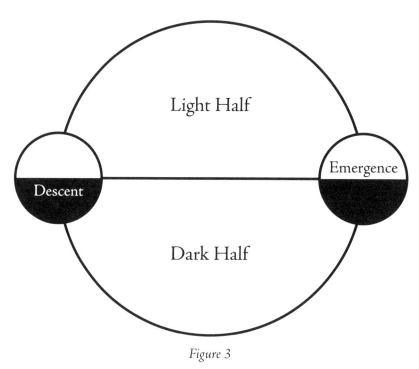

Figure 3

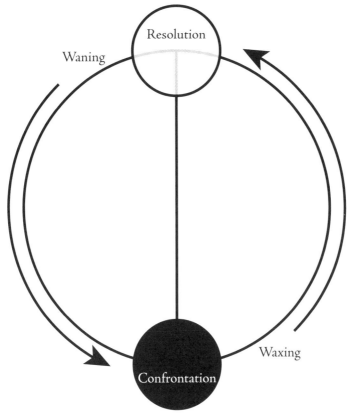

Figure 4

Dividing the year into threes permits us to see the overlay of the Avalonian Cycle Goddesses onto the twelve moons of the standard year; each of the three goddesses has four moons in her purview:

TIME OF CERIDWEN: Moons One–Four

TIME OF BLODEUWEDD: Moons Five–Eight

TIME OF RHIANNON: Moons Nine–Twelve

The Polarity Goddesses, as discussed above, are represented by the two moons that are less fixed, and so are outside of the division of the year. These moons are:

TIME OF BRANWEN: True Blue Moon—Moon of Reflection/Moon Thirteen

TIME OF ARIANRHOD: Total lunar eclipse—Moon of Cycle

As true Blue Moons only occur every two and a half or three years, the Moon of Reflection is not always present, but when it is, it inserts itself into the Cycle of Revealing wherever there is a second full moon in a sun sign, thereby adding a thirteenth moon to the year. For example, if one year there are two full moons that occur while the sun is in Gemini, the first of the two would be Moon Eight—the Moon of Liberation, and the second would be Moon Thirteen—the Moon of Reflection. The very next full moon, occurring while the sun is in Cancer, would be Moon Nine—the Moon of Dedication.

The Moon of Cycle, however, does not add a moon to the year, but instead, overlays itself onto any full moon that experiences a Total lunar eclipse; the energies of Arianrhod and the Moon of Cycle in essence overtake and augment a moon from whichever goddess would otherwise have been presiding over it. For example, if there was a total eclipse during Moon Nine—the Moon of Dedication—it would become the Moon of Cycle, and Arianrhod would take energetic precedent over Rhiannon for this month. Now, every Moon of Cycle is going to have a slightly different energy depending upon what other moon it overlays; the energy of the natural moon is modified by the lessons of the Moon of Cycle, so that when reflecting upon our inner patterns and the places we need to learn deep lessons, which is the core energetic of the moon of cycle, we should focus on the lessons of the overlain moon, examining our work in the context of the natural moon. This will be examined in greater detail in chapter 9.

Each of the moons in the Cycle of Revealing represents a specific energy on our path to wholeness, encapsulated in the energetics of its corresponding herb as well its associated portion of the presiding goddess's story. Within each of these moons, representing an entire lunar month, is also an iteration of the Cycle of Healing with its stations and goddess correspondences, aligning with the main phases of the moon:

Station	Moon Phase	Goddess Correspondence
Station of Descent	Third Quarter	Rhiannon
Station of Confrontation	Dark Moon	Ceridwen
Station of Emergence	First Quarter	Blodeuwedd
Station of Resolution	Full Moon	Arianrhod
Station of Integration	Sovereign Moon	Branwen

We can harness the work of the Cycle of Healing throughout the lunar month by using the tools of the five stations in alignment with the waxing and waning of the moon phases (Figure 5). Doing so brings us insight into the issue which is being examined through the filter of the energy of the current moon in the Cycle of Revealing. Using the smaller cycle (the Cycle of Healing through the phases of the moon) within the context of the larger cycle (the Cycle of Healing through the seasons of the year), which is concurrently broken down into the Lunar Keys of the Cycle of Revealing, provides us with a powerful system for self-examination, personal growth, and inner understanding.

Self-Reflective Questions for the Phases of the Moon

It can be helpful to guide our inner work by periodically examining the aspect of Self being focused on through the filter of the moon phase energetics. When considering the aspect of the Self that you are working on right now—either a sovereign aspect you wish to bring into greater manifestation or a shadow aspect you wish to heal and reclaim—what insights come up for you when viewed through the energetic filter of each moon phase?

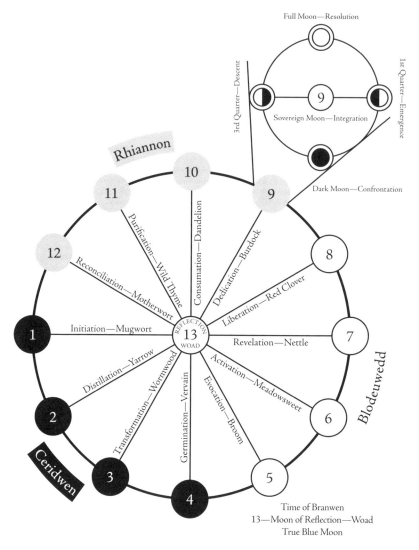

Full Moon—Resolution

3rd Quarter—Descent

1st Quarter—Emergence

9
Sovereign Moon—Integration

Dark Moon—Confrontation

Rhiannon

11   10   9

12

Reconciliation—Motherwort
Purification—Wild Thyme
Consumation—Dandelion
Dedication—Burdock
Liberation—Red Clover

1   Initiation—Mugwort   REFLECTION 13 WOAD   Revelation—Nettle   7

8

Distillation—Yarrow
Transformation—Wormwood
Germination—Vervain
Evocation—Broom
Activation—Meadowsweet

Blodeuwedd

2

Ceridwen

3   4   5   6

Time of Branwen
13—Moon of Reflection—Woad
True Blue Moon

Time of Arianrhod
14—Moon of Cycle—Queen Anne's Lace
(Overlays any Moon that is a Total Lunar Eclipse)

Figure 5

Third Quarter Moon

ELEMENTAL ALIGNMENT: Water

ASPECT OF BEING: Emotional

STATION IN THE AVALONIAN CYCLE OF HEALING: Descent

SELF-REFLECTIVE QUESTIONS FOR THIRD QUARTER
MOON WORK: What emotions does this issue trigger in you? How does it make you feel about yourself? What is your overall emotional state when this issue is triggered? Does this issue stem from or cause an imbalance of emotion—too much or too little? How connected are you to your emotions about this situation? How connected are you to your emotions in general? In what way are these affected by this issue? What insights can you gain by immersing yourself into the emotion of this issue?

Dark Moon

ELEMENTAL ALIGNMENT: Earth

ASPECT OF BEING: Physical

STATION IN THE AVALONIAN CYCLE OF HEALING: Confrontation

SELF-REFLECTIVE QUESTIONS FOR DARK MOON WORK: How does this issue manifest in your life? Can you pinpoint where this issue lives in your body? Where do you most carry its energy? In what ways does this issue affect your health? In what ways does this issue affect your abundance? What things in your environment contribute to this situation? What is your resistance to releasing or manifesting this aspect of yourself?

First Quarter Moon

ELEMENTAL ALIGNMENT: Air

ASPECT OF BEING: Mental

STATION IN THE AVALONIAN CYCLE OF HEALING: Emergence

Self-reflective Questions for First Quarter Moon Work: How are your perspectives influenced by this issue? How does this issue color how you think about yourself? What do you hold to be true about this issue? What do you suppose is actually true about it? What is the most logical way to approach this issue? What is a new way to think about this issue? How clear are you about the truth of this situation? What is a new way of thinking about this situation? How much of what you believe about this situation is something you were told by someone else? How would this situation change if you were to change your mind about it?

Full Moon

Elemental Alignment: Fire

Aspect of Being: Spiritual

Station in the Avalonian Cycle of Healing: Resolution

Self-reflective Questions for Full Moon Work: What stimulates a response about this issue? What form do these responses take? What are your immediate reactions to this issue when it is stimulated? How does this issue affect your energy? Is this a situation that saps your energy or leaves you with an abundance of energy? Does this situation prevent you from an action, or cause you to act? When you do act, do you regret that action at a later time? Does this issue stem from or cause an imbalance of will? Too much or too little? What actions can you take in your life to correct this issue? How would resolving this issue affect what you are able to do?

Working the Lunar Cycle

What follows is a way to approach the work of personal evolution and spiritual transformation from the perspective of the Avalonian Tradition, particularly as it concerns coming into alignment with the cycles of nature, building discernment, and learning to trust our inner wisdom. I like to refer to the entirety of the tradition as the loom upon which we weave our way to wholeness; what we create and the patterns we express are completely up to us, in accordance with our will and as an expression of our personal Sovereignty. The process outlined here is not meant to be constraining or inflexible; it is offered as a way to embrace a discipline using a structure follows the natural tides as a way of staying on track with our inner work. It's therefore possible to jump into the work at any time; there is no need to wait for the "beginning" of any cycle. It also accommodates the natural ebb and flow around personal work. We must remember to give ourselves permission to take time off to integrate what we have learned, adjust to the new energies we have opened, and acclimate to the changes we have made in our life. It is particularly important for us to honor where we are in our process and not punish ourselves for needing to take a break. This work is intense and sometimes life gets very full. After we acknowledge and honor this reality without judgment, we can go back to the work when we are ready.

The most important thing to understand about this template is that it harnesses the Cycle of Healing as it reveals itself through the year (the cycle of the sun) as well as how it unfolds each month (the cycle of the moon). The Cycle of Revealing connects these two iterations of theCycle of Healing; it is the string of pearls that encompasses the circuit of the year from a lunar perspective. What follows is an example of what working with these integrated cycles can look like. (Also refer to Figure 6 on the next page.)

We consider the full moon to be the moment that begins the new cycle: completely revealed, totally illuminated, and openly embodying

Monthly Guide to Daily Work for Each of the Lunar Keys

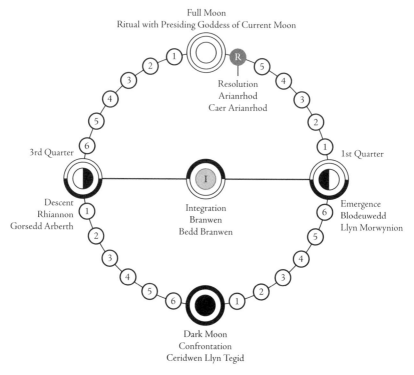

Key

Days 1–3: Process insights from previous Moon Phase and Station (For example, through meditation and doorway work.)*

Days 4–6: Immerse in energy for forthcoming Moon Phase and Station (For example, through trance postures and scrying.)*

Full Moon: Ritual Work with Presiding Goddess of current Moon (For example, using Avalonian Solitary Ritual.)*

Third Quarter: Engage in Station of Descent Work (Immram to connect with Rhiannon.)

Dark Moon: Engage in Station of Confrontation Work (Immram to connect with Ceridwen.)

First Quarter: Engage in Station of Emergence Work (Immram to connect with Blodeuwedd.)

R: Engage in Station of Resolution Work (Immram to connect with Arianrhod.)

I: Engage in Station of Integration Work (Immram to connect with Branwen; this can occur at any point in the month.)

*These tools are presented in detail in "Avalon Within"

Figure 6

the energy of the month. According to Caesar, the Celts of Gaul considered the setting of the sun to mark the ending of one day and the beginning of the next. We do not know for sure which lunar phase was considered to be the start of a new month for the Celts; however, since the full moon rises as the sun is setting and is a very clear and visible marker, this energetically feels like a good place to consider the beginning. And so it is at the full moon that those who follow the Avalonian Tradition do a working to connect with the goddess who presides over the current moon. For our example we'll use Moon Nine, the Moon of Dedication, occurring during the time of Rhiannon.

After meditating on the section of Rhiannon's story that corresponds with the Moon of Dedication (see chapter 7) and considering its lessons in the context of our own spiritual journey, we perform a full moon ritual to honor and connect with Rhiannon in order to seek out the wisdom and counsel of this goddess. The solitary ritual outlined in *Avalon Within* is ideal for making this connection. The guidance we obtain can come to us in several ways: we may see a symbol, hear words spoken, recall a memory, receive a vision, experience a shift of energy, or come into a place of knowing that has no direct sense associated with it. However it unfolds, this information is the seed of the work for the month to come, the thread that will be followed around the energetic loom formed by the phases of the moon.

Using tools such as the doorway, scrying, trance postures, and immrama to sacred sites on the island of Avalon (all of which are detailed in *Avalon Within*, although we will discuss a different iteration of the immram journey later in this chapter) the information received at the full moon is examined nightly as the moon cycles down into the third quarter, the waning half-moon aligned with the Station of Descent in the Cycle of Healing. At this time, the insights gained from the work between the full moon and the third quarter are brought in immram to Rhiannon, the goddess who holds energetic correspondence to the Station of Descent, to examine through the filter of the energies of

Descent. New symbols, visions, and working goals may be presented to us at this time, setting up the work between the third quarter and the dark moon, when the insights gained from these internal inquiries are brought before Ceridwen to be examined through the filter of the Station of Confrontation.

As polar opposite of the full moon, the dark moon is a time when we look into the deep mirror of our shadow and seek out the lesson in the challenge presented by the energies of the current moon cycle—again in our example, the Moon of Dedication. From this point, the lunar energies begin to wax once more, and using our tools, we unpack the insights received in our work with Ceridwen, until we reach the first quarter moon, the waxing half-moon associated with the Station of Emergence. At this time, we bring our work before Blodeuwedd to examine them from the perspective of Emergence and receive insights on how to affect the change we are called to manifest.

We work on these insights and any other symbols or visions we have received around them until we reach the night before the full moon to work with the energies of the Station of Resolution, at which point they are brought before Arianrhod. The full moon is properly the moon phase associated with the Station of Resolution, but as we will work with the goddess associated with next moon in the Cycle of Revealing at the full moon, we connect with Arianrhod the night before. This permits us to harness the insights of Resolution and build a relationship with Arianrhod while also honoring the goddess that presides over the next moon in accordance with the Cycle of Revealing.

The energies of the Station of Integration are not associated with any particular time in the cycle, and so we can bring our work before Branwen at any time during the month, particularly when we need to recenter ourselves, take a step back in order to look at the big picture of our process, and regain the perspective that comes with spending time at rest. Integration helps us to incorporate the insights we have received and changes we have made. Some women like to do the work of Integration on the night after the dark moon as a counterbalance to working with Arianrhod and the energies of Resolution on the night before the full moon. This is a good practice to adopt if you find yourself forgetting to take the time to Integrate or aren't feeling strongly drawn to do so internally. If you do choose to work with Branwen on the night after the dark moon, do so with the understanding that this isn't a proscribed practice or direct energetic correspondence, simply a matter of choice. It is also important to keep in mind that you can choose to work with the energies of Integration more than once a lunar cycle if you feel so drawn.

Coming around again to the full moon, we return to work with the goddess who presides over the next lunar cycle; in keeping with our example, the next night would begin the Moon of Consummation, which is the second moon in the time of Rhiannon. We go to the goddess once more with the insights, shifts, and changes we have set into motion when we examined the issue of focus from the last month through the Cycle of Healing based on the work she gave us at the last moon. At the present moon, we ask for the next step in our journey, and, open to her guidance, we start the process again, taking our work through the Cycle of Healing, but this time through the filter of the energies of Consummation.

Perhaps this entire process feels overly complicated or constraining; that is not its intention. Having a focus for every moon phase each month, and suggested work for the nights in between, helps us to build a consistent and dedicated practice. When we can determine exactly where we are in the cycle of the year and the cycle of the month, we can also identify the work we can be doing that will help us to align our personal work with the natural energetic tides around us.

The chart that follows gives a key to the work of focus for each of the moons of the Avalonian Cycle of Revealing, broken down into the composite moon phases corresponding with the Avalonian Cycle of Healing. More specific information is given for eaach of the Lunar Keys in part two of this book.

Full Moon	3rd Quarter Moon Descent Rhiannon Gorsedd Arberth	Dark Moon Confrontation Ceridwen Llyn Tegid	1st Quarter Moon Emergence Blodeuwedd Llyn Morwynion	Night Before Full Moon Resolution Arianrhod Caer Arianrhod	Monthly, Any Time Integration Branwen Bedd Branwen
Moon 1— Initiation Ceridwen Llyn Tegid *Holy Day: Calan Gaeaf Station of Descent*	Work of Initiation through the Emotional body: Attachments, hopes, fears	Work of Initiation in the Physical plane: Manifestation, embodiment	Work of Initiation through the Mental body: Perspectives, understandings	Work of Initiation through the Energy body: Actions, expressions of will	Work of Initiation through the Spiritual body: The big picture, soul purpose
Moon 2— Distillation Ceridwen Llyn Tegid	*Work of Distillation through the Emotional body: Attachments, hopes, fears*	*Work of Distillation in the Physical plane: Manifestation, embodiment*	Work of Distillation through the Mental body: Perspectives, understandings	Work of Distillation through the Energy body: Actions, expressions of will	Work of Distillation through the Spiritual body: The big picture, soul purpose
Moon 3— Transformation Ceridwen Llyn Tegid	Work of Transformation through the Emotional body: Attachments, hopes, fears	Work of Transformation in the Physical plane: Manifestation, embodiment.	Work of Transformation through the Mental body: Perspectives, understandings	Work of Transformation through the Energy body: Actions, expressions of will	Work of Transformation through the Spiritual body: The big picture, soul purpose

	Emotional body	Physical plane	Mental body	Energy body	Spiritual body
Moon 4—Germination Ceridwen Llyn Tegid *Holy Day: Gwyl Mair Station of Confrontation*	Work of Germination through the Emotional body: Attachments, hopes, fears	Work of Germination in the Physical plane: Manifestation, embodiment	Work of Germination through the Mental body: Perspectives, understandings	Work of Germination through the Energy body: Actions, expressions of will	Work of Germination through the Spiritual body: The big picture, soul purpose
Moon 5—Evocation Blodeuwedd Llyn Morwynion	Work of Evocation through the Emotional body: Attachments, hopes, fears	Work of Evocation in the Physical plane: Manifestation, embodiment	Work of Evocation through the Mental body: Perspectives, understandings	Work of Evocation through the Energy body: Actions, expressions of will	Work of Evocation through the Spiritual body: The big picture, soul purpose
Moon 6—Activation Blodeuwedd Llyn Morwynion	Work of Activation through the Emotional body: Attachments, hopes, fears	Work of Activation in the Physical plane: Manifestation, embodiment	Work of Activation through the Mental body: Perspectives, understandings	Work of Activation through the Energy body: Actions, expressions of will	Work of Activation through the Spiritual body: The big picture, soul purpose
Moon 7—Revelation Blodeuwedd Llyn Morwynion *Holy Day: Calan Haf Station of Emergence*	Work of Revelation through the Emotional body: Attachments, hopes, fears	Work of Revelation in the Physical plane: Manifestation, embodiment	Work of Revelation through the Mental body: Perspectives, understandings	Work of Revelation through the Energy body: Actions, expressions of will	Work of Revelation through the Spiritual body: The big picture, soul purpose

Full Moon	3rd Quarter Moon Descent Rhiannon Gorsedd Arberth	Dark Moon Confrontation Ceridwen Llyn Tegid	1st Quarter Moon Emergence Blodeuwedd Llyn Morwynion	Night Before Full Moon Resolution Arianrhod Caer Arianrhod	Monthly, Any Time Integration Branwen Bedd Branwen
Moon 8— Liberation Blodeuwedd Llyn Morwynion	Work of Liberation through the Emotional body: Attachments, hopes, fears	Work of Liberation in the Physical plane: Manifestation, embodiment	Work of Liberation through the Mental body: Perspectives, understandings	Work of Liberation through the Energy body: Actions, expressions of will	Work of Liberation through the Spiritual body: The big picture, soul purpose
Moon 9— Dedication Rhiannon Gorsedd Arberth	Work of Dedication through the Emotional body: Attachments, hopes, fears	Work of Dedication in the Physical plane: Manifestation, embodiment	Work of Dedication through the Mental body: Perspectives, understandings	Work of Dedication through the Energy body: Actions, expressions of will	Work of Dedication through the Spiritual body: The big picture, soul purpose
Moon 10— Consummation Rhiannon Gorsedd Arberth *Holy Day:* *Gwyl Awst* *Station of* *Resolution*	Work of Consummation through the Emotional body: Attachments, hopes, fears	Work of Consummation in the Physical plane: Manifestation, embodiment	Work of Consummation through the Mental body: Perspectives, understandings	Work of Consummation through the Energy body: Actions, expressions of will	Work of Consummation through the Spiritual body: The big picture, soul purpose

	Emotional body	Physical plane	Mental body	Energy body	Spiritual body
Moon 11—Purification Rhiannon Gorsedd Arberth	Work of Purification through the Emotional body: Attachments, hopes, fears	Work of Purification in the Physical plane: Manifestation, embodiment	Work of Purification through the Mental body: Perspectives, understandings	Work of Purification through the Energy body: Actions, expressions of will	Work of Purification through the Spiritual body: The big picture, soul purpose
Moon 12—Reconciliation Rhiannon Gorsedd Arberth	Work of Reconciliation through the Emotional body: Attachments, hopes, fears	Work of Reconciliation in the Physical plane: Manifestation, embodiment	Work of Reconciliation through the Mental body: Perspectives, understandings	Work of Reconciliation through the Energy body: Actions, expressions of will	Work of Reconciliation through the Spiritual body: The big picture, soul purpose
Moon 13—Reflection Blue Moon Branwen Bedd Branwen *Station of Integration*	Work of Reflection through the Emotional body: Attachments, hopes, fears	Work of Reflection in the Physical plane: Manifestation, embodiment	Work of Reflection through the Mental body: Perspectives, understandings	Work of Reflection through the Energy body: Actions, expressions of will	Work of Reflection through the Spiritual body: The big picture, soul purpose
Moon 14—Moon of Cycle Total Lunar Eclipse Ariarnhod Caer Arianrhod	Work of Soul Patterns and Lessons through the Emotional body: Attachments, hopes, fears	Work of Soul Patterns and Lessons in the Physical plane: Manifestation, embodiment	Work of Soul Patterns and Lessons through the Mental body: Perspectives, understandings	Work of Soul Patterns and Lessons through the Energy body: Actions, expressions of will	Work of Soul Patterns and Lessons through the Spiritual body: The big picture, soul purpose

Building Personal Relationships with the Divine

Consistent inner work brings the greatest insights and deepest changes. Harnessing the energies of the Cycle of Healing throughout the month provides a process that will also assist in building relationships with the goddesses Rhiannon, Ceridwen, Blodeuwedd, Arianrhod, and Branwen. In addition to catalyzing our personal work, engaging in the devotional practices further elaborated upon in part two of this book (as well as those discussed in greater detail in *Avalon Within*) helps us forge respectful and reverent connections with these ancient and powerful deities.

As part of establishing and developing authentic relationships with these divinities, it is a beautiful act of ongoing devotion to create either a single shrine to all of the Avalonian goddesses, or else create five separate spaces dedicated to each of them individually. A shrine, unlike a working altar for ritual, is a place where we can spend time in daily meditation, light a candle in support of the intention of our work, place offerings to honor the goddesses (things like apples, stones, feathers, mead, and bread are examples of types of offerings), and generally engage in mindfulness of practice with a visual reminder of the presence of the sacred in our everyday lives.

While we can make these shrines as large or small as we desire or have the space for, they need not be an elaborate undertaking. While niches filled with devotional statuary and beautiful images of the goddesses, their associated animals, and photos of their sacred sites are wonderful, a simple symbol and a heartfelt self-crafted representation is just as powerful … or perhaps even more so. As with all things, our intention counts for so much, and it is not the external manifestation of our devotion which helps us to build that bridge of relationship with these goddesses. It is the time spent in inner work, in study and contemplation of their myths, and the effort expended to connect with them through immrama and ritual that is the true measure of our devotion.

Beyond the Ninth Wave

In Celtic traditions, water has a very strong association with the Otherworld, serving as a boundary between the worlds, as well as a portal from one world to the next. When making a journey across the water, the ninth wave from the shore marks the boundary between known and unknown territory, and it is by crossing over the ninth wave that one can reach the islands of the Otherworld.

In Irish literary tradition, tales which feature journeys to the Otherworld over water are collectively known as immrama (singular *immram*), and although there are these types of tales in Welsh tradition, there is no corresponding term in Welsh. Because of this, in the Avalonian Tradition we have adopted the Irish term immrama to refer a specific type of inner journey that we perform to visit the Island of Avalon. When we seek to visit other islands in the Welsh Otherworld, we set up our immrama to take us over the sea, rather than across Avalon's lake.

A third variation of this journey is called the Ninth Wave immram; it is a very useful tool in general but is especially helpful to use when on pilgrimage to sacred sites. What makes it different is not only can we use this journey to visit places in the Otherworld, we can set it up so that we can journey anywhere through different layers of time, stopping at specific points to explore a landscape in different cultural and temporal contexts. Before beginning the journey work, the waves are set up to hold the energy of different time periods; we can set up any assignations we'd like beforehand, tailoring our work to suit our specific needs in the moment or aligning with particular areas of interest or study.

For example, if we were at Tomen y Mur, the modern-day site of Blodeuwedd and Lleu's court of Mur y Castell, and we wanted to journey to the site as it was during the Celtic Iron Age, we would assign ages to each of the waves and then undergo the journey in order to move back in time by counting back through the waves. When arriving at the time period of interest, we would simply stop the journey there, disembark, and explore the area in that temporal context. When we are done, we can return to the vessel and come back across the waves to the present, or else visit another time period by visualizing ourselves moving forward or backward over the waves as needed. When out in the sacred landscape with pilgrims, I generally set the waves up in the following manner, but as this is a flexible tool, we are able to assign the waves however we wish. What is most important is for us to have set the waves up ahead of time.

First Wave: Present

Second Wave: Pre-Industrial Period

Third Wave: Medieval Period

Fourth Wave: Dark Age

Fifth Wave: Roman Occupation

Sixth Wave: Celtic Iron Age

Seventh Wave: Bronze Age

Eighth Wave: Stone Age

Ninth Wave: Mythological

Beyond the Ninth Wave: The Otherworld

Throughout the course of this book, we will be journeying into the sacred landscapes of each of the goddesses: Llyn Tegid for Ceridwen, Llyn Morwynion for Blodeuwedd, Gorsedd Arberth for Rhiannon, Bedd Branwen for Branwen, and Caer Arianrhod for Arianrhod. As we are not on the sites in person, we will be journeying beyond the Ninth Wave to connect with each of the goddesses in the Otherworld. Once a degree of facility with this technique has been gained, exploring different waves is greatly encouraged.

The journeys presented in this book are specific and quite detailed in their guidance; once good discernment and clarity with this tool has been developed, I highly recommend using the induction and return for the Ninth Wave immram to journey to these sacred sites and connect with each of the goddesses without performing the specific working presented with the journeys in this book. For example, when traveling to Llyn Tegid to meet Ceridwen, the working intention can be set up to meet her on the shores of the lake in order to commune with her and receive her guidance rather than interact with her cauldron as directed in the working presented here.

We can also undertake these Ninth Wave immrama to connect with the goddesses in ritual during the times of their moons (see the Avalonian solitary ritual in *Avalon Within* for guidance) as well as each month during their particular moon phases. What follows is the procedure for embarking upon these journeys; until they are memorized, making an audio recording of someone reading the immram is recommended. (Alternatively, professionally produced downloadable files of these journeys will be available for purchase on my website as well; I know a lot of people are distracted by listening to the sound of their own voice.)

Tool: The Ninth Wave Immram

1. Be in a place and at a time when you are not likely to be disturbed.

2. Use your breath, visualization, and intention to cleanse and center. (See page 91 in chapter 4 for details).

3. Know where you are going, who you are visiting, and what you are seeking from them before you begin. (This will make sense once you have read all of the forthcoming chapters on the goddesses).

4. It is helpful to have looked at images of the site you are going to be visiting beforehand. You might want to print up a few so that you have a visual focus to start you on your journey.

5. When you are ready, perform the Ninth Wave induction below by listening to, or memorizing this working. This is the process

which will take you to the sacred site of the goddess you are currently working with; again, know the who, where, and why before you begin.

6. Next, follow the journey through the sacred landscape you are visiting; these can be found at the end of every goddess chapter.

7. Once you have done all of your work at the site and are ready to return, listen to or memorize the Ninth Wave immram return segment and bring yourself home.

8. As always, be sure to journal your insights and experiences.

Please note: if you are going to use a recording, it is helpful to create a playlist for each journey in your media player to give you a seamless experience. For example, a playlist for the journey to visit Ceridwen at Llyn Tegid would look like this:

1. Ninth Wave Immram Induction

2. Journey to Llyn Tegid

3. Ninth Wave Immram Return

Ninth Wave Immram Induction

Envision yourself standing on a rocky shoreline, looking west over the cold waters of the Atlantic Ocean. The sky is gray and the waters tumultuous; the waves hiss at you as they strike at the shore, over and over again. Match the rhythm of your breath with the rhythm of the tides and feel all resistance to this journey and the work you will be doing simply fall away.

You become aware that to the left of you, glinting and wet on a large stone boulder is a branch with nine cleverly wrought bells in the shape of small apples. You have a sense that you are being awaited, and with confidence you reach down to pick up the silver branch. You begin to shake the branch; nine times you ring it, and with each shake, you feel the bells take on a greater and deeper resonance. After the last shake rings out, you place the branch on the boulder again and fix your eyes on the horizon and wait.

It does not take long for your call to be answered. Moving more quickly than you could ever think a craft of this kind could, an enchanted boat comes into view. Within the space of three heartbeats, it comes to rest on the beach before you, in that place where the waves meet the sand. When you are ready, enter the craft and take the place in the boat that is waiting for you. As soon as you are settled, the boat begins to move again, this time out to sea. Become aware of the waves over which the small craft is sailing, and with your mind focused on your destination, begin counting down the nine waves that, when crested, will see you firmly in the Otherworld.

And so you sail over the first wave.

And now the second. All resistance falling away.

Smoothly you move, without hesitation over the third wave.

And now the fourth. You breathe into this journey, feeling yourself move deeper and deeper in.

Cresting the fifth wave. Feeling clear, feeling present, feeling safe.

Farther and farther away from the shore, you move over the sixth wave. The shore that you departed from is no longer in sight.

And now the seventh wave. Breathing deeply, you feel yourself getting lighter, moving farther.

You are completely surrounded by ocean as you go over the eighth wave.

And finally, the Ninth Wave.

You crest over the Ninth Wave.

And passing over the Ninth Wave, you feel yourself some-place altogether different.

Take three, deep, anchoring breaths. Feel yourself fully centered, fully present, and fully open.

The boat slides up onto a distant shore and comes to a full stop once more.

———————

Work with the goddess at her sacred site; the specific journeys can be found at the end of each goddess chapter. Once you have fully explored the directed journeys and lain the pathway through the mythic realms to connect with each of the goddesses and build relationships with them, you can use this Immram process to meet them in their sacred landscapes to connect with them about your personal work, as with each of the Stations of the Cycle of Healing during their corresponding moon phase each month. When you have completed your work at the sacred sites, and have thanked the goddess for her guidance, use the Ninth Wave Immram Return segment that follows to bring yourself home.

———————

Ninth Wave Immram Return

Take three deep centering breaths. Remember all that you have seen, and received, and committed to in this moment. When you are ready, follow the thread that connects you to the vessel which brought you to this Land Beyond Wave, taking your place in the boat once more, to begin the journey back over the nine waves.

And so you sail over the Ninth Wave.

And now the eighth. Remembering everything you experienced.

It's easy to pass over the seventh wave, releasing any excess energy as you go.

And now you crest over the sixth. You breathe into this journey, feeling yourself moving closer and closer to all that is familiar.

Cresting the fifth wave. Feeling clear, feeling present, feeling safe.

Closer and closer, you can make out the outline of the shore in the distance as you move over the fourth wave.

And now the third wave. Breathing deeply, you feel yourself getting lighter, returning home now ...

The shore where this journey began is so close now.

The whole of the beach where you began this journey is clearly in view as you pass over the second wave.

And finally, the first wave.

You crest over the first wave.

And passing over the first wave, you feel like you are back in familiar territory, with your mind and heart at ease.

The boat pulls up to the shore almost as if by magic, and comes to a full stop once more.

Take three deep, anchoring breaths. Feel yourself fully centered, fully present, and fully open.

And when you are ready, open your eyes ... return to the place that is here, and the time that is now.

Centering and Closing

Once you have returned from the immram, be sure that you are in a place of balance. With your breath and intention, put your hands on the ground and breathe out any excess energies or emotions that may have returned with you and potentially put you in a space of imbalance. If you still feel like you aren't centered and in your body, with your breath and intention visualize a clear and cleansing stream of rich, vital earth energy coming up from the planet that passes through the layers of the ground, moves through the floor, and enters into your energy field. Guided by your breath and intention, the stream of energy moves up through your seat, rises along your spine to revitalize your energy centers, before fountaining up through the top of your head, surrounding and filling your auric body. Continued to cycle the energy up, around, and through you until you find yourself in a place of centered and balanced clarity. As with all workings, be sure to journal your experiences.

Chapter 4

THE LUNAR KEYS

SOME HAVE SAID THAT HERBS are to Avalon what trees are to Druidry, and in today's Avalonian Tradition we have found this system of herbal immersion to be a powerful tool of connection with the energies of the Holy Isle, the lessons of her goddesses, and the corresponding energies within ourselves. This system of herbal moons or Lunar Keys that make up the Avalonian Cycle of Revealing is both a complement to, and a deepening of, the work of the Avalonian Cycle of Healing. Using both cycles concurrently will provide an empowering focus for our journeys into the realms of Avalon and along the pathways of the spirit.

Each herb in this system is connected to a specific month and corresponds energetically with an episode from the myths of the Welsh goddesses honored in the Avalonian Tradition. When we work with the energies of these herbs, they can open us to insights about the goddesses and the lessons presented in their stories. We can also receive assistance in reflecting these energies and insights within. Looking at ourselves and our personal journeys through the filter of these Lunar Keys can provide us with an understanding of where we have come from, a clear view of where we are now, and can help us to form a Sovereignty-centered vision of where it is we would like to go. In short, these thirteen moons can be used as mirrors of our soul which permit us to look at ourselves with new eyes and to bring aspects of ourselves into consciousness that we may never have seen before. Each of these Lunar Keys, therefore, can help the seeker open the door to understanding through three levels of engagement: goddess myth, lunar time, and herbal action.

The Mythic Map for Personal Transformation

An examination of the entire yearly cycle of moons taken as a whole reveals a step-by-step template for growth and transformation, one Lunar Key at a time:

1—The Moon of Initiation

Each new cycle begins with the quest for wisdom. It is here that we set the intention to seek out the treasure that can only be found in the shadowlands of the unconscious Self.

2—The Moon of Distillation

To accomplish this work, we are set to the task of personal contemplation and the development of inner discipline in order to receive the bounty of wisdom which emerges from the self-distillation catalyzed in the cauldron of the soul.

3—The Moon of Transformation

In order to fully integrate the lessons of these new-found wisdoms, we must engage in thorough self-exploration. This allows us to know ourselves well enough to see, with clarity, the ways in which our shadow tendencies manifest through all aspects of our being, and affect all parts of our life:

EARTH: Our physical health, environment, and material abundance.

WATER: Our emotional state, our spiritual lives, and our relationship to the past.

AIR: Our perspectives, assumptions, and our relationship with the future.

FIRE: Our creative resources, how and where we use our energy, and our ability to change.

4—The Moon of Gestation

Having reached the depths of our inner cauldron, the root of the shadow that dwells deep in the unconscious Self, we must surrender ourselves to the cycle of changes. This permits our outmoded ways of being to fall away and makes space for the wisdom we have earned to take root in our soul.

5—The Moon of Evocation

We must bring forth the wisdom we have found into the waxing light. Much like Gwydion and Math were able to call forth the essence of a goddess into physical manifestation, we must also learn how to incorporate the wisdom of the dark time into our lives and how to manifest the physical plane reflection of our higher self-potential.

6—The Moon of Activation

With these insights in place, we must commit ourselves to following a new course, one which is in greater alignment with our vision of personal authenticity. Like the movement of a flower that tracks the path of the sun across the sky, we must fix our sight upon the inner light of sovereignty—allowing nothing to deter us from our purpose.

7—The Moon of Revelation

The greater part of wisdom is coming to know how to live our truth. Once we have found who we are meant to be, it is up to us to make the choices that will allow us to actualize this potential. Sometimes the obstacles in our paths may seem insurmountable, but when we ask to know the way, it will be revealed to us.

8—The Moon of Liberation

Fully embracing one's truth is not without challenge. We may find ourselves taken to task for not conforming to others' expectations, or for daring to pursue our dreams when so many others have resigned themselves to never accomplishing their own. We cannot allow this lack of external support to dissuade us. Instead, we must heed the bardic call of *Y Gwir Yn Erbyn Y Byd*—the Truth Against the World—and commit to living from our center of truth, regardless of the opinions and actions of others. When we do so, our vision is expanded, our sight is sharpened, our actions are empowered, and we gain the wisdom we need in order to fly free.

9—The Moon of Dedication

Once we have claimed the truth of ourselves for ourselves, we are then faced with the trials that often accompany the choice to walking with integrity through our lives. There are many obstacles and distractions that we must navigate to ensure that we are not pulled off course on the journey to self-actualization. We must learn to maintain our focus on who we are, continue to make steady progress toward what we are striving to accomplish, and work to answer the call of the spirit. When we ask for what we need as we travel the path of sovereignty, Source responds in kind.

10—The Moon of Consummation

Remember too that the path within must be reflected in that which is without. The spiritual journey is not meant to take place on the subtler realms alone—it should find its partner in the physical plane as well. It is a powerful thing to be in active co-creation of a life we love, and there is much bounty to celebrate. We must learn to have patience with ourselves as well, should we falter; we must forgive ourselves, learn from our mistakes, and honor our responsibilities.

11—The Moon of Purification

As the cycle turns downward again, our commitment to our growth is challenged; difficulties arise to push our limitations and stretch our understanding. Painful lessons can yield great harvest if they are shouldered with patience, peace, and understanding. It is easy to give in to what is not true—but perseverance and dedication to right action in the face of adversity gives us the strength to see it through.

12—The Moon of Reconciliation

All of our strivings will be rewarded with our hearts desire, but only if we are able to see past our own shortcomings as well as the failings of others. Forgiveness is a powerful healing tool, not because it grants absolution to those who may have harmed us, but because it permits us to set down the emotional burdens that remove us from the sovereign order of our lives. Thus freed from anxiety, we reconnect with the truth of our wholeness, and are ready to enter the Cauldron of Wisdom anew. There's no end, but more room to grow.

13—The Moon of Reflection

The map of the spiritual journey is revealed: The soul becomes manifest on the physical plane. Experiencing wounding will cause our inner

Sovereignty to become imprisoned and isolated. The way back to a place of personal empowerment comes when all parts of the self are in clear communication with each other. When we can allow the inner/unconscious Self to clearly communicate with the outer/conscious self, we can set external change into motion based on internal need. Changes result in transformation, permitting the heart to open so that it may return to a state of conscious connection with Source. This is the work of a lifetime … or we can choose it in the now.

14—The Moon of Cycle

No matter where we are in our work, or how successful we have been in actualizing particular aspects of our Sovereignty, there is always more to be learned about ourselves and always more growing to be done. We will be presented with challenges to our personal power that will facilitate this growth and transformation, bringing us closer to the truth of who and what we are.

Identifying the Lunar Keys

The first thing that is necessary for undertaking this personal discipline, is to work out the dates of each of the Lunar Keys of the Avalonian Cycle of Revealing for the current year. This may at first feel like a daunting process, requiring specialized tables of planetary movements, moon phase calendars, and something that feels suspiciously like math, but it truly is easier than it may sound on the first go round. Being able to determine the dates of the Holy Days, the goddess times, and each of the moons is a powerful and empowering experience, and is outlined here:

1. Using a lunar calendar or ephemeris table for the present year, make a list of the full moon dates and times for the entire year. Be sure that the calendar or table you are using is specific for your

time zone; if you cannot find one, seek out a list that uses GMT and make the necessary conversions for where you live. For example, New York is −5 GMT, and so to get the local time, five hours must be subtracted to the list of times from the GMT list.

2. Be sure to make note of any total lunar eclipses which may be occurring in the year you are working on; this information is included on most lunar calendars. Note that because of the interplay of angles between the sun, the moon, and the Earth, every type of lunar eclipse (total, partial, and penumbral) occurs when the moon is full, while all types of solar eclipses occur (total, partial, annular, and hybrid) when the moon is dark. This is because when there is a dark moon, the moon is conjunct to the sun, which means that both celestial bodies are in the same area of the sky at the same time; they rise and set together, and are therefore in the same sign at the same time. It is this relationship that can result in a solar eclipse when the moon moves between the Earth and the sun, and appears to occlude the solar disk.

Conversely, when the moon is full, the sun and moon are in opposite sections of the sky, making an 180° angle to each other from the perspective of the Earth. On the night of the full moon, the moon rises as the sun sets, and both celestial bodies are in opposition to each other—that is, they are polar opposites or complementary pairings when it comes to their signs. This arrangement is also what leads to a lunar eclipse because the Earth moves between the opposing sun and moon, blocking the light of the sun and causing the planet to cast its shadow upon the surface of its satellite. (For more on lunar eclipses, see chapter 9).

3. The moon moves much more quickly than does the sun, and will pass through the entirety of the zodiacal round once every month, spending about 2.5 days in each sign, whereas it takes the sun an entire year to do the same; it is for this reason that

we talk about the Moons of the Cycle of Revealing in terms of sun sign and not moon sign. It is easier to find out the date of when the moon is going to be full during the time period the sun is in a particular sign than it is to determine *which* of the times the moon is in a particular house it is also a full moon. Remember, too, that the Blue Moon occurs when there are two full moons taking place during the period that the Sun is in a particular sign; when this phenomenon happens (once every 2.5 to 3 years), it is the second full moon that is the Blue Moon, and is Moon Thirteen, the Moon of Reflection.

Time Period	The Sun is in:	The Dark Moon is in:	The Full Moon is in:
Mar 21–Apr 19*	Aries	Aries	Libra
Apr 20–May 20	Taurus	Taurus	Scorpio
May 21–Jun 20	Gemini	Gemini	Sagittarius
Jun 21–Jul 22	Cancer	Cancer	Capricorn
Jul 23–Aug 22	Leo	Leo	Aquarius
Aug 23–Sep 22	Virgo	Virgo	Pisces
Sep 23–Oct 22	Libra	Libra	Aries
Oct 23–Nov 21	Scorpio	Scorpio	Taurus
Nov 22–Dec 21	Sagittarius	Sagittarius	Gemini
Dec 22–Jan 19	Capricorn	Capricorn	Cancer
Jan 20–Feb 18	Aquarius	Aquarius	Leo
Feb 19–Mar 20	Pisces	Pisces	Virgo

* *The beginning and end dates of the signs vary somewhat each year; this is because the run of the signs starts at the moment of the Vernal Equinox—which usually falls on March 20 or 21—and all other dates shift accordingly. To be certain of the dates, it is best to look them up annually in an ephemeris or a reliable online source.*

4. Once you have your list of full moons for the year, have noted any total eclipses or Blue Moons, and determined what house the sun is in for each full moon, you can match up each date on your list with its associated Lunar Key in the Avalonian Cycle of Reveal-

ing. I recommend that you begin with Moon One, identifying the date of Calan Gaeaf, and numbering the rest of the months from there. Once you have done so, double check that you have correctly determined the presence or absence of a Blue Moon or a total lunar eclipse, and indicate the location of Moon Thirteen and/or the Moon of Cycle on your list. Keep in mind that with this process we are overlapping several different calendar systems, so the beginnings of each system's cycle will not line up perfectly: the Gregorian year begins in January, the Celtic year begins at Calan Gaeaf or Samhain, and the astrological year begins at Spring Equinox with Aries.

Calendar Dates	Sun Sign	Lunar Key	Cycle of Revealing Names	Holy Days
Dec 22–Jan 19	Capricorn	Moon 3	Moon of Transformation	
Jan 20–Feb 18	Aquarius	Moon 4	Moon of Germination	Gwyl Mair
Feb 19–Mar 20	Pisces	Moon 5	Moon of Evocation	
Mar 21–Apr 19	Aries	Moon 6	Moon of Activation	
Apr 20–May 20	Taurus	Moon 7	Moon of Revelation	Calan Haf
May 21–Jun 20	Gemini	Moon 8	Moon of Liberation	
Jun 21–July 22	Cancer	Moon 9	Moon of Dedication	
Jul 23–Aug 22	Leo	Moon 10	Moon of Consummation	Gwyl Awst
Aug 23–Sep 22	Libra	Moon 11	Moon of Purification	
Sep 23–Oct 22	Virgo	Moon 12	Moon of Reconciliation	
Oct 23–Nov 21	Scorpio	Moon 1	Moon of Initiation	Calan Gaeaf
Nov 22–Dec 21	Sagittarius	Moon 2	Moon of Distillation	
Blue Moon/ 2nd FM in a Sun Sign		Moon 13	Moon of Reflection	
Total Lunar Eclipse			Moon of Cycle	

You should now have a reference detailing the specific dates and times of the forthcoming herbal moons. You can begin to work the Cycle of Revealing at any point; there is no need for you to wait until

Moon One rolls around again, although there is a progression of energy that moves through each of the Lunar Keys of this system, carrying the seeker from one area of growth and exploration to the next. Aim to begin this discipline at the next full moon, and use the time between now and then to gather all of your materials and familiarize yourself with this process so that you are ready to start when the moon waxes full once more.

The Herbal Connection

Plants and the moon are inextricably bound together; planting and harvesting crops according to moon phase is an ancient practice reflecting an understanding of the cyclic tides of life. Deeply entrenched in folk practice even to the present day, it is easy to imagine that even the earliest agriculturalists planted and harvested their crops in accordance with the phases of the moon. Modern science has studied the effect that the moon has on plants and has discovered that in much the same way it influences the tides of the ocean, the lunar cycle affects both the moisture in the soil as well as the amount of water that seeds and plants absorb; there is a measurable increase of each during the full moon. Leaf growth accelerates during the waxing moon, and slows down when the moon is waning, while the growth of roots exhibits the opposite pattern. Therefore, the time between the dark moon and the full moon is considered best for planting herbs whose aerial parts will be used for medicine making, while those planted during the waning period between the full and the dark moon should be herbs whose roots hold their medicinal qualities.

The harvesting of plants follows a similar pattern. Roots should be harvested on the dark moon in the autumn, once the plant has had the opportunity to go to seed in order to replenish itself; it is at this time that the life-force energy of the plant drops into the roots, so it will be more potent medicinally. The bark from woody plants and trees are best gathered at the third quarter moon; some feel this should happen in the early spring, while others feel that the late fall will cause less weeping of sap from the tree while still obtaining the same medicinal benefit. The aerial parts of a plant should be harvested on or near the full moon, preferably in the morning after the dew has evaporated off, but before the heat of the day causes the plants to wilt, in which case, it is best to wait until early evening to harvest. Generally, it is ideal to harvest leaves for medicine before the plant goes into flower, while flowers should be harvested before they have fully developed and become pollinated. If the whole plant is going to be used for medicine making, it will have the best potency when the flowers have just begun to bloom; but if the flower is not going to be used, harvest before the flower buds begin to appear, but after the leaves have come in.[5]

In much the same way, we can reflect these energies within; we can attend to our outward growth and the manifestation of personal Sovereignty during the light half of the cycle, while attending to our inner needs and seeking the root of our shadow during the cycle's dark half. There is, indeed, a time to sow and a time to reap—and the ancestral wisdoms which guided our agricultural pursuits for millennia can also be applied to personal growth and the soul's process. This is not to say that we need to feel constricted by lunar influences or fall into rote practices which could devolve into superstition. Rather, we seek instead to enter into conscious partnership with these cyclic natural forces, aligning ourselves with the greater pattern in order to harness the shifting turns of the great cycle in order to assist us in moving through our own changes, and to empower us in our own growth.

5. James Green, *The Herbal Medicine-Maker's Handbook: A Home Manual* (Berkeley: Crossing Press, 2000) 54–56.

Working With Plant Allies

Working in concert with plant allies on this quest makes sense in multiple ways. Seeking to be in balance with the green world can assist us in coming into positive relationship with the living land around us. Similarly, using the energetic and healing qualities of these plants can help us come to a place of inner balance. A sense of wholeness arises when we seek healing of body and spirit, both through an alignment with the rhythms of nature around us, as well as through the vibrational properties held by the plants which can help stimulate and support soul growth.

In this present work, we will explore the medicinal and energetic qualities of the herbs the comprise this Avalonian *materia medica,* but intrinsic to these tools for healing is a vitalistic consciousness that is deeply connected to planetary wisdom. Where others might consider plants and trees to simply be resources for us to collect and use as we will, opening ourselves up to work in concert with these beings is a richly satisfying experience that allows us to obtain a deeper connection to the world around us than we might ever have thought possible.

The idea that plants possess consciousness is not a new one, although in recent years science has made some exciting new discoveries about the Green World—including the process through which trees communicate with each other through fungi and underground networks—which validates this long-standing notion. Instead of thinking that there is something supernatural about the belief that humans have had all along based on their experiences of plants and their energies, there is a sense that these are natural and inherent phenomena which we are only just beginning to be able to observe and measure. Whether we call them devas, or nature spirits, or if we simply begin to see plants as living beings having as much right to a place here as we do in this planetary and energetic ecosystem of Earth, learning to enter into relationship with these beings can have an impact on our lives and in our work.

Finding ways to actively engage with plant allies in our daily lives is a powerful way to foster or deepen a relationship with the Green World. Planting gardens, practicing ethical harvesting, learning medicine making, and committing to the study of herbalism are ways that we can raise our consciousness of these beings, and integrate their wisdoms into our spiritual practices and the ways in which we walk upon this Earth.

Working: Communing with Plant Spirits

Plants are more than just tools we use on our journeys to physical wellness and spiritual wholeness; they are living entities with whom we can enter into conscious partnership. Whether we are growing herbs in a garden, caring for plants on our window sill, or seeking out nature spirits in their natural environments, fostering relationships with these Green Allies can yield a bountiful harvest of wisdom. Whether a mighty redwood tree or a sweetly scented lavender bush, what follows is a simple but effective process for establishing and building these relationships.

1. Prepare yourself for the connection by focusing on your breath and using it to bring yourself into a place of clarity and centeredness. As you inhale, gather up any energies that keep you from being clear and present in body, mind, or spirit. As you exhale, release these energies down through your feet and into the Earth below you, where they are received and absorbed. Engage in several cycles of this breath until you have released the energies which no longer serve you. Then, with your breath assisting you, visualize a pool of vibrant and revitalizing earth energy deep within the planet. As you inhale, breathe some of that energy up through the layers of the Earth, up through your feet, up along your spine, and through all of your energy centers to the crown of your head. As you exhale, allow that energy to fountain out from the top of your head, to cascade through and around you, and to fill in all of the places from which you released energy. Engage in

several cycles of this breath until you find yourself in a place of centered clarity and openness. You are now ready to begin.

2. As with any other energetic contact you may seek to make, approach the sacred life force essence of the plant (or the tree, or the fungus) with respect and openness.

3. In this place of openness, stand before or sit beside the plant, and take some time to experience the energy of the plant, just as it is.

4. Introduce yourself as a seeker and ask the plant if they are willing to connect with you. The response may come to you in many ways: you may "hear" a reply, see or feel a shift of energy around the plant, be filled with a sense of welcoming or experience what feels like a wall going up between you. Whatever the response, be sure to wait for it and to honor it.

5. When you are ready, and if you feel welcomed to do so, gently expand your energy field until it makes contact with that of the plant. With your breath, take in several cycles of the plant's energetic essence until you feel like your energy has shifted to match the vibration or energetic signature of the plant.

6. When you feel at one with the plant, take a moment to note how this energetic merger makes you feel: Is there an energy center within you that becomes more activated? Has your emotional state changed? Do you feel more energized or relaxed? Is there somewhere in your physical body that has somehow been affected by this connection?

7. Once you have observed your own changes, you can begin to ask your questions of the plant. Perhaps you'd like to learn something about its vibrational or medicinal qualities; in what ways does it affect physical or emotional healing? Or, you might ask something about its natural habitat: why does the plant grow where it does? What information can it share about the specific location

where it grows? Is there anything you can do to assist the plant or the area where it lives? This might be an especially interesting line of questioning if it grows on your own property or in a natural setting where you'd like to develop an ongoing working relationship with the area. And, finally, you can ask for insights about personal issues of a like energy. Just as the Hermetic Principle of Correspondence teaches us that like energies attract, so can the energies of the Green World act as bridges to obtain understanding of our own inner process. So, if while building a relationship with the spirit of a plant you begin to make connections about a shadow issue you are exploring, or start remembering long forgotten events from your childhood, then there is a good chance that the essence of the plant is aligned with the energies of these connections, and so can be used to help you process through and heal them.

8. Whatever your line of inquiry, when you are done communing with the plant, be sure to express your thanks, discharge and return the energy you've taken in, and leave an offering; charging up some water with energies of gratitude and then pouring it out as a libation is a powerful and welcome way to honor the plant and the spirits of place.

9. As always, journal your insights and experiences.

The Study and Practice of Herbalism

Reclaiming herbs as medicine is a powerful part of women's wisdom, and is a cornerstone of the Avalonian Tradition. There are few things that are more empowering than becoming an active partner in the maintenance and restoration of your health. Engaging in conscious eating, assessing your system's strengths and weaknesses, and choosing to commit to a healing protocol designed to balance your body's systems and bring you to a place of physical wholeness are all key elements to embracing a healthy lifestyle. Medicinal herbs are powerful allies in this process, and have been used to support and encourage the body's ability to heal since the dawn of time. How powerful is it when we recognize the benevolence of the land that provides us with what we need to maintain and regain our health—body, mind, and spirit!

We must, however, be mindful that harnessing the power of plants in this way requires research and respect. Herbalism as a healing modality requires depth of study; it must take into account a person's entire health history, requires an understanding of physiology and metabolic processes, and must consider contraindications with other medicines. If you are interested in working with herbs as a patient, always consult a trained herbalist with credentials you are comfortable with before undertaking any herbal regime, especially for long-standing health issues and those of a potentially serious nature.

The herbal information presented in this book is not meant to be used to address any health concerns. This is very basic information intended to catalyze further study of the medicinal, folkloric, and energetic traditions around each herb. If you are interested in using these or any other herbs as part of a healing procedure, it is important to consult with a well-trained herbalist or naturopath, as there are very many things to take into consideration when it comes to creating herbal protocols.

Certain herbs work synergistically with others to address particular aliments and situations in different parts of the body, so understanding both how herbs work alone (an herbal simple) and as part of a formula is required. Just as every plant is different, so must our approaches to them also differ. Depending on our healing goals, and the vital constituents of the plant in question, how we process an herb for use as medicine varies from plant to plant, and from part to part. Creating salves, ointments, oils, poultices, and washes are some ways to use herbs externally for healing. Tinctures, infusions, decoctions, capsules, boluses, and essences bring the herbal medicines into our bodies in different ways based upon how they can best affect change in the body's systems.

The ability to set dosage is critical, and the importance of this cannot be stressed enough. On the one hand, people erroneously believe that just because something is natural that it is safe; nothing could be further from the truth. Herbs are powerful medicine. Indeed, many of our modern pharmaceuticals are derived from plant sources, which underscores the need for herbal remedies to be treated with proper respect; taking the wrong part of a plant in too great of an amount can prove deadly.

On the other extreme, people who are accustomed to Western medicine's preference for standardized and concentrated dosages sometimes lose their patience with the comparatively gentle effect of herbal remedies, particularly where it concerns long-term, chronic conditions. A general yardstick for gauging the amount of time needed to affect a cure using herbs is that for every year a condition has been present, a month of herbal treatment will be necessary to address it. Patience and compliance are key when it comes to herbal medicines; it is important to follow herbal protocols consistently, and to allow sufficient time for them to take effect before deciding that they aren't working and giving up on the modality altogether.

All of this said, undertaking the study of herbalism is a powerful and empowering pursuit. There are many well-regarded herbal schools where one can engage in training, both in person and from a distance. Established local herbalists may teach classes, run training courses, and even offer apprenticeships which are an especially effective hands-on and traditional teaching model. Certainly, one need not become a practicing herbalist to acquire some herbal skills. Assembling an herbal first-aid kit, and learning how to make teas, tinctures, and salves to help fight colds, heal burns, and induce restful sleep naturally are incredible ways to reclaim some agency around the restoration and maintenance of our personal health.

Again, it is important to stress that a lay herbalist can be comfortable making fire cider to boost immunity, elderberry syrup to help fight the flu, and comfrey salves to treat bee stings. However, one should either consult a professional or else undertake a rigorous course of guided and evaluated study before attempting to treat things like heart conditions, diabetes, and cancer. Herbalism, like its related modalities of aromatherapy and homeopathy, is an excellent adjunct therapy for those working through intense health challenges. Be wary of supposed miracle cures or the well-meaning advice of your friends, and be sure to educate yourself as best as you can before considering switching away from allopathic medicine entirely when addressing potentially life-threatening health concerns—especially without the support of a credentialed alternative healthcare practitioner.

Energetic Healing

There is a model of the manifestation of illness in the physical body which believes that disease has its origin in energetic dis-ease; that is, an imbalance first exists in the subtle body of a person (for example, in their energetic or auric field), and when it is left unattended, it will eventually become manifest in the physical body. This physical expression of imbalanced energy is opportunistic; it will find the weakest point in a person's biological system and use that as the gateway through which it will express itself.

Energetic healing is an effective modality because it can identify areas of weakness, clear energetic blockages, and address imbalances before they manifest in the physical body. Many of the blocks and imbalances we carry with us are unexpressed energies generated by trauma; we can experience trauma mentally, emotionally, physically, environmentally, and even spiritually. Similarly, we can experience healing on all of those levels as well. Some energetic healing practices include: acupuncture and acupressure, reiki, crystal healing, sound therapy, reflexology, Polarity Therapy, Healing Touch, craniosacral therapy, vibrational essences, and so on. Other healing modalities can also have an effect on the energy body, among them are chiropractic, massage, psychotherapy, and medicinal herbalism.

Honoring an active disease process can be empowering when we ask ourselves what it is this situation has to teach us. Chronic issues and ongoing health challenges can illuminate life lessons for us when we see them as opportunities for learning, and indeed can facilitate needed healing on multiple levels. This is different from the kind of spiritual bypassing and toxic perspectives often found in new age and alternative spirituality teachings which engage in subtextual victim blaming by claiming that we call illnesses and challenging life situations to ourselves. No one asks to have cancer; no one invites sexual assault into their lives. The perspective I am championing here is centered on looking at the challenges that we experience in life as opportunities for learning, rather than as punishments for a failure to learn something.

Over the course of this thirteen moon immersion, we will be guided to engage with the herbal healing allies associated with each Lunar Key by creating and using lunar elixirs (vibrational essences potentiated by moonlight) for each of them, in addition to experiencing the energetics of the herbs directly. We are focusing on the vibrational qualities of these herbs because they are safe to work with for the vast majority of people, and we have found their use to be profoundly effective in supporting us through the challenges and triumphs we encounter as we engage in the inner alchemy of the Avalonian Cycle of Revealing.

Once we have completed the work of creating the elixirs associated with each of the Lunar Keys, we will spend time exploring their psychospiritual properties and identifying how their energies interact with our own. When we have worked through a complete turn of the cycle, and have created a full complement of lunar elixirs, we will have gifted ourselves with a set of tools that can be used in support of our spiritual work for years to come, each of which is a personal reflection of our own energetic relationship with cycle.

Exploring Herbal Energetics

There are few things more revelatory than connecting with the energies of the living essence of the planet and the energies of the great mother matrix than through partnering with our plant allies. Working with each herb directly is an effective way to connect with their energies from a physical, emotional, and spiritual perspective.

The following practices give us first-hand experience of how these herbs feel in our energy field, allow us to observe their vibrational actions, and teach us to recognize the connections they help us make between ourselves, our personal process, and the sovereign self we seek to birth. While building relationships with these herbal allies will result in our having excellent tools to support our inner work, the process outlined throughout this book has another benefit as well: it helps us to build discernment as we develop our intuitive abilities, a skill which ultimately teaches us to trust our inner wisdom—a key component in embracing our personal Sovereignty.

Because there are different ways of learning and different forms of knowing, to obtain the most broad-spectrum perspective of these Lunar Keys it is recommended that the exploration progress in this way every month:

> 1ST: INTUITIVE EXPLORATION—Obtain direct personal experience of each herb by working it energetically. Ideally, this would occur several times over a period of days in order to establish a solid connection to the energetics of each herb in order to come to an intuitive understanding of its relationship to the lessons of the goddess with which it is associated, and as well as its relevance to our own personal process.

2ND: SCHOLASTIC RESEARCH—Obtain solid information about the medicinal, energetic, and folkloric uses of each herb from reliable and well-researched sources. Part three of this book includes an Avalonian *materia medica* which discusses each of the fourteen Lunar Keys in some depth in order to get you started on this herbal immersion.

There are several reasons why it is always best to start off our explorations with intuitive work. First, it allows us a clear slate for journeying, so that we can follow the energetic thread of the herb without potentially being influenced by something we may have read beforehand. Second, and most importantly, once we have done the inner work, looking for the scholastic information afterwards can serve to validate our first hand experiences of the herbs as well as any information we may have received, which in turn helps us to build confidence in our abilities as well as our discernment skills.

The more we are able to trust our experiences and the messages we receive, the stronger the voice of the sovereign self becomes. This discernment is critical because as we go deeper into the work, we will begin to touch core shadow issues and the ways they manifest in our lives. When we are processing through these issues, it is vitally important that we are able to differentiate between the voices of our illusions—our fears, our hurts, and our anger—and those of our higher self, our guides, and our goddesses.

When we have lived for too long believing in the lies we have accepted about ourselves—that we are hopelessly flawed, unworthy of love, deserving of suffering, and that we will never be good enough—these self-deprecating voices become the loudest. Learning to be able to hear these voices for what they are, turning down their volume and rejecting their message, helps the often-stilled or much quieter voice of our connected and whole inner wisdom rise to the surface. This is the voice we must learn to hear and to trust. This is the voice of our sovereign self.

Experiencing Herbal Energies

A detailed guide for working with the Lunar Keys accompanies each of the moons of the Cycle of Revealing in part two of this book. It provides a week-by-week timeline for engaging in this energetic immersion using the specific herb for that month. What follows are detailed directions on how to prepare and engage with two approaches for experiencing these herbal energies: direct experience of the herbs, and the creation and use of lunar elixirs.

Working Directly with the Lunar Keys

This exercise illustrates many important principals central to the Avalonian Tradition:

1. It provides us with a model for coming to trust our own perceptions, allowing us to become independent of external sources of information.

2. It helps us to build vibrational associations by experiencing the herbal energies in our bodies and to recognize how we personally perceive these energies within our own energy fields, in accordance with the Hermetic Principles of Vibration and Correspondence.

3. It helps us to identify any elemental or energetic blockages we might have, a key piece of information in our quest to understand the self.

4. It teaches us to engage in the practice of merging, an effective tool for coming to know and understand something.

5. It is a method through which the inner "muscles" of discernment can be flexed and our ability to discriminate between different kinds of energies can be exercised.

The following supplies are necessary for this exercise:

+ A package of self lighting charcoal.

+ A small cast iron cauldron or other such heat resistant vessel to hold the ignited charcoal.

+ One ounce of each of the fourteen herbs of the Cycle of Revealing, organic if possible: mugwort, yarrow, wormwood, vervain, broom, meadowsweet, nettle, red clover, burdock, dandelion, wild thyme, motherwort, woad, and Queen Anne's lace. (You will not be using a full ounce of the herb for this exercize, but can use the rest for making the lunar elixirs, described later on in this work.)

+ A dedicated herbal journal.

Once you have gathered these items, begin the process of connecting with the herbs, one a month, on an intuitive level; do not yet research their energetic properties, folkloric associations, or medicinal uses—that will come later. Instead, focus on the plant or plant matter directly and take the time to get to know the herb physically: what does it look like, smell like, feel like, taste like? (Don't eat it, just place a small amount on the tongue, unless otherwise cautioned.)

If you have access to a living example of the month's plant ally, sit in its presence and introduce yourself to its essence, asking to learn more about it and how to build a relationship with it; detailed guidance for this process appears earlier in this chapter on page 91. If you are working with dried herbs, once you have made these connections, place a pinch of the solitary herb on a lit charcoal disk burning in a cast iron cauldron or other vessel (if ceramic, fill with sand first). Stand over the smoke and breathe it up into your energy field, from the base of your spine through to the top of your head and fountaining out again.

Take note of where the energies of the herb seem to concentrate in your body, how it makes you feel, and how it may have affected your energy level. Keep in mind the five energy centers from Western tradition that we sometimes work with in the Avalonian Tradition (Root, aligned with Earth, at base of spine and seat; Womb, aligned with Water, in lower abdomen and back; Heart, aligned with Fire, through the center of the chest; Throat, aligned with Air, centered around your vocal chords; and Third Eye, aligned with Spirit, which is through and above your head, focused at the center of your forehead) and see if the herbal energies have an affinity for any one area. What does this tell you about the herb? What might this tell you about yourself and where you are at this moment on the path to Sovereignty?

Once you feel that you have completely filled yourself with the energy of the herb, take notice of how your energy may have shifted. What differences can you note between how you felt before breathing in the energy and after having done so? While taking in the energy, did you "see" any colors or symbols or scenes behind your closed eyes? What thoughts, feelings, or memories came up for you when you brought this energy into your auric space? Be sure to record any and all of these observations in your journal.

As always, when you have completed this exploration, be sure to discharge all of the energies you have brought into your energy field. Breathing them out, and directing them down, and feeling them sink into the Earth as an energetic offering. Do this until you feel clear, and have returned to a place of center and clarity. Be sure to journal your experiences and insights each time.

Lunar Vibrational Elixirs

Another effective way to work with the energies of these Lunar Keys is to create a set of lunar elixirs. These are vibrational essences which are made by utilizing the activating power of the full moon to imbue pure spring water with the energies of the herb that corresponds to that specific full moon. Unlike herbal tinctures, there are no chemical constituents actually present in the elixir; it is only the energy of the plants that become fixed in the spring water. Traditionally, vibrational essences are created from the flowering portion of the plant or tree, however it is possible to create essences with leaves, seeds, fruits, berries, roots and bark. Ideally, each essence is created in concert with living plants, potent in their vitality and in partnership with the intention of the elixir. However, should this not be not possible, essences can be made from other substances as well; several options are offered to insure that everyone has access to the use of vibrational essences as an energetic support of the work

One of the key methods for coming to understand something is through the process of merging with it—to match our energies with its own. Becoming one with something is a very potent tool of the feminine energetic; seeking power with something rather than power over it. The Lunar Keys presented in this book are effective ways of connecting to the Avalonian Cycle of Revealing. Further, because the elixirs help us to match our personal vibration to that of the work and lessons of each Lunar Key, the corresponding energy within us rises to the surface of our psyche and allows us to explore and work on understanding this aspect of ourselves. The more our vibrational state matches the frequency of something we seek to understand, the easier it will be to connect with it and see it clearly. This principle applies to the outer work of understanding Avalon and aspects of her mysteries and tradition, as well as the inner work of personal growth and spiritual transformation—that process by which the inner landscape is cleared, allowing an increased range of sight—both within and without.

The practice of making and using a lunar elixir for each of the Lunar Keys of the Avalonian Cycle of Revealing is presented here as a tool to augment personal growth, to facilitate our understanding of the disparate energies of the Thirteen Moons, and to assist in the integration of the lessons contained in the myths of the goddesses of Avalon. To create a full set of fourteen (the thirteen moons plus the Moon of Cycle) will take a little more than a year, but it is well worth the time and energy to do so; indeed, it is a beautiful devotional practice to take the time to create these elixirs each month, and the experience that working with these vibrational essences can bring is priceless and is helpful on several levels:

- They tie us into the energy of each Lunar Key as we simultaneously ride the Avalonian Cycle of Healing throughout the year.

- They stimulate the corresponding energies within us so that we may examine them and consider their relevance and impact on our work.

- They facilitate the work of the cycles and support our striving to align with them.

- They aid in connecting with the goddesses of Avalon through a deep examination of their stories and the lessons they hold in our own lives.

- They help us to gain an understanding of the energetic of each of the herbs themselves, bringing us into direct experience of their vibrational actions, lessons, and gifts.

These elixirs can last for many years, and once you understand through personal experience of working with these elixirs what each of their energies stimulates within you, you will have at your disposal an energetic toolkit that you can use to support your work whenever you have the need. For example, if you have found from your time working with the vervain elixir you created during the Moon of Germination that this vibrational essence helps you to move past the illusions generated by your fear to see the heart of the matter at hand, you can then take some whenever you find yourself paralyzed by fear to help shift your energy to bring you to a more centered place.

Creating the Elixirs

Supplies:

+ One ounce each of the fourteen herbs of the Avalonian Cycle of Revealing (shared with the herbal explorations detailed earlier in this chapter).

+ Small clear glass or plain silver bowl.

+ Spring water.

+ Brandy (80 proof). Alternatively, organic apple cider vinegar may be used for those who have a sensitivity to alcohol, but elixirs made in this way should be kept refrigerated as they do not last as long.

+ Fine mesh or paper filter (unbleached, preferably).

+ Fourteen sterilized storage jars or bottles, pint sized—Blue or brown glass is preferred, but clear mason jars will also work.

+ Fourteen sterilized glass bottles (blue or brown) with droppers.

+ Funnel, preferably sterilized glass or Pyrex.

Step 1

Before the night of the full moon, find a safe outdoor space where you can create your elixir without it being disturbed. If you do not have a yard where you can put your bowl in direct moonlight, you can put it on your windowsill to good effect instead. In either case, keep your intention focused on the devotional work at hand as you put the components together.

Please note: for the Moon of Cycle, you will want to create two separate elixirs—one using Queen Anne's lace, the herb of the Moon of Cycle, and the other using the herb for the moon that is being overlain by the Moon of Cycle. As like calls to like, the dual energies of the moon will separate out and each will be drawn to empower the herb with which it holds correspondence.

Step 2

On the night of the full moon, fill your glass or silver bowl with spring water and place a small amount of the month's herb in the water. Do this with clear intention, perhaps chanting the name of the Moon as you do so. Fresh cut flowers are traditionally used in the creation of a vibrational essence, but you may use about a teaspoon of dried herbs in lieu of these, knowing that your intention will empower your work. Should an herb not be available to you, you can create an elixir using a clear glass bowl without any etching or ornaments, and below it put a picture of the herb and the name of the Moon, so that these can be seen through the bottom of the bowl.

Step 3

Leave your prepared bowl in direct moonlight for at least three hours. If it is a cloudy night, you can still create the elixir because the energies of the full moon are still present, even when she is not seen.

Step 4

After the allotted time has passed, keep a clear focus, and strain your moon-empowered water into one of your larger storage bottles or jars, making sure to remove the plant material. Do your best to not touch the liquid.

Step 5

Into the same storage bottle or jar, pour enough brandy or apple cider vinegar to double the contents of the liquid. Cap the bottle tightly and, keeping your focus on the work at hand—again, perhaps chanting the name of the Moon over and over again in your head—set the elixir by shaking and swirling the contents of bottle ninety-nine times, in a counterclockwise motion. This is now the Mother Elixir from which you will make your individual working elixirs. Be sure to label and date your elixir, and store it in a cool, dark place. If you used apple cider vinegar, you should keep it in your refrigerator. Depending upon how much you made, this Mother Elixir should last you for years.

Step 6

To create your individual working elixir, or Daughter Elixir, fill a glass dropper bottle half way with spring water and half way with brandy or apple cider vinegar, leaving some room at the top so that the contents do not overflow when you put the dropper back in. To this water/brandy mixture, add nine drops of the Mother Elixir. Cap and shake as directed above. Label your dropper bottle with the name of the Herb and the name of the Moon. It is now ready to use both for your exploration of the energetics of this Avalonian Herbal Moon as well as for future use in bringing the vibrational influence of this energy into your life whenever you need it.

As an optional aside, should you have access to Red and White Spring water from Glastonbury, a town in England strongly associated with the real world location of Avalon, you may consider adding three or nine drops of Red Spring water to the Mother Elixirs created during the dark half of the year, and three or nine drops of White Spring water to the Mother Elixirs created during the light half of the year. Add both to the Mother Elixirs for the Blue Moon and for the Herb of Cycle.

Working with the Elixirs

Once you have created a Daughter Elixir, begin engagement with the energetics of the herb in the following way:

Week One

- Take a daily inner inventory to see where you are with your inner work, and how you feel in this moment: physically, emotionally, energetically, mentally, and spiritually. Cleanse and center.

- Place three drops of the elixir under your tongue. Sit in silence, and engage in nine deep cycles of breath, paying close attention to any shifts of energy which may occur as you do so. Let the energies settle within you, and open yourself to the experience of the herb.

- Sit with how this shifts your energy and meditate on what the elixir contributes to your understanding of what the herb does and what it has to teach you.

- You may choose to use a live specimen of the herb or a photograph of it as a focus for journeying; focus on your breath, perhaps using the name of the herb as a mantra, and be open to the experience that comes to you.

- In all things, pay attention to any and all symbols, feelings, memories, energy shifts, or visions which may come up for you while working with the herb. Be sure to write these down for future reference. A journal dedicated to this herbal work is recommended, so that your thoughts, insights, and experiences are all in one place.

Week Two

- Continue to immerse yourself in the vibrational energies of the herb by using the Daughter Elixir daily, as outlined in Week One, steps 1–3 above, being sure to journal all of your insights and experiences.

- After the first week of simply experiencing the energies of the elixir and exploring how it makes you feel—being sure to take note of what guidance comes to you during this time—consider comparing the energetics of the elixir to the direct experience of the herbs themselves.

+ Using self-lighting charcoal to burn some of the dried herb, use the technique outlined in the magical herbalism working earlier in this chapter to explore the herb associated with the month.

+ Make note of how the herb makes you feel. What are the differences and similarities between burning the herb and ingesting the elixir? Why do you think this may be?

Week Three

+ Continue to immerse yourself in the vibrational energies of the herb by using the Daughter Elixir daily, as outlined in Week One, steps 1–3, being sure to journal all of your insights and experiences.

+ Research traditional, medicinal, and folkloric uses of the month's herb. An overview of these streams of information are presented in this book, but it is enthusiastically recommended that you use this information as a jumping off point to research deeper. Again, record your findings in your journal.

+ Begin to compare your intuitive insights from the week before to the information you are gathering about the month's herb. Are there similarities in what you saw and experienced and what you discovered and read? How does your research compare to your experiences of the vibrational properties of the herb? In what ways does it differ? In what ways does one validate the other? Use your journal to archive these connections and insights as well.

+ Beginning to make connections between the objective information you've gathered from solid sources about these plants, and the information you intuited—through meditating, journeying, and taking in the energetics of the plant through the herbs themselves or their vibrational essence—is a powerful way to foster trust in your innate wisdom as well as an excellent way to build discernment around the information you have received.

Week Four

- Continue to immerse yourself in the vibrational energies of the herb by using the Daughter Elixir daily, as outlined in Week One, steps 1–3, being sure to journal all of your insights and experiences.

- Explore the mythic portion of the goddess' story that is related to the work of the Moon. The tales of the five goddesses of the Avalonian Tradition contain a trove of guidance and wisdom, and while each of their stories will be retold in this book, it is recommended that you read the source material as well, in order to have access to details that the redactors of the stories felt were important, but may not be present in the retellings. Be sure to write down dialog, narrative imagery, plot lines, and characterizations which stand out to you—both positively and negatively.

- Examine the mythic portion of this moon from the perspective of the lunar herbal energetics. How does the energy of the herb relate to this part of the myth? How does it help you connect, if at all, with the presiding goddess? How does it help you relate, if at all, the mythic portion with your present personal process? As always, journal your insights and connections.

As the month draws to a close, begin to integrate the information gathered through these streams of wisdom and consider whatever parallels you may find between the mythic portion, the medicinal and folkloric uses of the herb, and your perceptions and insights about the energy of the herb as you have experienced them. In what way do these commonalities connect with your life's story? How does this Lunar Key relate to your personal process?

Further, under what circumstance or circumstances could you see yourself reaching to use this moon's elixir in support of your work and personal process? If you had to describe the actions of this lunar elixir using one word, what would it be? What about using one sentence? What about using a whole paragraph? Again, be sure to journal everything.

Beginning the Immersion

Part one of this book has presented foundational information and key tools for doing the work of the Avalonian Cycle of Revealing as a monthly immersion and spiritual discipline. Part two details the application of these tools, and presents a step-by-step process of engagement to support this immersion and assist in the exploration of each of the fourteen Lunar Keys. For every moon of the year, we will be presented with opportunities to interact with the energies of its Lunar Key in several ways:

1. Through direct exploration of the herb associated with that Key, which includes the creation of, and experiential engagement with, the lunar elixir of that month's herb.

2. Through the study of, and reflection on, the mythic portion of the goddess story associated with that moon.

3. Through immram journeys to the sacred landscape of the goddess associated with that Lunar Key.

4. Through undertaking a practice guided by the interwoven Cycle of Healing and Cycle of Revealing.

Following this process will aid us in making connections, deepening relationships, and furthering our understanding both of Self and

- Source through the lessons each of these goddesses, their stories, and the energetics of their Lunar Keys can bring.

Please keep in mind that this system of practice is intended to be cyclic and ongoing. We need not feel like we must always engage with every aspect of the work at any given time. The different elements of practice are presented as portals of entry into the inner work of the Avalonian Tradition. They are intended to catalyze shifts of energy, facilitate changes in perspective, and magnify the growing relationship between the Self and the Divine. We can choose to engage only with the goddesses and their stories, or to work solely with the herbal energetics, or to focus on our personal work as we weave around the Wheels of the Sun and Moon—or we may integrate some or all of these things, as they each support and reinforce the work of the others.

To assist you in this process, each Moon of the Avalonian Cycle of Revealing explored in part two of this book is accompanied by an immersion guide entitled "Seeking Sovereignty Within—Journaling Prompts and Self-Reflective Questions." This guide presents a weekly focus for the suggested work of each Moon, both as it concerns connecting with the goddesses around our personal work at each moon phase, as well as keeping us on track with the various suggested methods for exploring the energetics of the month's herbal correspondence.

Finally, it is important to keep in mind that we can start to do the work of the Avalonian Cycle of Revealing at any time; we need not wait until Calan Gaeaf or Moon One to come around again in order to begin. It is also critical that we enter into this immersion with the intention to embrace it as a spiritual discipline, but to also give ourselves permission to take some time away if we need to, and to give ourselves room to make a sovereign choice to pause our work and to take it up again when we are ready to do so. While we should always explore our motivations, and seek out the reasons that we engage in self-sabotage, especially as it concerns our personal growth, spending time in cycles of guilt and punishing ourselves with self-recrimination is not a constructive use of our energy.

Perhaps instead, we could strive to acknowledge the challenges that prevented us from continuing with our discipline, resolve to work through whatever roadblocks that got in our way, and turn the page on what was by committing to take up the work once more. No one is perfect, and even the smallest steps toward our goal of increased self-knowledge and connection with goddess will help us to manifest that intention. Give yourself permission to ebb and flow with the work; if it is the nature of Nature to wax and wane like the moon, why should we expect anything different from ourselves? What is important is that we do the work as we can, when we can, to the degree we can.

And so, with these things in mind, let us begin our immersion into the Avalonian Cycle of Revealing.

Part Two
IMMERSION

Chapter 5

THE TIME OF CERIDWEN

CERIDWEN IS AN ENIGMATIC FIGURE for whom we have very little traditional lore, but who has nevertheless captured the imagination of modern Pagans to become one of the most well-known and widely honored Celtic divinities. Today, she is predominantly considered a goddess of magic, but to the bards of medieval Wales, she was their primary Muse; from her cauldron she bestowed upon them the gifts of Awen (divine inspiration), and these bards considered themselves the children of Ceridwen—the Cerddorion. Although Ceridwen is mentioned in several medieval Welsh poems, chiefly in her role as muse and mother to Taliesin, the only tale we have about her is found in a work called *Ystoria Taliesin* (*The Story of Taliesin*). The earliest extant version we have of the story comes from a sixteenth-century manuscript, however, linguistic analysis of the story has determined that it dates back to the ninth century, at least in its written form..

The meaning of Ceridwen's name is not entirely clear, in part because of all of the variant spellings of her name in early Welsh poetry, which leave us with several possible etymologies. Some possible meanings of her name include: "Holy Song," "Crooked Woman," or "Bent White One." "Holy Song" is clearly in alignment with Ceridwen's role as muse, with *cerdd* meaning "song, poetry," while "Crooked Woman" has connotations perhaps of a bent-backed crone or one who is stooped over to gather herbs. Interestingly, the Welsh *cwr*, which means "hooked" or "crooked," has a common root with the Irish *corrán*, which means "hook" or "sickle"—the sickle being a tool used for the harvesting of herbs.[6] The meaning of "Bent White One," similar in energy to "Crooked Woman," also suggests the shape of the crescent moon, leading some to believe that she may have been a goddess with lunar associations. In *Ystoria Taliesin*, Ceridwen is not identified as a goddess at all but rather as a sorceress or a witch. However, the etymology of her name and the description of her nature play an important role in reclaiming Ceridwen's divinity. In this case, the presence in her name of the feminine terminal deific *-wen*, which means "bright, shining, holy," makes a strong argument that this shape-shifting woman who dwelt on an island in (or perhaps under) a lake, with the power to brew elixirs of wisdom and dispense Awen from her cauldron, had likely once been somewhat more than a sorceress.

---

6. Rachel Bromwich, ed. and trans., *Trioedd Ynys Prydein: The Welsh Triads* (Cardiff: University of Wales Press, 2006), 312–313.

Moon 1

THE MOON OF INITIATION

Moon One of the Avalonian Cycle of Revealing is called the Moon of Initiation and is associated with the herb mugwort (Artemisia vulgaris). The lunar month begins on the first full moon when the sun is in Scorpio; the full moon is in Taurus. It is the first of four moons during the Time of Ceridwen. This full moon corresponds with the Station of Descent in the Avalonian Cycle of Healing, and it is the holy day of Calan Gaeaf.

It is here the journey begins, standing on the rim of the Cauldron of Transformation. Just as summer shifts into winter, just as night is birthed by day, it is by entering the shadow that we find the seeds of Sovereignty within. We pause here at this threshold place, straddling the light and dark halves of the cycle and the light and dark halves of the self. We pause to look behind us to see the path that has led us to this moment, to acknowledge all that we have accomplished, to take stock of the resources we have at our disposal, and to identify the places where our life's harvest has not yet been abundant. And then, knowing where we have come from, we turn to set course to where we wish to go. We turn our sight inward and seek out the places of challenge, the places that hold pain, the places that know fear. We commit ourselves to the work ahead and set our intention for change...and then dive head first into the cauldron.

It begins.

The Mythic Portion

On an island in the middle of Lake Tegid lived Ceridwen with her husband, Tegid Foel ("Tegid the Bald") and their two children. Her daughter Creirwy was the most beautiful of maidens, and her son Morfran was the most hideous of youths. Determined to help Morfran compensate for his appearance and be able to take his place in the world, Ceridwen immersed herself in study of the alchemical arts, at last discovering a formula which would gift her son with wisdom and the powers of prophecy.

The Work of the Moon of Initiation

In her tale, we learn that Ceridwen has two children: a daughter named Creirwy ("the Purest," "Lively Treasure," or "Dear One") and a son named Morfran ("Sea Crow/Cormorant" or "Great Raven"). Creirwy was accounted to be one of the most beautiful women who ever lived, while Morfran was so hideously ugly and deformed he was given the name *Afagddu*, which means "Utter Darkness." Ceridwen believed her son would never be accepted into society because of his fearsome visage and so became determined to help him by brewing a Draught of Wisdom and Prophecy that would grant him extraordinary abilities that would compensate for his appearance.

In the language of mythic symbolism, Llyn Tegid (possibly from the word *teg*, meaning "fair" or "beautiful") can be seen to represent the deep Otherworld of the intuitive Unconscious, which holds at its center the elusive home of Ceridwen, that island-core of our being centered in and at one with the Divine. Her two children represent the dual aspects of the Self: that which is sovereign and Conscious (Creirwy) and that which is shadow (*Afagaddu*), the wounded part of Morfran, who represents the Unconscious. Through the process of rarefaction and transformation as represented by her study and undertaking of the discipline of alchemy, Ceridwen seeks to bring that which is in shadow into the light of wisdom, to spin gold from the dross.

Ceridwen's children embody beauty and ugliness. Wholeness and woundedness. Light and darkness. We too are her children, and like them, we are made of shadow and Sovereignty—the hidden and Unconscious, and the revealed and Conscious. Ceridwen can be seen to represent our Higher Self or what connects us to Source. This part of us knows the truth of our greatest potential as well as what prevents us from actualizing it.

In the Avalonian Tradition, the dark half of the year symbolically represents the Cauldron of Transformation within which we engage in the inner shadow work that will ultimately bring us deep soul healing; we use the Moon of Initiation to begin this process. Like Ceridwen, we must assess our needs with clarity, find the place where our shadow is most in need of attention, and begin to make our way down the inner path leading us to what is most in need of illumination. It is only when we bring the light of recognition into the utter darkness of our fear, pain, and embraced limitations that we can claim the wisdom that awaits us in the bottom of our cauldron.

Ceridwen didn't look upon her son, recoil in horror, and dismiss him from her sight. Instead, fueled by the power of a mother's unconditional love, she embarked upon a lengthy and difficult process to help her son achieve his greatest potential; she sought to gift him with what would allow him to overcome his greatest challenges—the gift of wisdom. Our shadows need mothering, and with the assistance of allies like Ceridwen and the healing energies of mugwort, we can give it— and ourselves—the gifts of transformation and rebirth.

Searching Deeper

Ceridwen makes her home on an island in Llyn Tegid, a glacial lake of great depth found in the Penllyn region of northern Wales, near the present-day town of Bala. There are no islands in Llyn Tegid, which seems to orient the island-home of Ceridwen firmly in the realm of the Otherworld or else put it in line with the many instances of submerged residences so prevalent in Celtic myth. However, local folk tradition recounts two separate origin tales for Llyn Tegid, both of which include the inundation and drowning of an old town or castle.

In the first tale, the old town of Bala was ruled by a cruel prince who mistreated his people; every day he heard a voice say, "*Dial a ddaw, dial a ddaw!*" ("Vengeance will come, vengeance will come!"), but he mockingly dismissed the voice every time. One day, the prince's grandson was born and there was a celebration in the town. A young harpist from a neighboring village was hired to entertain the guests during the feasting, during which the people engaged in wild excess. Taking a short break at midnight, the harpist heard a voice in his ear saying, "*Dial a ddaeth, dial a ddaeth!*" (meaning "Vengeance has come, vengeance has come!"). A small bird appeared to the harpist, and it led him out of the palace and into the hills where he promptly fell asleep. When he awoke the following morning, he saw that where before there had been a town was now only a large lake with his harp floating on the water's surface.[7]

The lake was henceforth called Llyn Tegid, after the cruel prince whose name was Tegid Foel, the same as Ceridwen's husband. She does not appear at all in this tale, nor is Tegid himself present in *Ystoria Taliesin*, only named, in the same way he is mentioned in the Welsh Triads and the court list of Culhwch ac Olwen—primarily to establish a lineage for named warriors and courtiers. Perhaps in the same way that Ceridwen is not named a goddess in her tale and is presented only as a witch, the mythic memory of an Otherworldly being named Tegid Foel may have attached itself to this inundation myth; there is nothing in any of the Arthurian references to Tegid Foel which marks him

---

7. Robin Gwyndaf, *Welsh Folk Tales* (Cardiff: National Museums and Galleries of Wales, 1999), 55.

as being a cruel prince who terrorized his people before perishing in a flood as punishment.

The other inundation tale concerns a well at the center of the ancient village of Bala, called Ffynnon Gywer or Gower's Well. The well was in the care of a guardian whose duty it was to cover the well with its lid every night, lest the spirit of the well grow angry and vengeful. One night, alas, the guardian was distracted by some festivities in town and forgot to secure the well cover. When the last villager had gone to bed, water began to spew out of the well and the village began to flood. Desperate, the people of Bala tried to correct the guardian's oversight, but it was too late. Realizing what he had done, the guardian ran away but was quickly overtaken by the angry waters, which drowned him. The residents of Bala did what they could to escape the rising waters, but nothing could save their village, and by the time the sun had risen, the whole of it was underwater. Today, it is said, when the surface of the lake is still, one can see the ruins of the drowned village . . . but the spirit of the well is said to still not be appeased. There is yet another prophecy, remembered in a rhyme, which says:

> *Y Bala aeth a'r Bala aiff*
> *A Llanfor aiff yn llyn*

("Bala has gone, and Bala will drown again, and Llanfor will become a lake." Llanfor is another town a few miles away from Llyn Tegid.)[8]

There doesn't appear to be any historic foundation for these inundation tales, and similar stories exist in a few Welsh coastal towns, but none have to do with a freshwater lake like Bala. A sad aside, in 1965 the Welsh village of Capel Celyn was evacuated and purposefully flooded to create a reservoir for the English city of Liverpool. There were many protests and acts of civil disobedience, but the British government in London went through with the plan regardless of local sentiment.

---

8. Gwyndaf, *Welsh Folk Tales*, 55.

These tales aside, Llyn Tegid has another unusual property in addition to being the largest natural lake in Wales: the Afon Dyfrdwy, also known as the River Dee, runs through it; it is said that the current of the river causes the waters of the lake to churn and rock in such a way that the abundance of slate that makes up much of the lake bed is shaped by the water to form long, slender pieces of stone. To me, these have always been suggestive of the arthritic digits on the hands of a crone. I remember once while deep in work on the shores of Llyn Tegid, the words "Ceridwen's fingers" came into my mind. In sharing this flash of Awen with others, this name has become increasingly attached to these naturally shaped pieces of slate ever since. And how fitting, because just as the landscape shifts to accommodate the needs and challenges of the environment, so are we changed when we enter the alchemical vessel of Ceridwen's cauldron, constantly becoming shaped and smoothed and rarefied in the wake of this magical current, in the ebb and flow of our own inner light and shadow.

Seeking Sovereignty Within:
Journaling Prompts and Self-Reflective Questions

Moon One
The Moon of Initiation
The Time of Ceridwen

Mythic Focus: Ceridwen begins to gather the herbal components needed to create the Elixir of Wisdom for her son Morfran, who was also called Afagaddu—a name that means "Utter Darkness."

Personal Insights Around This Moon's Mythic Portion: *Meditate upon the portion of Ceridwen's story associated with this moon, and reflect it within yourself. Her story is your story.*

The Focus of the Moon of Initiation by Phase

Seek the lessons of the Moon of Initiation at each moon phase by using the stations of the monthly Cycle of Healing; be sure to journal all of the insights, symbols, and guidance you receive from each goddess at each moon phase. As you work with the information you receive between each phase, perhaps following the daily process outlined in chapter 3 of this book, and using tools such as trance postures and doorways as detailed in *Avalon Within*, be sure to record those insights in your journal as well.

Full Moon: Connect with Ceridwen, as this is one of the four moons that make up her time, to set up your work for the month and to receive insight on the issue of focus. This is also the **Station of Descent** in the cycle of the sun, marked by the holy day of **Calan Gaeaf**, and so will establish the work of the dark half of the year.

Third Quarter: Station of Descent in the cycle of the moon. Bring the issue of focus to Rhiannon to explore through the filters of the Station of Descent and the Moon of Initiation.

Dark Moon: Station of Confrontation in the cycle of the moon. Bring the issue of focus to Ceridwen to explore through the filters of the Station of Confrontation and the Moon of Initiation.

First Quarter: Station of Emergence in the cycle of the moon. Bring the issue of the focus to Blodeuwedd to explore through the filters of the Station of Emergence and the Moon of Initiation.

Night before the Full Moon: Station of Resolution in the cycle of the moon. Bring the issue of focus to Arianrhod to explore through the filters of the Station of Resolution and the Moon of Initiation.

At any point in the month, bring the issue of focus to Branwen to explore through the Station of Integration and the Moon of Initiation. Some women will do this on the night after the dark moon in counterpoint to working with Arianrhod on the night before the full moon.

Herbal Ally for the Moon of Initiation
Mugwort (*Artemisia vulgaris*)

Creating the Mother Elixir: On the night of the full moon, create your Mugwort Lunar Elixir using the directions found on page 105 of chapter 4. Be sure to label and date the bottle you are using to store the Mother Elixir. Journal your experiences around the creation of the Mugwort Elixir.

Prepare the Daughter Elixir: After you have made the Mother Elixir, use the directions found on page 107 of chapter 4 to prepare a dosage bottle for use in the daily experience of this elixir throughout the month. Remember to use a blue or amber dropper bottle for this purpose, and to clearly label your Daughter Elixir.

Daily Work with the Mugwort Elixir: As discussed in chapter 4, begin your daily exploration of the Mugwort Elixir. Be sure to journal everything you can about how the elixir makes you feel, what you think its energetic actions are, where it sits in your energy body, and any and all impressions, insights, symbols, visions, and memories it presents to you:

WEEK ONE OF MOON ONE: Immerse yourself in the lunar elixir by taking it every day, reflecting upon how it makes you feel, and journaling all of the insights that come to you when you meditate upon the energies of the elixir.

WEEK TWO OF MOON ONE: Continue to take the lunar elixir daily, but this week spend time experiencing and comparing the energetic impact of mugwort as an essence, and mugwort as a magical herb that you burn, as detailed in chapter 4. Again, reflect upon how each makes you feel, and journal all of the insights that come to you when you meditate upon the energies of the elixir and the energies of the herb itself.

WEEK THREE OF MOON ONE: Continue to take the lunar elixir daily, but this week spend time researching the medicinal, folkloric, and magical uses of mugwort, beginning with the information provided in Part Three of this book. Compare your findings this week with your direct experiences, being sure to journal all of the insights and connections you've made.

WEEK FOUR OF MOON ONE: Continue to take the lunar elixir daily, but this week meditate upon the mythic portion of the month and reflect upon the ways in which the energies of mugwort are related to the present portion of Ceridwen's tale, and how it helps you to build a relationship with Ceridwen herself.

End of Moon Reflections: Under what circumstances could you see yourself using the Mugwort Elixir in support of your work and personal process? If you had to describe the actions of this lunar elixir using one word, what would it be? What about using one sentence? What about using a whole paragraph? Again, be sure to journal everything.

Moon 2

THE MOON OF DISTILLATION

Moon Two of the Avalonian Cycle of Revealing is called the Moon of Distillation, and is associated with the herb yarrow (Achillea millefolium). It is the second of four moons during the Time of Ceridwen, and the lunar month begins on the first full moon when the sun is in Sagittarius; the full moon is in Gemini.

The unconscious self is a vast and mysterious vessel, filled with all manner of things. It serves as an archive of our memories, a catalog of our experiences, and a storehouse of treasures awaiting discovery. It is also the abode of the shadow: the place where we file away all the things we don't like about ourselves, all the things we were told are unacceptable about who we are and what we desire, and all the things that happened to us which are simply too painful to keep in our consciousness. As we explore the nature of our soul's cauldron, part of our task is to identify as best we can the component ingredients that have become part of our innate brew. This deep inventory permits us to see the building blocks that form our perspectives about ourselves, our worth, and our relationship with others and the world. The process of inner distillation uses the alembic of our intention to seek out the outdated energetic patterns actively at work in our lives, so we may know them for what they are, liberate the lessons they hold for us, and move forward with clarity—leaving the poison of our pain behind.

The Mythic Portion

Much work and preparation are required to brew the Draught of Wisdom. Ceridwen gathers many different herbs at their magically auspicious times and sets them to boil in her cauldron where they must be constantly stirred, and the water within constantly replenished, for a year and a day. At the end of this time, three drops of liquid will separate from the poisonous brew and emerge from the cauldron. Whomever these drops fall upon will receive the gift of all wisdom. Ceridwen enlists the help of an old blind man named Morda to stir the bubbling liquid, and charges a young boy named Gwion Bach to keep the fire aflame.

On the last day of the process and weary from her labors, Ceridwen sets Morfran before the cauldron to await the drops should they emerge before she returned from her much-needed rest. Not long after this, the elixir is at last complete, and as the three drops leap from the cauldron, Gwion Bach pushes Morfran out of the way and receives the Draught of Wisdom intended for Ceridwen's son. The cauldron shatters with a terrible shriek, its foul-smelling liquid befouling the hearth before oozing out the door to poison the surrounding landscape. Ceridwen is awakened from her sleep.

The Work of the Moon of Distillation

The great labor involved in creating the Elixir of Wisdom teaches that our path to wholeness is one that takes time, patience, and endurance. The Wise Old Man Morda ("Great Good") and the child Gwion Bach ("Little Innocent") can be seen to represent the wise old man (the *senex*) and the Eternal Child (the *puer eternus*), Jungian archetypes that are in opposition to each other, creating fundamental psychological tension. The senax represents measured caution, discipline, and strict adherence to rules and tradition, whereas the puer is impulsive, chaotic, and acts from a place of pure instinct. Experience is what stirs the pot, even when we are blind to what is contained within and must coax it to the surface through this inner agitation. The energy of potential is what keeps it boiling. Everything must be added in its time and in its place, and the journey within must be one of dedication and discipline. The year and a day is a Celtic measurement of time where the day is a liminal period that brings the entire endeavor out of time and places it firmly in the Otherworld—the inner realm.

After all the work involved in the seeking of wisdom, at last the goal has been reached in the form of the three drops. These drops separate themselves from the rest of the brew, although they came from the same liquid in much the same way that wisdom is a gift that originates in our darkness. The energy that liberates this wisdom is the same that breaks the container that has held all the darkness for so long; the poison is released and washes away in the face of the newfound knowledge. The innocent, the wonder child, the potential or unrealized Self pushes aside the darkness to receive the drops of wisdom.

This process of inner distillation is difficult work. It requires a commitment to uncovering the nature of our shadow, as well as the courage to accept responsibility for the ways in which our shadow tendencies have made themselves manifest in our lives. It's not enough to say that we have been hurt by others; we must also accept that in this place of hurt and arising from our desire to keep ourselves from experiencing further hurt, we have also hurt others. Perhaps perpetuating the cycle of hurt has not been our intention; perhaps inflicting pain was an unconscious reaction to situations that feel like the ones our original woundings arose from initially. However, intention and impact are two very different things. It is said that hurt people hurt people; while we are not responsible for having been hurt, we must still aim to own the ways in which we have acted out from that place of hurt.

It is this hard-won understanding of the self which are the drops of wisdom that arise from the shadow work process of self-distillation. Likewise, the shadow compensations that we gradually learn to leave behind are what make up the poison that breaks open the vessel of our old limitations. What was, no longer defines us.

Only we can know what ingredients must be brought to the inner cauldron which will yield our personal wisdom. Examining one aspect of the self at a time and placing it into our soul's crucible for distillation will bring us closer to the root of our inner woundings. The closer we get to the foundation or origination of our shadow-self manifestations, the more potent will be the three drops of wisdom produced by the cauldron's overflow. We must be diligent in our seeking and disciplined in our work if we wish to obtain our desire. Sometimes we must work blindly and with a child's trust, remembering always that the goddess is overseeing our process. In the end, however, she must set us before the cauldron alone, for only we ourselves can make the changes that will bring us to greater wholeness.

Searching Deeper

Ceridwen is the keeper of the Cauldron of Inspiration, and it is from this cauldron that she bestows the gift of Awen—Divine Inspiration. Awen has been represented symbolically by the Three Rays of Illumination, written like so: /|\ . A symbol created by Iolo Morganwg during the Druidic Revival movement of the eighteenth and nineteenth centuries, one interpretation of the Three Rays is that it describes the radiating creative energy of the Divine flowing down from Source to become manifest in the physical world. The Three Drops of prophetic wisdom derived from Ceridwen's cauldron can be seen as represented by the rays of the Awen as well.

When Gwion obtained the Three Drops, he started down a path of transformation that changed his destiny forever. He would go on to become Taliesin, the greatest bard ever known to the Island of the Mighty and the paragon to which all other bards aspired. His name, which means "shining brow," was a mark of Taliesin's wisdom; the gift of Awen was said to cause a 'Fire in the Head,' certainly a testimony to the illuminating wisdom Gwion had received from the Cauldron of Ceridwen. Taliesin goes on to have incredible adventures and to serve as a bard in the courts of kings and chieftains. He is considered to be a semi-historical personage, in part because there is the mythological Taliesin who appears in stories such as *Ystoria Taliesin* and Geoffrey of Monmouth's *Vita Merlini*, as well as a sixth-century bardic figure of the same name who counted as his patrons Brochfael Powys, Urien Rheged, and Maelgwn Gwynedd. It is the historic Taliesin who ostensibly wrote the poems collected in the *Llyfr Taliesin*, the earliest extant version of which comes to us from the early fourteenth century.[9]

Much is known about Taliesin … but what became of Morfran?

While nothing more is said of him in this tale—it is the *Story of Taliesin*, after all—there are references to Morfran elsewhere in Welsh lore. He is immortalized in the *Trioedd Ynys Prydein* as one of the Three Slaughter-Blocks of the Island of Britain and is also there accounted as one of the Three Irresistible Knights of Arthur's Court; irresistible because it was repugnant for anyone to refuse him anything because of his ugliness. In *Culhwch ac Olwen*, the earliest surviving Arthurian prose tale, Morfran is named as one of the three survivors of the Battle of Camlan; he was covered in hair like that of a stag and was so ugly that no one dared attack him during the battle, believing him to be some manner of demon. In the end, Morfran was able to take what Ceridwen thought was his greatest weakness and turn it into his greatest asset, becoming a warrior of renown and one of Arthur's best knights.

9. John T. Koch, "Taliesin" in *Celtic Culture: A Historical Encyclopedia* (Oxford: ABC-CLIO, 2006), 1655.

Seeking Sovereignty Within:
Journaling Prompts and Self-Reflective Questions

Moon Two
The Moon of Distillation
The Time of Ceridwen

Mythic Focus: Ceridwen sets Gwion Bach to stirring the cauldron for a year and a day. When the brew is ready, he takes the three drops meant for Morfran for himself.

Personal Insights Around This Moon's Mythic Portion: *Meditate upon the portion of Ceridwen's story associated with this moon, and reflect it within yourself. Her story is your story.*

The Focus of the Moon of Distillation by Phase

Seek the lessons of the Moon of Distillation at each moon phase by using the Stations of the monthly Cycle of Healing; be sure to journal all of the insights, symbols, and guidance you receive from each goddess at each moon phase. As you work with the information you receive between each phase, perhaps following the daily process outlined in chapter 3 of this book, and using tools such as trance postures and doorways as detailed in *Avalon Within*, be sure to record those insights in your journal as well.

Full Moon: Connect with Ceridwen at the full moon. Review the work of the previous month and the insights it brought to you, set up your work for the coming month, and ask for insights on the issue of focus which may have shifted or deepened due to the work you have done.

Third Quarter: Station of Descent in the cycle of the moon. Bring the issue of focus to Rhiannon to explore through the filters of the Station of Descent and the Moon of Distillation.

Dark Moon: Station of Confrontation in the cycle of the moon. Bring the issue of focus to Ceridwen to explore through the filters of the Station of Confrontation and the Moon of Distillation.

First Quarter: Station of Emergence in the cycle of the moon. Bring the issue of the focus to Blodeuwedd to explore through the filters of the Station of Emergence and the Moon of Distillation.

Night before the Full Moon: Station of Resolution in the cycle of the moon. Bring the issue of focus to Arianrhod to explore through the filters of the Station of Resolution and the Moon of Distillation

At any point in the month, bring the issue of focus to Branwen to explore through the Station of Integration and the Moon of Distillation. Some women will do this on the night after the dark moon in counterpoint to working with Arianrhod on the night before the full moon.

Herbal Ally for the Moon of Distillation
Yarrow (*Achillea millefolium*)

Creating the Mother Elixir: On the night of the full moon, create your Yarrow Lunar Elixir using the directions found on page 105 of chapter 4. Be sure to label and date the bottle you are using to store the Mother Elixir. Journal any of your experiences around the creation of the Yarrow Elixir.

Prepare the Daughter Elixir: After you have made the Mother Elixir, use the directions found on page 107 of chapter 4 to prepare a dosage bottle for use in the daily experience of this elixir throughout the month. Remember to use a blue or amber dropper bottle for this purpose and to clearly label your Daughter Elixir.

Daily Work with the Yarrow Elixir: As discussed in chapter 4, begin your daily exploration of the Yarrow Elixir. Be sure to journal everything you can about how the elixir makes you feel, what you think its energetic actions are, where it sits in your energy body, and any and all impressions, insights, symbols, visions, and memories it presents to you:

WEEK ONE OF MOON TWO: Immerse yourself in the lunar elixir by taking it every day, reflecting upon how it makes you feel, and journaling all of the insights that come to you when you meditate upon the energies of the elixir.

WEEK TWO OF MOON TWO: Continue to take the lunar elixir daily, but this week spend time experiencing and comparing the energetic impact of yarrow as an essence, and yarrow as a magical herb that you burn, as detailed in chapter 4. Again, reflect upon how each makes you feel, and journal all of the insights that come to you when you meditate upon the energies of the elixir and the energies of the herb itself.

WEEK THREE OF MOON TWO: Continue to take the lunar elixir daily, but this week spend time researching the medicinal, folk-loric, and magical uses of yarrow, beginning with the information provided in Part Three of this book. Compare your findings this week with your direct experiences, being sure to journal all of the insights and connections you've made.

WEEK FOUR OF MOON TWO: Continue to take the lunar elixir daily, but this week meditate upon the mythic portion of the month and reflect upon the ways in which the energies of yarrow are related to the present portion of Ceridwen's tale, and how it helps you to build a relationship with Ceridwen herself.

End of Moon Reflections: Under what circumstances could you see yourself using the Yarrow Elixir in support of your work and personal process? If you had to describe the actions of this lunar elixir using one word, what would it be? What about using one sentence? What about using a whole paragraph? Again, be sure to journal everything.

Moon 3
THE MOON OF TRANSFORMATION

Moon Three of the Avalonian Cycle of Revealing is called the Moon of Transformation, and is associated with the herb wormwood (Artemesia absinthium). *It is the third of four moons during the Time of Ceridwen, and the lunar month begins on the first full moon when the sun is in Capricorn; the full moon is in Cancer.*

Although hidden in the depths of our unconscious mind, the workings of shadow affect every aspect of our being. As we undertake to understand the ways in which our shadow tendencies manifest in our lives by recognizing patterns of behavior and taking note of external challenges which trigger unconscious reactions, we must follow the flow of energy through every layer of our existence. From the Earthen matters of physical health, safety, and abundance, to the Watery realms of our emotional state and degree of trust in our intuition, to the Airy concerns of our perspectives, assumptions and thought patterns, and at last through to the Fiery affairs of our reactions, use of energy, and ability to change. However, it is not enough to know something about ourselves; we must also act to set change into motion. Knowledge applied is Wisdom obtained. Life brings with it many challenges, and one way or another, we are changed by them.

The Mythic Portion

Having received the three drops which bestowed upon him all Wisdom, Gwion knows that Ceridwen will want to destroy him for what he has done, and so runs away. Ceridwen is in quick pursuit, however, and Gwion seeks to evade her. He uses his newfound knowledge to shapeshift, and transforms into a hare. She, in turn, transforms into a greyhound, and just as she is about to catch him, Gwion leaps into the water in the shape of a salmon. Ceridwen follows as an otter, but again he eludes her by flying away in the form of a wren. Ceridwen chases him as a sharp-taloned hawk, and he falls to ground as a piece of grain, lost in the chaff of a winnowing floor. Ceridwen becomes a black hen, and scratches and pecks at the ground until she finds Gwion and devours him.

The Work of the Moon of Transformation

The transformational journey through the five elements can be a map for us to follow in our search for true Wisdom.

Earth—Hare/Greyhound

To seek the origins of the shadow we must first identify the ways in which it manifests in our lives. What does it prevent us from doing or being? How does it keep us from being whole? What destructive patterns do we find ourselves caught in? How do these wounds bleed away our life force and wear away our vital essence? In what ways do we carry our issues in our bodies? Are there chronic health issues to contend with or do they flare up acutely in times of stress as a reflection of an active manifestation of shadow? Do these issues affect particular systems of the body? Can these areas of physical weakness be clues to the nature of the fundamental issue—the core of the shadow?

Water—Salmon/Otter

Examining our emotional reactions to situations can provide us with very important information about ourselves in this quest for self-knowledge. What specific external situations tend to trigger unconscious reactions in us? What makes us feel anxious? Fearful? Worthless? Lost? What is the nature of this reaction? Do we act out? Back down? Withdraw? Fight back? Is the type of reaction dependent upon what triggers us? That is, does it differ depending on the particulars of the activating situation? How do we care for ourselves when we have been in situations that make us feel unsafe? What practices do we engage in which can help us to come back to a state of balance after the trigger is gone? How do we fortify ourselves from within so that our emotional reactions do not throw us off our mark? How do we establish good emotional boundaries with others? What is the baseline state of health, energy, or mental load that we need to maintain in order bring our best and most centered selves to any given situation?

Air—Wren/Hawk

An objective look at our preconceived ideas or perspectives about our life and the situations in it can yield great treasure. Many times, just shifting how we look at a situation will bring us to a different level of understanding, which in turn opens the way to a more positive relationship with the self and others. What have you accepted to be true about you and your life, without engaging in truly objective analysis? Where, how, and from whom did you come to learn what you believe to be true? Do these beliefs still hold true for this situation? Can you relate the formation of these outdated and potentially problematic perspectives back to the core issue you are exploring? How can you change the way this issue affects your life? Are you bringing a bias to this situation which has nothing to do with what is actually going on? How can you shift the situation by learning to change your mind about it?

Is there another way to see this situation? How can you shift your attention to something else in order to disempower problematic thought processes by withdrawing your energy from them?

Fire—Grain/Hen

Becoming conscious of the ways in which we express ourselves in the world, and taking stock of the things upon which we expend our energy can give us some means of measuring the efficacy of our energetic investment in ourselves, our goals, and our life's purpose. "If we always do what we've always done, we'll always get what we've always gotten," the old saying goes. Fire is the will to act—we can chose a different route, or we can continue to participate in our patterns. Sometimes it takes making a break in the established energy to be able to see a situation clearly. In this way, fire catalyzes the changes we are seeking. Is there a different option that you can choose? One that may have seemed impossible before?

Searching Deeper

The magical sequence of transformations which make up the chase between Ceridwen and Gwion have long been believed to be a symbolically encoded Druidic initiatory rite. Although the ancient Celts are not known to have used a five element system, the classic elements present in the tale are a reflection of the medieval time period in which the story was committed to writing. As many modern Western spiritual and occult systems do work with the five elements, it can be meaningful to meditate upon the transformations of Ceridwen and Gwion as representing a series of changes through each of the elements:

Earth	Hare	Greyhound
Water	Salmon	Otter
Air	Wren	Hawk
Fire	Grain	Hen

The overarching element of Spirit or Aether can be seen as being represented by the ultimate transformation of Gwion: the old self—the "small innocent"—dies in order to be reborn of the goddess as the enlightened Taliesin. That the transmutation results from Ceridwen the Hen devouring and, ostensibly, ending the life of Gwion the Grain, a resonance with the theme of the harvest sacrifice is revealed. We can also find a reflection in the ritualistic death that some British bog bodies appear to have experienced. Lindow Man, for example, was believed to have been hit in the head with a blunt object, strangled with a garrote, and drowned in a bog, in what is seen as an example of what has come to be called "the threefold death." This method of death may have represented a ritual sacrifice which took place in each of the Three Realms—that Celtic triune cosmological division of Land, Sky, and Sea, respectively.

Whether or not the myth of Ceridwen is a symbolic encoding of Druidic initiatory rites or is a guide to the bardic art of obtaining Awen, it comes to us today as a symbol system brimming with wisdom applicable and relevant to the life of the spiritual seeker. The pathway to wisdom is the pathway to the Divine—the pathway to wholeness. In its simplest terms, the spiritual path can be conceived as the movement from a place of disconnection to one of connection, from darkness into light, from individuality into unity, and from woundedness into wholeness.

Ceridwen's knowledge of herbcraft suggests that she is a healer as well as the mistress of Awen. True healing is a function of the soul. In the end, there are no shortcuts to wisdom. As Gwion discovered, he needed to earn that which he had taken, and Ceridwen saw to it that he would experience all and integrate all through every level of being. She is the loving Great Mother, seeking what is best for her son, but she is also the Terrible/Devouring Mother—guiding Gwion out of his naive innocence into the death of the self which is the true initiation that bestows the gifts of Wisdom.

Seeking Sovereignty Within:
Journaling Prompts and Self-Reflective Questions

Moon Three
The Moon of Transformation
The Time of Ceridwen

Mythic Focus: Ceridwen pursues Gwion Bach in a shape-changing chase through the elements until she consumes him as a grain of wheat.

Personal Insights Around This Moon's Mythic Portion: *Meditate upon the portion of Ceridwen's story associated with this moon, and reflect it within yourself. Her story is your story.*

The Focus of the Moon of Transformation by Phase

Seek the lessons of the Moon of Transformation at each moon phase by using the Stations of the monthly Cycle of Healing; be sure to journal all of the insights, symbols, and guidance you receive from each goddess at each moon phase. As you work with the information you receive between each phase, perhaps following the daily process outlined in chapter 3 of this book, and using tools such as trance postures and doorways as detailed in *Avalon Within*, be sure to record those insights in your journal as well.

Full Moon: Connect with Ceridwen at the full moon. Review the work of the previous month and the insights it brought to you, set up your work for the coming month, and ask for insights on the issue of focus which may have shifted or deepened due to the work you have done.

3rd Quarter: Station of Descent in the cycle of the moon. Bring the issue of focus to Rhiannon to explore through the filters of the Station of Descent and the Moon of Transformation.

Dark Moon: Station of Confrontation in the cycle of the moon. Bring the issue of focus to Ceridwen to explore through the filters of the Station of Confrontation and the Moon of Transformation.

1st Quarter: Station of Emergence in the cycle of the moon. Bring the issue of the focus to Blodeuwedd to explore through the filters of the Station of Emergence and the Moon of Transformation.

Night before the Full Moon: Station of Resolution in the cycle of the moon. Bring the issue of focus to Arianrhod to explore through the filters of the Station of Resolution and the Moon of Transformation.

At any point in the month, bring the issue of focus to Branwen to explore through the Station of Integration and the Moon of Transformation. Some women will do this on the night after the dark moon in counterpoint to working with Arianrhod on the night before the full moon.

Herbal Ally for the Moon of Transformation
Wormwood (*Artemesia absinthium*)

Creating the Mother Elixir: On the night of the full moon, create your Wormwood Lunar Elixir using the directions found on page 105 of chapter 4. Be sure to label and date the bottle you are using to store the Mother Elixir. Journal any of your experiences around the creation of the Wormwood Elixir.

Prepare the Daughter Elixir: After you have made the Mother Elixir, use the directions found on page 107 of chapter 4 to prepare a dosage bottle for use in the daily experience of this elixir throughout the month. Remember to use a blue or amber dropper bottle for this purpose, and to clearly label your Daughter Elixir.

Daily Work with the Wormwood Elixir: As discussed in chapter 4, begin your daily exploration of the Wormwood Elixir. Be sure to journal everything you can about how the elixir makes you feel, what you think its energetic actions are, where it sits in your energy body, and any and all impressions, insights, symbols, visions, and memories it presents to you:

WEEK ONE OF MOON THREE: Immerse yourself in the lunar elixir by taking it every day, reflecting upon how it makes you feel, and journaling all of the insights that come to you when you meditate upon the energies of the elixir.

WEEK TWO OF MOON THREE: Continue to take the lunar elixir daily, but this week spend time experiencing and comparing the energetic impact of wormwood as an essence, and wormwood as a magical herb that you burn, as detailed in chapter 4. Again, reflect upon how each makes you feel, and journal all of the insights that come to you when you meditate upon the energies of the elixir and the energies of the herb itself.

WEEK THREE OF MOON THREE: Continue to take the lunar elixir daily, but this week spend time researching the medicinal, folkloric, and magical uses of wormwood, beginning with the information provided in Part Three of this book. Compare your findings this week with your direct experiences, being sure to journal all of the insights and connections you've made.

WEEK FOUR OF MOON THREE: Continue to take the lunar elixir daily, but this week meditate upon the mythic portion of the month and reflect upon the ways in which the energies of wormwood are related to the present portion of Ceridwen's tale, and how it helps you to build a relationship with Ceridwen herself.

End of Moon Reflections: Under what circumstances could you see yourself using the Wormwood Elixir in support of your work and personal process? If you had to describe the actions of this lunar elixir using one word, what would it be? What about using one sentence? What about using a whole paragraph? Again, be sure to journal everything.

Moon 4

THE MOON OF GERMINATION

Moon Four of the Avalonian Cycle of Revealing is called the Moon of Germination and is associated with the herb vervain (Verbena officinalis). It is the last of four moons during the Time of Ceridwen, and the lunar month begins on the first full moon when the sun is in Aquarius; the full moon is in Leo. This full moon corresponds with the Station of Confrontation in the Avalonian Cycle of Healing, and it is the holy day of Gwyl Mair.

From the smallest of seeds held in Earth's rich soil to the embryonic stars forming in the dense stellar nurseries of deep space, the greatest growth occurs in darkness. It is here at the deepest point of the great cycle and the bottom of the Cauldron of Transformation where we must fully embrace our darkness. It is in this place we must embrace the ultimate trust in ourselves and our process. We do this by letting go of our attachment to outmoded ways of seeing ourselves and the world, by releasing our illusions of control over anything or anyone but ourselves, and by surrendering ourselves to the process of inner alchemy that we have set into motion when we undertook this journey into Sovereignty.

It is the shedding of the confines and limitations of our old life that permits us to drink deeply from the vessel of rebirth. It is by emptying ourselves of what was that we are able to glimpse the possibilities of what may yet be. When we are as fully conscious of the dark as we can be … when we are able to look at the places where we have been broken, or have fallen short of our goals, or have otherwise not actualized the potential that lies dormant within us … we can then see the light that has always been there within us. It is then that we can discover the treasure awaiting release—the Fire in the Head, the Shining Brow that will lead us with compassion and true wisdom up and out of the cauldron as the cycle waxes anew.

The Mythic Portion

It is not long after her shape-shifting pursuit that Ceridwen discovers the piece of wheat that had been Gwion Bach has taken root in her womb. After the passage of nine moons, she gave birth to a boy child. As angry as she was at Gwion, she found that she couldn't do the babe any harm. She instead wrapped him in a leather bag and set him adrift on the sea in a coracle. Some say that forty years passed before the coracle made its way into a salmon weir where it was found by a Welsh prince named Elphin on Nos Calan Gaeaf—the Eve of the First of Winter. The prince cut open the leather and revealed the infant within, exclaiming at the sight of him, "Behold, this radiant brow!" And so the child receives the name Taliesin. Raised by Elphin and his wife, Taliesin grew to become the most gifted and renowned of all Welsh bards.

The Work of the Moon of Germination

The Moon of Germination is the same moon as the Holy Day of Gwyl Mair ("The Festival of Mary" or "The Festival of the Mother"), both of which correspond to the Station of Confrontation in the Avalonian Cycle of Healing. It is the time which marks the very bottom of the cauldron of the dark half of the year—the deepest depths of winter.

And yet it is here, in this darkness, that new growth takes place.

Gwion as the devoured seed spends nine moons planted in Ceridwen's womb and in doing so, reveals the reflective nature of the process of becoming conscious of the most hidden parts of ourselves. Nine is the number of the Moon, that archetypal symbol of the Unconscious realm. The journey into wisdom is the great initiation which makes one Twice Born: once of the womb (physical birth), and once of the cauldron (spiritual birth), each a symbolic resonance of the other.

Though this gestational period appears like a fallow time from the outside, a great deal is happening in the darkness. Our inner potential begins to pierce through the hull of its seed, sending shoots of new growth up toward the surface of consciousness, seeking discovery…awaiting our attention. When this deep wisdom is at last revealed, when the reborn child is discovered and freed from the leather bag—another womb-symbol, rendering us Thrice Born (the new Self that arises from the union of Consciousness and Unconsciousness)—the hard-earned Wisdom that illuminates the path of our inner process becomes plain to see.

Oftentimes the things we most deplore bring with them our life's greatest blessings. Within the shadow of our fear lies the beauty of our strength. Our gifts are often realized through the harnessing of our flaws; they are intimately related, two extremes of the same whole. Releasing these things into the void by relinquishing our control over the outcome is a part of the work of the Station of Confrontation. We must learn to see the root of our issue for what it is and then change our lives by letting it go. Transformation will come.

When we learn to trust in the process of the Universe, when we release ourselves from the bonds of our outmoded beliefs, we enter into a place of true wisdom. Immersing ourselves as fully and as openly as possible into the deepest depths of shadow will result in our ability to emerge from these dark inner waters with new perspective and clarity; we will have become the Radiant Brow. We are a different person than the one who first entered the cauldron, and though it may have been difficult to face or accept what was contained within, we are better for having dared to make the journey … and that much more wise.

Searching Deeper

Ceridwen was the patroness and muse of the bards, the bestower of gifts from the Pair Awen, her Cauldron of Poetic Inspiration. As Taliesin was accounted to be the greatest of all bards, having attained enlightenment and been reborn from the Cauldron of Ceridwen, he became the paragon to which all bards aspired as they too sought to be considered Cerddorion, the children of Ceridwen.

It is not an accident that the infant Taliesin was found in a salmon weir on Calan Gaeaf—a holy day and threshold time that marked the beginning of winter—the Welsh equivalent of Samhain and the Celtic new year. Further, salmon has strong associations with wisdom in the myths of the Celts, and it is interesting to note that Ceridwen's home of Llyn Tegid—a deep glacial lake through which the River Dee runs—is the only known home in Wales to a species of fish called gwyniad, which are in the salmon family. The salmon is also one of several connections between the story of Gwion Bach, who transformed himself into one while being chased by Ceridwen, and the Irish tale of a youth named Demne, who would become the great hero, Finn Mac Cumaill.

Demne was apprenticed to a druid poet named Finnegas, who dwelt on the banks of the River Boyne. For many years, Finnegas made a daily visit to the Well of Segais, the source of the Boyne, which formed a pool surrounded by nine hazel trees upon which grew the nuts of wisdom. In this pool dwelt wondrous salmon that ate the hazelnuts that fell into the water, and Finnegas sought to catch one, as there was a legend that whomever caught and ate one of these salmon would obtain the art of poetic prophecy. After five years of Demne's service, Finnegas was at last successful in catching one of the salmons of wisdom.

He set Demne to the task of cooking the fish with the command that the youth not eat any of it while Finnegas went to fetch more firewood.

The boy agreed, for he held his master in great regard, and set about cooking the salmon in a way that would best honor this wondrous fish. During the cooking, Demne noticed that a bubble was forming under the skin of the salmon, and he used his thumb to press it flat again; as he did so, he burned himself, and in an unthinking reaction to the pain, Demne popped his thumb into his mouth to soothe it. Too late, Finnegas returned, finding that the prophecy he had tried to circumvent—that he was destined to catch the Salmon of Wisdom, but someone else was destined to eat it—had nonetheless come to pass, for the wisdom had flowed into his apprentice. And so it was that Demne received the name Finn, which means "fair, blessed, enlightened," and he would go on to become a renowned warrior-poet and leader of the Fianna, a noble war band, whose adventures are told in the Fenian cycle of stories. Finn was able access the powers of prophecy for the rest of his life simply by putting the thumb he had burned in his mouth.

The similarities between the two tales is striking, from the youth employed as an assistant obtaining the wisdom intended for another, to the acknowledgment of their enlightened state with a name that speaks of their newly acquired radiant brightness. The Irish name *Finn* is etymologically connected to the Welsh name *Gwyn*, both meaning "bright, white, holy"; we also see it in the terminal form *-wen* in the names of mythic personages believed to have once been deities such as Ceridwen and Branwen. Although it is uncertain, it is also believed that the name Gwion is related to Gwyn and may share the same meaning.

What is the significance of these two tales being so similar? We cannot be certain, but it could mean that both the Irish and the Welsh tales are drawing upon an earlier, common tradition that may have roots in the Celtic mother culture that arose on the European continent, or that in the inevitable cultural exchanges that occur with neighboring peoples, the tale of Finn or Gwion (or someone else they were based upon) passed from one place to another. We must also remember that although these tales were written down during the medieval period, they likely have their origins centuries earlier, and were preserved in bardic oral tradition. While the Irish and the Celtic Britons were two different cultural groups, albeit related, the druids were an important part of every Celtic society, and it may be that these two tales have a common origin story that would have been a feature of Druidic teaching.

Seeking Sovereignty Within:
Journaling Prompts and Self-Reflective Questions

Moon Four
The Moon of Germination
The Time of Ceridwen

Mythic Focus: After nine moons in Ceridwen's womb, Gwion is reborn as Taliesin, the fully realized Shining Brow. She casts him into the waters and he is found in a salmon weir.

Personal Insights Around This Moon's Mythic Portion: *Meditate upon the portion of Ceridwen's story associated with this moon, and reflect it within yourself. Her story is your story.*

The Focus of the Moon of Germination by Phase

Seek the lessons of the Moon of Germination at each moon phase by using the stations of the monthly Cycle of Healing; be sure to journal all of the insights, symbols, and guidance you receive from each goddess at each moon phase. As you work with the information you receive between each phase, perhaps following the daily process outlined in chapter 3 of this book and using tools such as trance postures and doorways as detailed in *Avalon Within*, be sure to record those insights in your journal as well.

Full Moon: Connect with Ceridwen, as this is one of the four moons that make up her time, to set up your work for the month and to receive insight on the issue of focus. This is also the **Station of Confrontation** in the cycle of the sun, marked by the holy day of **Gwyl Mair**, and so will acknowledge the potential found in the depths of the darkness.

Third Quarter: Station of Descent in the cycle of the moon. Bring the issue of focus to Rhiannon to explore through the filters of the Station of Descent and the Moon of Germination.

Dark Moon: Station of Confrontation in the cycle of the moon. Bring the issue of focus to Ceridwen to explore through the filters of the Station of Confrontation and the Moon of Germination.

First Quarter: Station of Emergence in the cycle of the moon. Bring the issue of the focus to Blodeuwedd to explore through the filters of the Station of Emergence and the Moon of Germination.

Night before the Full Moon: Station of Resolution in the cycle of the moon. Bring the issue of focus to Arianrhod to explore through the filters of the Station of Resolution and the Moon of Germination.

At any point in the month, bring the issue of focus to Branwen to explore through the Station of Integration and the Moon of Germination. Some women will do this on the night after the dark moon in counterpoint to working with Arianrhod on the night before the full moon.

Herbal Ally for the Moon of Germination
Vervain (*Verbena officinalis*)

Creating the Mother Elixir: On the night of the full moon, create your Vervain Lunar Elixir using the directions found on page 105 of chapter 4. Be sure to label and date the bottle you are using to store the Mother Elixir. Journal any of your experiences around the creation of the vervain elixir.

Prepare the Daughter Elixir: After you have made the Mother Elixir, use the directions found on page 107 of chapter 4 to prepare a dosage bottle for use in the daily experience of this elixir throughout the month. Remember to use a blue or amber dropper bottle for this purpose, and to clearly label your Daughter Elixir.

Daily Work with the Vervain Elixir: As discussed in chapter 4, begin your daily exploration of the Vervain Elixir. Be sure to journal everything you can about how the elixir makes you feel, what you think its energetic actions are, where it sits in your energy body, and any and all impressions, insights, symbols, visions, and memories it presents to you:

WEEK ONE OF MOON FOUR: Immerse yourself in the lunar elixir by taking it every day, reflecting upon how it makes you feel, and journaling all of the insights that come to you when you meditate upon the energies of the elixir.

WEEK TWO OF MOON FOUR: Continue to take the lunar elixir daily, but this week spend time experiencing and comparing the energetic impact of vervain as an essence, and vervain as a magical herb that you burn, as detailed in chapter 4. Again, reflect upon how each makes you feel, and journal all of the insights that come to you when you meditate upon the energies of the elixir and the energies of the herb itself.

WEEK THREE OF MOON FOUR: Continue to take the lunar elixir daily, but this week spend time researching the medicinal, folkloric, and magical uses of vervain, beginning with the information provided in Part Three of this book. Compare your findings this week with your direct experiences, being sure to journal all of the insights and connections you've made.

WEEK FOUR OF MOON FOUR: Continue to take the lunar elixir daily, but this week meditate upon the mythic portion of the month and reflect upon the ways in which the energies of vervain are related to the present portion of Ceridwen's tale, and how it helps you to build a relationship with Ceridwen herself.

End of Moon Reflections: Under what circumstances could you see yourself using the vervain elixir in support of your work and personal process? If you had to describe the actions of this lunar elixir using one word, what would it be? What about using one sentence? What about using a whole paragraph? Again, be sure to journal everything.

Working: Journey Into the Sacred Landscape of Ceridwen

Llyn Tegid

Please perform the induction to travel over the Ninth Wave, as found on page 74, and then proceed with the working below. When you have completed it, be sure to return from across the Ninth Wave, using the visualization found on page 76.

Having crossed the Ninth Wave into the Otherworld, disembark and envision a silver tether that extends from the center of your torso to the vessel which bore you here; it is of endless length and will expand and retract as necessary as you explore this Realm Over Waves, while keeping you connected to the boat in order to facilitate your return.

Take three deep, anchoring breaths, and immerse yourself in the energies of this place. It is the reflection of Llyn Tegid, the home of Ceridwen, here in the realm of the Mythic Otherworld. Standing on shore of the lake in the fading twilight, you are greeted by a strange, almost acrid scent borne upon the breeze. You follow it, and it leads you along the edge of the water taking you from the open beachfront at the foot of the long, glacial lake up along the eastern shoreline. You enter into an overgrowth of spiral-limbed and moss-covered trees that make a lush canopy that forms a living tunnel along the water's edge. The scent becomes stronger as you continue to walk carefully in the dim light of the gloaming to step over the trunks of fallen trees and exposed roots lifting out of the ground like the gnarled fingers of ancient and arthritic hands.

At last you find yourself in a sheltered alcove, open to the waters of the lake but protected all around by a dense tangle of brush and trees. The scent is overwhelmingly strong here, and in the center of the wooded grotto you see a large cauldron hanging by a chain from a tripod over a slowly dying fire. Smoke rises from the mouth of the vessel, but no one appears to be tending this brew. Noticing a pile of neatly-stacked wood nearby, you feel called to add some fuel to the fading flames. You select a log and carefully place it among the embers and the half-burned wood underneath the cauldron. Squatting beside the fire, blow below the new wood three times to encourage the fire to catch; your effort is rewarded almost immediately—hungry tongues of flame begin to greedily devour the new wood.

You stand once more and see in the accompanying brightness that the cauldron is filled with a thick dark substance that roils into a boil as the fire crackles below it with increased vigor. The acrid stench fills your nostrils as large bubbles rise to the surface of the liquid, and belch odor into the darkness as they break. You notice a long-handled spoon hanging from one of the legs of the tripod. Take it and begin to stir. The liquid gets hotter and hotter as the boiling continues. The bubbles are smaller now but more numerous and frequent, and the steam rising from the of the brew shifts suddenly—it feels like the mixture has begun to coalesce. The bubbles come faster and faster.

And then, as if by magic, it is done.

There is a stillness…a silence…and then a bright and blinding light. Before you can react, three drops of shining liquid leap from the cauldron and land on your thumb. Instinctively, you pop your thumb into your mouth, expecting the heat of the brew to burn your skin, but this is not the case. Instead, you experience a warmth spreading from your hand, an almost ecstatic joy that rushes up your arm and fills the whole of your being with a radiant brilliance that infuses every cell and vibrates through every part of you. Pause now and fully experience this moment as you give yourself over to this energy that washes over your being, opens your heart, and brings illumination to your spirit. Filled in this way, you find that you now have full knowledge of what has just happened—you have received three drops of the Elixir of Wisdom from the Cauldron of Ceridwen, here on the shores of Llyn Tegid, her home. Take three deep and centering breaths as you anchor yourself in this new understanding.

Suddenly, your attention is brought back to the alcove when you hear a deep and resonant rumbling; the cauldron begins to shake and shudder. You back away from the unstable vessel and watch as it cracks in two, its dark and syrupy contents spill upon the ground, burning grass and the roots of shrubs and trees like a powerful acid.

In that moment, you sense that something is coming and you know that it is time. A light flashes inside you, the same light that emerged from the cauldron when the drops flew forth; you know it is a sign arising from your newly-gained Wisdom. Almost immediately, you sense a rustling in the underbrush and hear the low growl of what sounds to be a dog…and you know that you must run. With swift thought and an even swifter body, you sprint away and find that you somehow know how transform yourself into a hare. Bounding away into the brush, you run and run…pursued by a fleet-footed greyhound snarling and snapping at your tail. You dart left and right but cannot lose her. She closes in behind you, barking at you as her jaws seek to catch you. Your heart beating quickly, you continue to evade her.

A light flashes within you again, and suddenly you find that you are able to understand the meaning behind the greyhound's growls—another side effect of the cauldron's brew. She speaks: "I hold the challenges of the energies of Earth! What aspects of your physical self—your body, your health, your environment and access to resources—are holding you back in the here and now? How can these be transformed?"

Call upon the wisdom of the three drops and seek the answers to these questions as you continue to run from the greyhound…and when you feel you have received the answers you need, take three deep, centering breaths to integrate this understanding. And just as you feel these deeply rooted patterns that you're connecting with here and now are about to slow you and restrict you from moving forward, you become aware of the hot breath of the dog upon your back legs…a light within you impels you to move in a way you haven't before … to turn and leap, now jump, now dive into the water to escape the greyhound's jaws.

As you dive, the blinding light within you makes you know how to shift and change, and as you hit the water you become a shining silver salmon. Your slim body slices through the water as if it's something you've done your entire life. As you go down into the unfathomable depths of the deep glacial lake, you hear a large splash behind you. Turning your body so that you can look behind you, you realize you are still being pursued; the greyhound has also changed, becoming a swiftly swimming otter.

And even as its sharp claws brush dangerously close to the filaments of your delicate tail as you dart this way and that in your desire to get away, you experience that bright flash of inner light, and get a sense of what the otter is seeking to ask you: "I hold the challenges of the energies of Water! What aspects of your emotional self—your fears, your pain, your attachments—are holding you back in the here and now? How can these be transformed?"

Call upon the wisdom of the three drops and seek the answers to these questions as you continue to swim away from the otter … and when you feel you have received the answers you need, take three deep, centering breaths to integrate this understanding. And just as you feel these emotions you're connecting with are about to overwhelm you, you find the strength to lift yourself above them … to get the perspective you need to prevent them from pulling you down deeper and deeper into the well of what no longer is … and with a burst of strength, and a flash of light within, you throw yourself high above the surface of the water, entering the realm of air. As you do so, you realize that your fins have become wings, your scales have become feathers, and you have become a tiny wren whose beating wings take you high above the water to soar on the wake of the wind.

But the pursuit is not over—although you have taken flight and left the lake below you, you look down to see the otter leap out of the water. As she hits the air, she transforms into a sharp-taloned hawk who spreads her wings and closes the distance between you. Still you fly, and still the hawk pursues you, screeching. Up and around, darting left, veering right, you try to avoid her powerful beak and razor-like claws, but she remains close behind. Once more, the light shines within you, and in that moment of brightness you find that you can understand the hawk's screeching.

She asks: "I hold the challenges of the energies of Air! What aspects of your mental self—your perspectives, your illusions, how you communicate—are holding you back in the here and now? How can these be transformed?"

Call upon the wisdom of the three drops and seek the answers to these questions as you continue to fly away from the hawk … and when you feel you have received the answers you need, take three deep, centering breaths to integrate this understanding. And just as you feel the clarity of mind and the multitude of possibilities arising you're connecting with are about to overwhelm you, you find the focus to channel your energy to formulate a plan. Filled now with insight, you also find it increasingly difficult to elude the grasp of the hawk. Trying not to panic, you center and breathe. The light of understanding blazes inside of you, and in your mind you know at last what it is you must do.

Below you and not far from the long and shining body of Llyn Tegid, you see a farm. You fly toward it as quickly as your tired wings can take you and you catch sight of a mill as you draw close. Everywhere on the ground you see scattered seeds of wheat, and so you drop to the earth and you hide yourself among the grains there on the threshing floor. You only have a moment to breathe when you find again that you are not alone. The hawk has followed you, and as she glides to the ground, she transforms into a hungry black hen who pecks and scratches at the grains of wheat. Lying there still and silent, you listen to the scratching of the hen draw near, then far, then closer once more.

A flash of light fills your mind, and you find you can understand the clucking of the hen.

She asks: "I hold the challenges of the energies of Fire! What aspects of your creative self—your motivations, your obsessions, how you express your will—are holding you back in the here and now? How can these be transformed?"

Call upon the wisdom of the three drops and seek the answers to these questions as you continue lie still, hiding from the hen…and when you feel you have received the answers you need, take three deep, centering breaths to integrate this understanding. Deep recognition dawns on you at the same moment the hen's beak hovers above you. She tilts her head to look at you with one steady eye, and you know what you are meant to do. You take another three centering breaths and surrender yourself to the moment. The beak comes down and devours you…

And you know nothing but darkness…

Unsure of how much time you have spent in the stillness of the darkness, you become vaguely aware of a growing light coming from within you and around you all at once. In this faint glow, you slowly realize that you are surrounded by water and you feel yourself being held in the deep curve of the bottom of Llyn Tegid, feeling so much like the Cauldron of Ceridwen. Experience yourself being rocked back and forth…back and forth…back and forth…and as you are rocked, you are shaped and you are shifted and you are changed. You are like the many pieces of slate that are smoothed and formed by the rhythms of Llyn Tegid as its waters are churned by the currents of the River Dee as it flows through this glacial lake. You too are shifted…you too are held…you too are rocked and formed and smoothed like one of Ceridwen's fingers, the long and thin pieces of slate birthed by this lake and its current.

The light within you flashes stronger than ever, and you know that you are in a place of renewal and rebirth…the womb of the goddess.

You know, too, that when you are ready, you will emerge from these maternal waters. Take some time now, to reflect upon your life. Think about the person you would like to be. Think about what it would be like to go through life with the certainty that you are now, and always have been, connected to goddess, connected to the Divine… and that you are her child, being reborn with every breath.

It is time now to reemerge from the lake, from the womb, from the Cauldron of Ceridwen. Leaving behind the energies that interfere with you knowing your wholeness and keep you from acknowledging your holiness, you emerge from the water and find yourself once more on the shores of Llyn Tegid. Take a moment and look at yourself in the mirror-like surface of the water. You see a shining face different from before but somehow also the same. How have these drops of wisdom shifted you? How can you better do your work in the world? How does it feel to have reclaimed some of the energies locked up in shadow while looking forward to doing more work in the light of Sovereignty?

Take three deep, centering breaths. Remember all that you have seen, and received, and committed to in this moment. And when you are ready, follow the thread that connects you to the vessel which took you to this Land Beyond Wave, taking your place in the boat once more, to begin the journey back over the Nine Waves, to the place that is here and the time that is now.

Chapter 6

THE TIME OF BLODEUWEDD

THERE ARE FEW FEMALE CHARACTERS in Welsh Mythology who present as great a moral challenge to modern readers as Blodeuwedd, who appears in the Fourth Branch of *Y Mabinogi*. A face-value reading of her tale paints her as a shallow and faithless woman originally made of flowers, an adulteress who plots with her lover to murder her husband, and a fleeing woman who is ultimately punished for her crimes by being transformed into an owl for all eternity. How could she be anything but a villain? Who would look up to this wicked woman, much less honor her as a goddess? Clearly, there is more going on in her story than meets the eye, and the key to understanding requires some context from medieval Welsh culture, as well as the inherent symbolism of the story with roots that go back further still.

Magically created from the flowers of oak, broom, and meadowsweet she is first called *Blodeuedd*, which simply means, "flowers." Later, when she is transformed into an owl, her name also changes, becoming *Blodeuwedd*—"flower face"—which describes the flower-like face of the owl she has become. Blodeuedd is created for one purpose: to be the bride of Lleu Llaw Gyffes, who has had a destiny lain upon him that prevented him from marrying a human woman. Soon after they are wed, for the first time acting with any agency in the tale, Blodeuedd falls in love with Gronw Pebyr, the lord of a neighboring land, and the resulting love triangle that unfolds in the story is deeply symbolic. Lleu, whose name potentially means "light," can be seen as the Solar Hero who represents the light half of the year while Gronw, who we meet as a hunter, is associated with chthonic symbols that hint at his status as the Otherworldly Champion who represents the dark half of the year. The two faces of Blodeuwedd underscore this polarity; she is an owl when mated with the Otherworldly Champion, and a Flower Bride when wed to the Solar Hero.

There is therefore potential that the tale of Blodeuwedd in the Fourth Branch is a medieval Welsh resonance of an international folk motif depicting a symbolic reenactment of the endless struggle between light and dark or between summer and winter. It is significant that Blodeuwedd is the pivot around which the balance shifts. This may be an indication of her former status as a tutelary deity—a goddess of the land—and indeed she is literally made of nature. By extension, she may well have been a Sovereignty goddess of the seasonal variety. As such, she has the right to choose her mate, and who she chooses becomes king. This may be why she could not simply have run away with Gronw—only one king can reign at a time.

Whether she is simply a legendary figure from medieval Welsh lore, or is in truth a Sovereignty goddess once worshiped in Celtic Britain, there is no doubt that Blodeuwedd is celebrated and honored in modern times as a divinity in her own right. After dwelling for centuries in darkness and flying on owl wings along the liminal boundary that straddles superstition and sacred symbol—this world and the Otherworld, archetype and divinity—the essence of all that is Blodeuwedd is venturing once more into the light of consciousness. Simultaneously Flower Bride and Owl of Wisdom, Unfaithful Wife, and Lady of Sovereignty, this complex figure holds many lessons for those who seek to know her; through her, we may learn to shed the fragile petals of illusion wrought by the expectations of others, in order to birth the authentic self that is able to see truth with owl-wise eyes.

Moon 5

THE MOON OF EVOCATION

Moon Five of the Avalonian Cycle of Revealing is called the Moon of Evocation and is associated with the herb broom (Cytisus scoparius). It is the first of four moons during the Time of Blodeuwedd. The lunar month begins on the first full moon when the sun is in Pisces; the full moon is in Virgo.

It is the time of Blodeuwedd. Just as the mysteries of the dark moon give way to the marvel of the first silvered crescent of the new moon, so must we begin the work of bringing the reclaimed seeds of wisdom from out of the fallow darkness up into the waxing light. While we are still in the process of coming to a deep understanding of these seeds and the matrix of shadow which held the treasure of them for so long, we pivot from being fully receptive in our search for meaning to considering new ways of being which will bring about lasting change. This is indeed an evocation, a calling forth of new beginnings from out of the slowly weakening entanglements of shadow. We may not yet have the complete blueprint that will guide us from our present state of being to a place of greater balance and consciousness of Self, but we can start the process of change by harnessing the upward swing of the newly waxing cycle to commence creating a container to hold and concentrate the energies of our sovereign intention.

The Mythic Portion

Forbidden by his mother Arianrhod to take a wife from among the women of the Earth, the guardians of Lleu Llaw Gyffes—his uncle Gwydion and great-uncle Math—use their magic to create a bride for him out of the flowers of oak, broom, and meadowsweet. Conjuring forth the most beautiful woman anyone had ever seen, the magicians name her *Blodeuedd*, whose name means "flowers."[10]

The Work of the Moon of Evocation

Just as Math and Gwydion call Blodeuedd forth from the Otherworld, we are charged to bring the changes demanded by the revelations of Confrontation into manifestation. The lunar cycle has begun to wax, moving back up toward the light half of the cycle, and bringing with it the renewed energy reclaimed from the darkness. Possessing this new wisdom and increased clarity, we must now find the strength of purpose needed to call forth the potential revealed in the reflection at the bottom of the cauldron. Much like Gwydion and Math were able to call forth the essence of a goddess into physical manifestation, we must also learn how to incorporate the wisdom of the dark time into our lives in order to become the physical plane reflection of our Higher Self potential. Remember to appreciate the sweetness and beauty of this renewal, but know that there is more that needs to change than what is apparent on the surface.

The shift in energy between the Time of Ceridwen and the Time of Blodeuwedd is a powerful one—a jump from the emptiness of the Void to the promise of renewal. Here we see mirrored the transformation of the Loathly Lady from hag to beauty when she is given what

---

10. Blodeuedd's name changes at the end of the tale, becoming the more familiar Blodeuwedd, "flower-face," as a reflection of her transformation into an owl.

she most desires—Sovereignty. Indeed, finding the root of the shadow in the darkness is the key to self-mastery.

Searching Deeper

Blodeuedd is conjured into being through the enchantments of Math, Lord of Gwynedd, and his nephew Gwydion, both of whom are powerful magicians. She is created in order to circumvent the third *tynged*, meaning "destiny" or "fate," placed upon Lleu by his mother, Arianrhod; this *tynged* declared that he was forbidden to marry a woman of the race of the Earth. As Lleu's manhood and future kingship depended on his taking a wife, it was critical for his uncles to secure one for him, even in the face of his mother's prohibition. (Arianrhod's tale is covered in detail in chapter 9).

The tale was very specific about the flowers used to create Blodeuedd; these particular blooms may well have held a significance that would have been immediately understood by the contemporary medieval audience—a significance we can only guess at but which may well have influenced specific information about the nature of Blodeuedd's character. The oak is a tree closely associated with the Solar Hero in many cultures, and it is this very tree which houses the wounded Lleu when he is in eagle form (yet another solar association) later on in the tale. The oak was, of course, sacred to the Celts and holds strong druidic associations; its inclusion may reflect a druidic origin of the magics of Math and Gwydion.

The broom is used as a descriptor for Olwen's yellow hair in the medieval Welsh tale *Culhwch ac Olwen*, and while it may be mentioned to likewise allude to Blodeuedd's hair color, it is also a herb used in the *materia medica* of the Physicians of Myddfai to cool fevers. Broom was used to cleanse the house on May Day and was often included in brides' bouquets, as was meadowsweet (which is also known by the name "bridewort"). Interestingly, meadowsweet has also been used as a funerary herb; perhaps its presence here presages the role Blodeuedd will play in Lleu's "death."

The fourteenth-century Welsh manuscript *Llyfr Taliesin* (*The Book of Taliesin*) contains a poem called "Cad Goddeu" ("The Battle of the Trees"), which has several lines that appear to refer to the creation of Blodeuedd by Math and Gwydion:

> *When I was made,*
> *Did my Creator create me.*
> *Of nine-formed faculties,*
> *Of the fruit of fruits,*
> *Of the fruit of the primordial God,*
> *Of primroses and blossoms of the hill,*
> *Of the flowers of trees and shrubs.*
> *Of earth, of an earthly course,*
> *When I was formed.*
> *Of the flower of nettles,*
> *Of the water of the ninth wave.*
> *I was enchanted by Math,*
> *Before I became immortal,*
> *I was enchanted by Gwydyon*
> *The great purifier of the Brython*

If this poem, said to be written by the historic bard Taliesin, does indeed refer to the creation of Blodeuedd, he includes some alternative components in her creation. The nettle plant that grows so wild and abundantly in Britain is also called "stinging nettle" due to the painful reaction caused by the venom on its hair-like spines when it comes into contact with skin. It is a plant with powerful healing qualities with the ability to cause hurt as well—an apt representation of the darker side of Blodeuedd.

One of the recurring themes in the Fourth Branch of *Y Mabinogi* is circumventing expected gender roles, especially where it comes to birth.

The first part of the Fourth Branch sees Gwydion and his brother Gil-faethwy punished by their uncle Math for starting an unjust war and committing rape; for three years they are transformed into different animals, taking turns swapping genders, and bearing each others' sons while in animal form. Later, their sister Arianrhod rejects the role of mother of the children she was forced to birth, and Gwydion takes what the text describes to be a "small thing" that falls from Arianrhod's body to place it in a chest at the foot of his bed. There it incubates and becomes an infant boy, who would later be named Lleu. Finally, to overcome the last of the *tynghedau* put upon Lleu by his mother, Math and Gwydion work together to create life, "birthing" Blodeuedd out of flowers, thereby completely claiming the progenitive powers of women for their own.

Seeking Sovereignty Within:
Journaling Prompts and Self-Reflective Questions

Moon Five
The Moon of Evocation
The Time of Blodeuwedd

Mythic Focus: When Arianrhod prohibits her son, Lleu, from marrying a woman of any race on the Earth, Blodeuwedd is "created" from the flowers of oak, broom, and meadowsweet by the magicians Gwydion and Math.

Personal Insights Around This Moon's Mythic Portion: *Meditate upon the portion of Blodeuwedd's story associated with this moon, and reflect it within yourself. Her story is your story.*

The Focus of the Moon of Evocation by Phase

Seek the lessons of the Moon of Evocation at each moon phase by using the Stations of the monthly Cycle of Healing; be sure to journal all of the insights, symbols, and guidance you receive from each goddess at each moon phase. As you work with the information you receive between each phase, perhaps following the daily process outlined in chapter 3 of this book, and using tools such as trance postures and doorways as detailed in *Avalon Within*, be sure to record those insights in your journal as well.

Full Moon: Connect with Blodeuwedd at the full moon. Review the work of the previous month and the insights it brought to you, set up your work for the coming month, and ask for insights on the issue of focus which may have shifted or deepened due to the work you have done.

3rd Quarter: Station of Descent in the cycle of the moon. Bring the issue of focus to Rhiannon to explore through the filters of the Station of Descent and the Moon of Evocation.

Dark Moon: Station of Confrontation in the cycle of the moon. Bring the issue of focus to Ceridwen to explore through the filters of the Station of Confrontation and the Moon of Evocation.

1st Quarter: Station of Emergence in the cycle of the moon. Bring the issue of the focus to Blodeuwedd to explore through the filters of the Station of Emergence and the Moon of Evocation.

Night before the Full Moon: Station of Resolution in the cycle of the moon. Bring the issue of focus to Arianrhod to explore through the filters of the Station of Resolution and the Moon of Evocation.

At any point in the month, bring the issue of focus to Branwen to explore through the Station of Integration and the Moon of Evocation. Some women will do this on the night after the dark moon in counterpoint to working with Arianrhod on the night before the full moon.

Herbal Ally for the Moon of Evocation
Broom (*Cytisus scoparius*)

Creating the Mother Elixir: On the night of the full moon, create your Broom Lunar Elixir using the directions found on page 105 of chapter 4. Be sure to label and date the bottle you are using to store the Mother Elixir. Journal any of your experiences around the creation of the broom elixir.

Prepare the Daughter Elixir: After you have made the Mother Elixir, use the directions found on page 107 of chapter 4 to prepare a dosage bottle for use in the daily experience of this elixir throughout the month. Remember to use a blue or amber dropper bottle for this purpose, and to clearly label your Daughter Elixir.

Daily Work with the Broom Elixir: As discussed in chapter 4, begin your daily exploration of the broom elixir. Be sure to journal everything you can about how the elixir makes you feel, what you think it its energetic actions are, where it sits in your energy body, and any and all impressions, insights, symbols, visions, and memories it presents to you:

WEEK ONE OF MOON FIVE: Immerse yourself in the lunar elixir by taking it every day, reflecting upon how it makes you feel, and journaling all of the insights that come to you when you meditate upon the energies of the elixir.

WEEK TWO OF MOON FIVE: Continue to take the lunar elixir daily, but this week spend time experiencing and comparing the energetic impact of broom as an essence, and broom as a magical herb that you burn, as detailed in chapter 4. Again, reflect upon how each makes you feel, and journal all of the insights that come to you when you meditate upon the energies of the elixir and the energies of the herb itself.

WEEK THREE OF MOON FIVE: Continue to take the lunar elixir daily, but this week spend time researching the medicinal, folkloric, and magical uses of broom, beginning with the information provided in Part Three of this book. Compare your findings this week with your direct experiences, being sure to journal all of the insights and connections you've made.

WEEK FOUR OF MOON FIVE: Continue to take the lunar elixir daily, but this week meditate upon the mythic portion of the month and reflect upon the ways in which the energies of broom are related to the present portion of Blodeuwedd's tale, and how it helps you to build a relationship with Blodeuwedd herself.

End of Moon Reflections: Under what circumstances could you see yourself using the Broom Elixir in support of your work and personal process? If you had to describe the actions of this lunar elixir using one word, what would it be? What about using one sentence? What about using a whole paragraph? Again, be sure to journal everything.

Moon 6
THE MOON OF ACTIVATION

Moon Six of the Avalonian Cycle of Revealing is called the Moon of Activation, and is associated with the herb mead-owsweet (Filpendula ulmaria). It is the second of four moons during the Time of Blodeuwedd, and the lunar month begins on the first full moon when the sun is in Aries, with the full moon in Libra.

Cultivating an honest understanding of ourselves is a critical part of our soul work. With increased clarity comes greater discernment, and both are crucial for an honest evaluation of the longstanding circumstances of our lives, as well as our most deeply held beliefs and perspectives—whether about the world or about ourselves. When we start to question some of our beliefs, or feel resistance to meeting certain expectations, or begin making choices that cause others to feel challenged and defensive, it is the sap of our personal agency which is beginning to arise within us. This is a powerful place to be as it permits us to evaluate our choices, our lives, and the people in it from a more authentic place—a place that is increasingly centered in our growing understanding of the person we have become, as well as the person we know that we are able and destined to be.

The Mythic Portion

The marriage of Blodeuedd and Lleu permits him to enter fully into manhood, bestowing upon him the ability to rule in his own right. Now that he has a wife, the last of Arianrhod's three *tynghedau* has been overcome. His great-uncle Math gives him lands to rule, and Lleu, whose name potentially means "light," is diligent in his care of them, often leaving his court at Mur Castell in Ardudwy to oversee his other holdings, as well as to visit Math at his court of Caer Dathyl. Blodeuedd is the very paragon of the perfect and dutiful wife, caring for the court in her husband's absence, and extending the expected hospitality to the neighboring lord, Gronw Pebyr of Penllyn, when his hunting party tarries late on Lleu's lands. However, the two of them fall in love, and sleep with each other for three nights; Gronw at last departs before Lleu returns.

The Work of the Moon of Activation

Since ancient times, humanity has taken notice of flowers which track the motion of the sun as it moves across the sky. Tenacious in their pursuit of the light, these open blossoms absorb the rays of the sun, which warms their pollen and attracts the pollinators needed to fertilize the plant. As beautiful as flowers are, and as sweet as their fragrance may be, they exist to serve a very specific and powerful task, and the rest of the plant relies upon them to accomplish it. Creating a woman made from flowers to marry a being with authority over the light was a very shrewd thing for Gwydion and Math to do on Lleu's behalf; she could not help but be drawn to him, attentive to his every move.

Similarly, from a very young age we are groomed to believe we have a particular role to play in society that is oftentimes related to our gender presentation. Further, it is during this formative time, before we have any concept that we possess any personal agency, that the foundation is lain for social and familial expectations to which we will be held accountable. And, for many of us, it is during this time that the filters through which we will view the world for the rest of our lives is formed, and the perspectives we hold about many things is set, unless we deliberately choose otherwise.

Some of these perspectives are actively transmitted to us by our families of origin, by our faith communities, in our educational systems, through our civic requirements, and from our understanding of the law. We adopt other perspectives in a more passive manner: unconsciously receiving instruction about societal standards, cultural taboos, and social expectations from the media, through observation of others, and from personal experience of what happens when and if we deviate from the norm in any given way. As a survival mechanism, we learn to reflect the world around us onto the world within us. Driven by these cultural forces, therefore, the development of this inner adaptation is supported by our being rewarded for conformity to external expectations and punished for transgressing against these expectations.

As a consequence, many of our views on the world—for example, the things we consider "normal," the behaviors we deem to be morally correct, the elements we feel are necessary to have a good life, the metrics we use to determine success—are often those that have been taught to us from a young age, rather than ones that we have developed for ourselves. These aren't necessarily bad things *per se*, but they are unconscious things that greatly influence our choices in life. When we believe that life is supposed to look a certain way and meant to include certain experiences and follow a specific trajectory, we reject opportunities that present themselves to us simply because they do not conform with this unconscious model.

Unfortunately, there are those who follow the pre-plotted map, and get to the point in their lives where they have checked all of the boxes of what a well-lived life is supposed to look like, only to realize that they are not truly happy. They may come to recognize that the life they have lived followed someone else's model instead of being an authentic reflection of the person they truly are. This is why working to know ourselves as best as we can—our hurts, our gifts, our fears, our desires—is such a key part of living a life of Sovereignty. No choices are "wrong"—instead, it is critical that we understand the reasons *why* we make the choices that we do, and armed with this knowledge, we can move forward on a path of authenticity.

To this end, questions we can ask ourselves include: In our lives, what are the garments we that we wear and the roles we play? How in sync are these roles with our divine purpose? What *is* our divine purpose? How can we bring forth the changes required by the cauldron's insights? What aspects of our lives make us happy? What fulfills our life's purpose? What is simply present because it is what is expected of us? What must we change to live a life of authenticity?

Searching Deeper

Medieval Welsh law contains an entire section detailing the rights of women where it concerns marriage, divorce, and inheritance. These laws specify that a woman cannot be given into marriage by her kin without her consent: "…a woman must be a free consenting party to her marriage and could not be disposed of against her will … there was no selling of a woman in marriage."[11]

We see the dynamic of consent at work in *Y Mabinogi* in several places. In the First Branch, it is Rhiannon who pursues Pywll so as not to marry a man she does not love, and in the Third Branch, Rhiannon consents to marry Manawydan at the suggestion of Pryderi, her son. In the Second Branch, Branwen agrees to marry Matholwch, the King of Ireland, after conferring with her family, and it is her family who comes to her aid when she is mistreated by her husband. Yet, in the Fourth

---

11. T.P. Ellis, "Legal references, terms and conceptions in the Mabinogion," *Y Cymmrodor* 39 (1928): 124–125.

Branch, Blodeuedd is not shown to give her consent to the marriage, nor does she have a family to advocate for her and to make the marriage arrangements. Because of this, it is possible that her marriage to Lleu was not a legal one—a fact that would have likely been understood by the tale's medieval Welsh audience.

She has been created for one purpose only—to marry Lleu so that he can obtain his status in the world, despite the prohibitions placed upon him by his mother. The perfect bride, Blodeuedd is everything a man of this time could want: beautiful, attentive, and compliant. The creation of Blodeuedd out of flowers not only bypassed—or perhaps if considered in another way, fulfilled—Arianrhod's requirement for her son, it also represented the well-established Celtic folkloric motif that required the king to make a sacred marriage with the land in order to claim his right to rule.

The motif of the Flower Bride has many resonances in Celtic mythology. She is the vessel of Sovereignty—she who bestows kingship with her body through the sympathetic union of the king and the land. How better to illustrate this than by manifesting a woman made completely from flowers—a component of the land? If Blodeuedd is a Sovereignty figure, then she is already divine when she is called through the veil to take form on the physical plane by Math and Gwydion.

Seeking Sovereignty Within:
Journaling Prompts and Self-Reflective Questions

Moon Six
The Moon of Activation
The Time of Blodeuwedd

Mythic Focus: Blodeuwedd is wed to Lleu, and he comes into his power as an adult man, ruling over lands granted by Math.

Personal Insights Around This Moon's Mythic Portion: *Meditate upon the portion of Blodeuwedd's story associated with this moon, and reflect it within yourself. Her story is your story.*

The Focus of the Moon of Activation by Phase

Seek the lessons of the Moon of Activation at each moon phase by using the Stations of the monthly Cycle of Healing; be sure to journal all of the insights, symbols, and guidance you receive from each goddess at each moon phase. As you work with the information you receive between each phase, perhaps following the daily process outlined in chapter 3 of this book, and using tools such as trance postures and doorways as detailed in *Avalon Within*, be sure to record those insights in your journal as well.

Full Moon: Connect with Blodeuwedd at the full moon. Review the work of the previous month and the insights it brought to you, set up your work for the coming month, and ask for insights on the issue of focus which may have shifted or deepened due to the work you have done.

3rd Quarter: Station of Descent in the cycle of the moon. Bring the issue of focus to Rhiannon to explore through the filters of the Station of Descent and the Moon of Activation.

Dark Moon: Station of Confrontation in the cycle of the moon. Bring the issue of focus to Ceridwen to explore through the filters of the Station of Confrontation and the Moon of Activation.

1st Quarter: Station of Emergence in the cycle of the moon. Bring the issue of the focus to Blodeuwedd to explore through the filters of the Station of Emergence and the Moon of Activation.

Night before the Full Moon: Station of Resolution in the cycle of the moon. Bring the issue of focus to Arianrhod to explore through the filters of the Station of Resolution and the Moon of Activation.

At any point in the month, bring the issue of focus to Branwen to explore through the Station of Integration and the Moon of Activation. Some women will do this on the night after the dark moon in counterpoint to working with Arianrhod on the night before the full moon.

Herbal Ally for the Moon of Activation
Meadowsweet (*Filpendula ulmaria*)

Creating the Mother Elixir: On the night of the full moon, create your Meadowsweet Lunar Elixir using the directions found on page 105 of chapter 4. Be sure to label and date the bottle you are using to store the Mother Elixir. Journal any of your experiences around the creation of the Meadowsweet Elixir.

Prepare the Daughter Elixir: After you have made the Mother Elixir, use the directions found on page 107 of chapter 4 to prepare a dosage bottle for use in the daily experience of this elixir throughout the month. Remember to use a blue or amber dropper bottle for this purpose, and to clearly label your Daughter Elixir.

Daily Work with the Meadowsweet Elixir: As discussed in chapter 4, begin your daily exploration of the meadowsweet elixir. Be sure to journal everything you can about how the elixir makes you feel, what you think its energetic actions are, where it sits in your energy body, and any and all impressions, insights, symbols, visions, and memories it presents to you:

WEEK ONE OF MOON SIX: Immerse yourself in the lunar elixir by taking it every day, reflecting upon how it makes you feel, and journaling all of the insights that come to you when you meditate upon the energies of the elixir.

WEEK TWO OF MOON SIX: Continue to take the lunar elixir daily, but this week spend time experiencing and comparing the energetic impact of meadowsweet as an essence, and meadowsweet as a magical herb that you burn, as detailed in chapter 4. Again, reflect upon how each makes you feel, and journal all of the insights that come to you when you meditate upon the energies of the elixir and the energies of the herb itself.

WEEK THREE OF MOON SIX: Continue to take the lunar elixir daily, but this week spend time researching the medicinal, folkloric, and magical uses of meadowsweet, beginning with the information provided in Part Three of this book. Compare your findings this week with your direct experiences, being sure to journal all of the insights and connections you've made.

WEEK FOUR OF MOON SIX: Continue to take the lunar elixir daily, but this week meditate upon the mythic portion of the month and reflect upon the ways in which the energies of meadowsweet are related to the present portion of Blodeuwedd's tale, and how it helps you to build a relationship with Blodeuwedd herself.

End of Moon Reflections: Under what circumstances could you see yourself using the meadowsweet elixir in support of your work and personal process? If you had to describe the actions of this lunar elixir using one word, what would it be? What about using one sentence? What about using a whole paragraph? Again, be sure to journal everything.

Moon 7

THE MOON OF REVELATION

Moon Seven of the Avalonian Cycle of Revealing is called the Moon of Revelation and is associated with the herb nettle (Urtica dioica). It is the third of four moons during the Time of Blodeuwedd, and the lunar month begins on the first full moon when the sun is in Taurus; the full moon is in Scorpio. This full moon corresponds with the Station of Emergence in the Avalonian Cycle of Healing, and it is the holy day of Calan Haf.

It can be a shock when at last we discover our soul's purpose. It can be a profoundly life-changing event that may dissemble our sense of self down to the core of us in anticipation of our building it up again, centered around this new understanding of who we are and what we are meant to be. Sometimes this revelation is catalyzed by someone or something in our lives, while other times it comes as a result of the inner work that we are doing and the way we have begun to walk in the world as a result of it. The work has just begun, however, and this precious, tiny sapling of the authentic you has a lot of growing to do. At this time and in this place, which is neither a time nor a place, commit to manifesting this deep soul desire out into the world. Begin to chart the path you will take, outline the real-world steps you will make, and remember to be patient with yourself and your process. The bridge from one state of being to the next can be a long one, especially if you've not journeyed down this pathway before.

Breathe. Envision. Become.

The Mythic Portion

On one occasion of Lleu's absence from court, Gronw Pebyr, the lord of the neighboring land of Penllyn, was hunting a stag on Lleu and Blodeuedd's lands. He brought it down on the banks of the River Cynfal. He was tarrying to skin the stag and bait his dogs, so it was almost nightfall by the time he and his retinue passed by the gate of the court. Not wanting to dishonor a neighboring lord, Blodeuedd offered Gronw Pebyr hospitality with the support of her household servants. At the feast she laid before him, Blodeuedd and Gronw were infused with love for each other, and slept together that night. He tried to leave in the morning, but Blodeuedd bade him remain with her, so he did. He tried to leave again the next morning, but she asked him to stay one more night with her, saying she would let him go the next day. On the third morning before Gronw departed, the couple planned how they could remain together, and determined that Blodeuedd would discover how it was that Lleu could be killed under the guise of being concerned for his well-being.

When Lleu returns that night, Blodeuedd tells him she is worried about what would happen if he should die before her. Trying to set her mind to rest, Lleu confides in Blodeuedd that the only way he can be killed is under very specific circumstances: he cannot be indoors nor outdoors, nor can he be on horseback or on foot, and he can only be killed by a spear that was crafted over the course of a year and a day, and only worked on during mass on Sundays. Expressing relief to Lleu in the moment, she nevertheless sends this information to Gronw, and he sets to work on creating the spear.

When the year and the day has passed and the spear is ready, she prepares for Lleu a bath in a large cauldron on the banks of the River Cynfael, and above it constructs a structure consisting of a thatched roof with no walls. Blodeuedd brings a buck beside the bath, and after Lleu has bathed, she asks him to show her how he would have to stand in order to fulfill the requirements that would bring about his death—

neither indoors nor outdoors, not on foot nor on horseback—just to reassure her it could never happen. He puts on his trousers and places one foot on the edge of the tub and the other on the back of the buck, standing beneath the wall-less roof. Immediately Gronw rises from his hiding place and casts his spear, striking Lleu in the side. Instead of dying, Lleu is transformed into an eagle that flies off, wounded. Now free to be together, Blodeuedd and Gronw return to Mur Castlle. Adding them to his own, Gronw takes over all of Lleu's lands and rules them with Blodeuedd

The Work of the Moon of Revelation

Changing your life to obtain that which you most desire is a noble pursuit, especially when what you want is in alignment with the person you are actively working to become. The more you change, the more you pull away from people and situations that have become toxic to you and your goals, the more centered in authenticity you become. In the face of the difficulties you may be encountering from others around the positive changes you are making, you must learn to set good boundaries for yourself, lest you allow others to push you off your mark.

Do not be surprised when the people in your life object to a path you have chosen, the changes you have made, or the things you no longer do because they only ever existed to meet the expectations of others. Unless you are embarking upon a dangerous journey, or else are in the grip of shadow illusions so strong that you are being reckless, these objections are often rooted in others' own fears and wounds and their inability to see themselves with clarity.

People sometimes get angry, feel hurt, and don't know how to relate with someone they've known for a long time who has made significant changes in their life—particularly when it affects the relationship. Often they will pull away, especially if you refuse to stop becoming someone they no longer recognize; sadly, you may be the one they blame for pushing them away.

The greater part of wisdom is coming to know how to live your truth. Once you have found who you are meant to be, it is up to you to make the choices that will allow you to manifest this potential. Sometimes the obstacles in our paths seem insurmountable—all you need to do is ask the way and it will be revealed to you.

Searching Deeper

There is more to Blodeuedd's betrayal of Lleu than what meets the eye; in order to see the underlying themes, we must consider the cultural context of the story and not read it from a modern perspective. Blodeuedd acts with personal agency for the first time when she meets Gronw. She offers him hospitality, as would be expected of her, but when the two fall in love, she boldly asks him to remain with her for three nights. Each night he asks permission to leave, but she refuses and instead asks him to stay another night. Although this is not made explicit in the text, it is likely that the medieval audience would have recognized this to be one of the legal unions provided for by Welsh law which recognized nine different types of marriage. Each union held a different status ranked by the degree of honor each held and the amount of protection each afforded the woman in terms of property, dowry, and compensation during divorce.

The most respected form of marriage was called *priodas*, which was a union of two people of equal rank and financial stature; examples of priodas is illustrated in *Y Mabinogi* by the marriages of Branwen and Rhiannon. In contrast, Blodeuedd and Gronw engaged in a *llathlud twyll* (false or secret elopement), a type of marriage called *caradas* (marriage for love), wherein a woman chose a man without the permission of her family and slept publicly with that man for three nights in a row.

Whoever sleeps with a woman for three nights from the time when the fire is covered up until it is uncovered the next day, and wishes to repudiate her, let him pay her a bullock worth twenty pence and another worth thirty and another worth sixty. And if he takes her to house and holding, and she is with him until the end of the seven years, he shares with her as with a woman who had givers.[12]

While this was a legally recognized marriage, it did not carry the same respect and legal protection afforded by priodas until seven years into the union, after which it would hold the same legal standing as *priodas*. If Lleu and Blodeuedd's marriage was not lawful, as she is not shown to give her consent to the union as mentioned earlier during our discussion of the Moon of Activation, then perhaps it would have been clear to a medieval audience that her elopement with Gronw was within her legal rights to make—a fact that would change the tenor of the affair completely.

12. Jane Cartwright, *Feminine Sanctity and Spirituality in Medieval Wales* (Cardiff: University of Wales Press, 2008), 169.

Seeking Sovereignty Within:
Journaling Prompts and Self-Reflective Questions

Moon Seven
The Moon of Revelation
The Time of Blodeuwedd

Mythic Focus: Blodeuwedd falls in love with Gronw Pebyr, and chooses him over Lleu.

Personal Insights Around This Moon's Mythic Portion: *Meditate upon the portion of Blodeuwedd's story associated with this moon and reflect it within yourself. Her story is your story.*

The Focus of the Moon of Revelation by Phase

Seek the lessons of the Moon of Revelation at each moon phase by using the Stations of the monthly Cycle of Healing; be sure to journal all of the insights, symbols, and guidance you receive from each goddess at each moon phase. As you work with the information you receive between each phase, perhaps following the daily process outlined in chapter 3 of this book, and using tools such as trance postures and doorways as detailed in *Avalon Within*, be sure to record those insights in your journal as well.

Full Moon: Connect with Blodeuwedd at the full moon. Review the work of the previous month and the insights it brought to you, set up your work for the coming month, and ask for insights on the issue of focus which may have shifted or deepened due to the work you have done. This is also the **Station of Emergence** in the cycle of the sun, marked by the holy day of **Calan Haf**, and so will establish the work of the light half of the year.

Third Quarter: Station of Descent in the cycle of the moon. Bring the issue of focus to Rhiannon to explore through the filters of the Station of Descent and the Moon of Revelation.

Dark Moon: Station of Confrontation in the cycle of the moon. Bring the issue of focus to Ceridwen to explore through the filters of the Station of Confrontation and the Moon of Revelation.

First Quarter: Station of Emergence in the cycle of the moon. Bring the issue of the focus to Blodeuwedd to explore through the filters of the Station of Emergence and the Moon of Revelation.

Night before the Full Moon: Station of Resolution in the cycle of the moon. Bring the issue of focus to Arianrhod to explore through the filters of the Station of Resolution and the Moon of Revelation.

At any point in the month, bring the issue of focus to Branwen to explore through the Station of Integration and the Moon of Revelation. Some women will do this on the night after the dark moon in counterpoint to working with Arianrhod on the night before the full moon.

Herbal Ally for the Moon of Revelation
Nettle (*Urtica dioica*)

Creating the Mother Elixir: On the night of the full moon, create your Nettle Lunar Elixir using the directions found on page 107 of chapter 4. Be sure to label and date the bottle you are using to store the Mother Elixir. Journal any of your experiences around the creation of the Nettle Elixir.

Prepare the Daughter Elixir: After you have made the Mother Elixir, use the directions found on page 110 of chapter 4 to prepare a dosage bottle for use in the daily experience of this elixir throughout the month. Remember to use a blue or amber dropper bottle for this purpose and to clearly label your Daughter Elixir.

Daily Work with the Nettle Elixir: As discussed in chapter 4, begin your daily exploration of the nettle elixir. Be sure to journal everything you can about how the elixir makes you feel, what you think its energetic actions are, where it sits in your energy body, and any and all impressions, insights, symbols, visions, and memories it presents to you:

WEEK ONE OF MOON SEVEN: Immerse yourself in the lunar elixir by taking it every day, reflecting upon how it makes you feel, and journaling all of the insights that come to you when you meditate upon the energies of the elixir.

WEEK TWO OF MOON SEVEN: Continue to take the lunar elixir daily, but this week spend time experiencing and comparing the energetic impact of nettle as an essence, and nettle as a magical herb that you burn, as detailed in chapter 4. Again, reflect upon how each makes you feel, and journal all of the insights that come to you when you meditate upon the energies of the elixir and the energies of the herb itself.

WEEK THREE OF MOON SEVEN: Continue to take the lunar elixir daily, but this week spend time researching the medicinal, folkloric, and magical uses of nettle, beginning with the information provided in Part Three of this book. Compare your findings this week with your direct experiences, being sure to journal all of the insights and connections you've made.

WEEK FOUR OF MOON SEVEN: Continue to take the lunar elixir daily, but this week meditate upon the mythic portion of the month and reflect upon the ways in which the energies of nettle are related to the present portion of Blodeuwedd's tale, and how it helps you to build a relationship with Blodeuwedd herself.

End of Moon Reflections: Under what circumstances could you see yourself using the nettle elixir in support of your work and personal process? If you had to describe the actions of this lunar elixir using one word, what would it be? What about using one sentence? What about using a whole paragraph? Again, be sure to journal everything.

Moon 8

THE MOON OF LIBERATION

*Moon Eight of the Avalonian Cycle of Revealing is called the
Moon of Liberation and is associated with the herb red clover
(Trifolium pratense). It is the last of four moons during
the Time of Blodeuwedd, and the lunar month begins on the
first full moon when the sun is in Gemini; the full moon is in
Sagittarius.*

What is the nature of freedom? Is it something someone gives you,
or is it something you claim for yourself? Freedom of choice is a precious gift and a true privilege, but it must be underwritten by our Sovereignty or else it is just another illusion. If we make choices based on
unconscious fears and half-healed wounds, we are still locked in a cage
of illusion, often without even knowing it. Look to the treasures un-
earthed from the darkness of shadow. These hard-earned truths and
understandings about ourselves, our lives, and our world are what give
us the wings we need to fly and grant us the sight that allows us to see
what we need to see. Do not be satisfied with someone else's version of
who you are. Take what is true and leave the rest behind. Let no one
define you but you!

The Mythic Portion

Distressed by the news of Lleu's betrayal and wounding, Gwydion set off to look for his beloved nephew. After searching far and wide, the magician followed a sow that led him to a tall oak tree; in its uppermost branches was a wounded eagle that shook off maggots and rotting flesh, thus attracting the sow every day. Believing it to be Lleu, Gwydion sang three *englynion*, or metered verses. The eagle responded to him in three stages, descending from the tree and into Gwydion's lap. With his wand, Gwydion transformed his wounded nephew back to his human form and took him to Math's court at Caer Dathyl. There, Lleu was nursed back to health and was fully restored by the end of the year.

When he was whole once more, Lleu sought justice from Gronw Pebyr, demanding that he be able to cast a spear at Gronw in the same way it had been hurled at him. When none of Gronw's men would volunteer to stand in for their lord, he agreed to Lleu's conditions, asking to be able to hold a stone between them since it was for the sake of a woman that all of this had occurred. Lleu agreed, and in the same place on the banks of the River Cynfal where he was ambushed by Gronw, Lleu cast a spear at his adversary which passed through the stone and into Gronw's heart, killing him. To this day, a holed stone called *Llech Ronw* (Gronw's Stone) stands on the banks of that river. Lleu became lord over his lands once more, and in time would come to rule all of Gwynedd in Math's place.

In the meantime, Gwydion went to Mur Castell seeking to punish Blodeuedd for her betrayal of Lleu. When she heard that he had come, Blodeuedd and her maidens took flight in search of safety at another court on a mountain. As they ran, the terrified women kept looking behind them to see if Gwydion was catching up with them. In their haste through the hilly terrain, all the women except Blodeuedd fell into a lake and drowned because they kept looking back; to this day, the lake bears their name: Llyn Morwynion, the Lake of the Maidens. At last overtaking Blodeuedd, Gwydion passes judgment upon her for her shaming of Lleu, saying that instead of killing her, he was going to do worse. She would be transformed into an owl and would never be able to show her face in the light again; instead, she was cursed to forever hunt in the night and be hated by all other birds. Yet, she would keep her name, now *Blodeuwedd*, a Welsh word for "owl."

The Work of the Moon of Liberation

Fully embracing one's truth has many ramifications. At times, society will demonize us for not conforming to its expectations and for daring to do that which so many have resigned themselves to never accomplish. We must overlook this lack of external support; living in right action will reap its own rewards from the Universe. We must seek to embrace the bardic axiom, *Y Gwir yn Erbyn y Byd*, "the Truth Against the World." More than this, living from one's center grants expanded vision, sharpened sight, powerful tools, and the ability to fly free. There is much to be gained.

Although Blodeuwedd is demonized in myth, she serves as an example and role model for women and anyone fighting for their true desire and seeking to live their life on their own terms. She teaches us to achieve our goals based upon the recognition of our true will regardless of the expectations of others and no matter what the cost. Blodeuwedd's tale illustrates many things for us, among them that wisdom comes from our being able to see in the darkness as well as from daring to grow while we are in the light. Sometimes flowers and sometimes feathers, there are many ways to address the choices before us; we can be flexible and adaptable, using different tools at different times depending on what is needed.

Searching Deeper

From a mythological perspective, the rivalry between Lleu and Gronw has much deeper meaning than a simple love triangle or tawdry affair.

To understand its full significance, we need to explore the tale's cultural context. In Wales and some other Celtic lands is a winter tradition called the Hunting of the Wren. Although differing from region to region, this folk practice typically occurred sometime between Winter Solstice and New Year's Day, with an occasional outlier happening as late as Gwyl Mair. The time period is significant, as traditions surrounding the new year (however it was measured) in almost every culture saw it as a dangerous time. Indeed, any threshold time carried the potential for disaster as the transition place between the old and the new was considered to be outside time and so did not conform to the natural order of things.

The wren hunt reflects time's liminality. Except for the one day when it was hunted, the wren was considered a sacred bird, and it was bad luck to even disturb the nest of a wren much less kill it. Indeed, in the British Isles and Ireland, the wren was considered the king of the birds, and throughout Europe, its name reflected its royalty: in Greek (*basiliskos*, "little king"), Latin (*regulus*, "king"), French (*roitelet*, "little king"), Spanish (*reyezuelo*, "little king"), Italian (*reatino*, "little king"), Danish (*elle-konge*, "alder king"), and so on.[13] However, during the time of reversals, bands of young men would engage in the hunting of the wren; whomever killed or captured the small bird would become the "king" for the year; that man would oversee the feasting and be paraded around the village, bringing good fortune and abundance to each household he visited.

While the origins and full meaning of the practice is not entirely clear, some scholars believe that the killing of the wren in the darkest part of the year was a sacrifice of the king by proxy; that is, the bird was a symbolic stand-in for the actual king or a priest-king who may once have been chosen to rule for a year before being willingly sacrificed in

---

13. Elizabeth A. Lawrence, *Hunting the Wren: Transformation of Bird to Symbol* (Knoxville, TN: University of Tennessee Press, 1997), 23.

exchange for the renewal of the Earth and rebirth of the sun in winter.[14]

While seeking to overcome the three prohibitions placed upon him by his mother, Arianrhod, the yet-unnamed Lleu kills a wren while disguised along with Gywdion as a shoemaker in the Fourth Branch of *Y Mabinogi*. His unsuspecting mother observes the boy casting and hitting the famously small bird with a stone and exclaimed, "the fair one has a steady hand!" In this way, she unknowingly named him—Lleu Llaw Gyffes—and fulfilled one of the *tynghedau* she placed upon him, that he would not have a name save the one she gave him. This act takes greater significance in light of the context given above; the medieval Welsh audience would likely have understood that by hitting the wren with a stone, Lleu had effectively established himself as a seasonal king. After likewise obtaining his arms through the help of Gwydion's trickery, Lleu is prohibited by Arianrhod against marrying a woman of the race that dwells on the Earth, so he must therefore make the sacred marriage to the land with the goddess of Sovereignty in order to take his place as king.

When we first encounter Gronw, he is hunting a stag he had pursued onto Lleu's land; it is late in the day when he finally overcomes the animal, killing and dressing it on the banks of the River Cynfal. While this may not seem like much to the eyes of the modern reader, to the contemporary medieval audience this was a highly significant act in several respects. First, there are several instances where the presence of the Otherworld has made itself known through liminality: the crossing of borders by Gronw from his own lands into Lleu's is one, the killing and dressing of the stag on the banks of the river is another, and the time of day—sunset—is yet another. Second, the presence of water

---

14. Karl Wentersdorf, "The Folkloric Symbolism of the Wren," *The Journal of American Folklore*, vol. 90, no. 358 (Apr–Jun 1977): 192-198.

is a hallmark of the Otherworld, and rivers are especially symbolic of shifts of status between heroes, as we shall see.

The pursuit of the stag itself is deeply meaningful. In medieval Wales and elsewhere, the hunting of stags was highly regulated; it was royal game, and hunting it was considered the sport of kings. From a literary perspective, "The Chase of the White Stag" is narrative motif that served as a readily recognizable marker heralding the entrance into or involvement with the Otherworld; often the presence of this chase leads to an encounter between the hero and a woman who is a representative of the Sovereignty of the land.[15] In addition to being royal animals with Otherworldly associations, stags are symbolic of death and rebirth and are strongly connected to the seasonal round, in part because of their annual shedding and regrowth of their antlers. Therefore, not only can Gronw be seen as having strong connections with the Otherworld, his role as hunter and connection to stags can be seen to confer powerful chthonic associations on him as well.

If we consider the magical or Otherworldly elements of the narrative to be signposts for the former Pagan Celtic culture, the entire love triangle between Lleu, Blodeuwedd, and Gronw—and its attendant deaths and transformations—may represent a memory of a year myth. Much like the battle at the ford between Pwyll and Hafgan in the First Branch that saw the victorious Pwyll become Pen Annwfn (chief of the Otherworld), the back and forth defeat and victory of Lleu and Gronw for the hand of the Flower Bride may be another iteration of this mythic motif. The alternating casting of the spear occurs on the banks of a river—the same river where Gronw killed the stag and later cast his spear at Lleu—a liminal place symbolizing the presence of the Otherworld. The indication is that the action takes place between the

---

15. Will Parker, *The Four Branches of the Mabinogi* (Oregon House, CA: Bardic Press, 2005), 233.

worlds, straddling them as with the great festivals of Calan Gaeaf and Calan Haf—gateways between the dark and light halves of the year.

In time, the Lord of the Light (one of the most accepted etymological glosses for the name Lleu is "light") must make way for the Lord of the Dark, just as the light half of the year gives way to the dark half. Similarly, the hunter Gronw kills Lleu with a holy spear and becomes the new consort of the Sovereignty goddess. Gronw is then in turn killed by the spear of Lleu when the cycle comes around again; whomever has the favor of Sovereignty's representative is who reigns. We cannot of course ignore the sexual symbolism of the holey stone and spear of kingship, nor the cycle of light and dark that revolves around the axis of Sovereignty that is Blodeuwedd, both Flower Bride and Keen-Eyed Hunter in the Night.

Taken in light of the stories' cyclical nature, can we finally consider the truth of Blodeuwedd to be laid bare? No longer a betraying adulteress, she is instead revealed as a seasonal Sovereignty figure, she who is wed in turn to the Solar Hero and the Otherworldly Champion. Twice a year, the Lord of Summer and the Lord of Winter battle for her favor in a threshold place and at liminal times, Calan Haf and Calan Gaeaf, when the veil between the worlds is thin. Her aspect changes to reflect the energies of her mate: when she is wed to Lleu, the Solar Hero, she is the Flower Bride; when she is wed to Gronw, the Otherworldly Champion, she is the owl. What a powerful reclamation of this misunderstood goddess!

Seeking Sovereignty Within:
Journaling Prompts and Self-Reflective Questions

Moon Eight
The Moon of Liberation
The Time of Blodeuwedd

Mythic Focus: Lleu reclaims his lands by killing Gronw. Blodeuwedd transforms into an owl.

Personal Insights Around This Moon's Mythic Portion: *Meditate upon the portion of Blodeuwedd's story associated with this moon, and reflect it within yourself. Her story is your story.*

The Focus of the Moon of Liberation by Phase

Seek the lessons of the Moon of Liberation at each moon phase by using the Stations of the monthly Cycle of Healing; be sure to journal all of the insights, symbols, and guidance you receive from each goddess at each moon phase. As you work with the information you receive between each phase, perhaps following the daily process outlined in chapter 3 of this book, and using tools such as trance postures and doorways as detailed in *Avalon Within*, be sure to record those insights in your journal as well.

Full Moon: Connect with Blodeuwedd at the full moon. Review the work of the previous month and the insights it brought to you, set up your work for the coming month, and ask for insights on the issue of focus which may have shifted or deepened due to the work you have done.

Third Quarter: Station of Descent in the cycle of the moon. Bring the issue of focus to Rhiannon to explore through the filters of the Station of Descent and the Moon of Liberation.

Dark Moon: Station of Confrontation in the cycle of the moon. Bring the issue of focus to Ceridwen to explore through the filters of the Station of Confrontation and the Moon of Liberation.

First Quarter: Station of Emergence in the cycle of the moon. Bring the issue of the focus to Blodeuwedd to explore through the filters of the Station of Emergence and the Moon of Liberation.

Night before the Full Moon: Station of Resolution in the cycle of the moon. Bring the issue of focus to Arianrhod to explore through the filters of the Station of Resolution and the Moon of Liberation.

At any point in the month, bring the issue of focus to Branwen to explore through the Station of Integration and the Moon of Liberation. Some women will do this on the night after the dark moon in counterpoint to working with Arianrhod on the night before the full moon.

Herbal Ally for the Moon of Liberation
Red Clover (*Trifolium pratense*)

Creating the Mother Elixir: On the night of the full moon, create your Red Clover Lunar Elixir using the directions found on page 105 of chapter 4. Be sure to label and date the bottle you are using to store the Mother Elixir. Journal any of your experiences around the creation of the Red Clover Elixir.

Prepare the Daughter Elixir: After you have made the Mother Elixir, use the directions found on page 107 of chapter 4 to prepare a dosage bottle for use in the daily experience of this elixir throughout the month. Remember to use a blue or amber dropper bottle for this purpose, and to clearly label your Daughter Elixir.

Daily Work with the Red Clover Elixir: As discussed in chapter 4, begin your daily exploration of the red clover elixir. Be sure to journal everything you can about how the elixir makes you feel, what you think its energetic actions are, where it sits in your energy body, and any and all impressions, insights, symbols, visions, and memories it presents to you:

Week One of Moon Eight: Immerse yourself in the lunar elixir by taking it every day, reflecting upon how it makes you feel, and journaling all of the insights that come to you when you meditate upon the energies of the elixir.

Week Two of Moon Eight: Continue to take the lunar elixir daily, but this week spend time experiencing and comparing the energetic impact of red clover as an essence, and red clover as a magical herb that you burn, as detailed in chapter 4. Again, reflect upon how each makes you feel, and journal all of the insights that come to you when you meditate upon the energies of the elixir and the energies of the herb itself.

Week Three of Moon Eight: Continue to take the lunar elixir daily, but this week spend time researching the medicinal, folk-loric, and magical uses of red clover, beginning with the information provided in Part Three of this book. Compare your findings this week with your direct experiences, being sure to journal all of the insights and connections you've made.

Week Four of Moon Eight: Continue to take the lunar elixir daily, but this week meditate upon the mythic portion of the month and reflect upon the ways in which the energies of red clover are related to the present portion of Blodeuwedd's tale, and how it helps you to build a relationship with Blodeuwedd herself.

End of Moon Reflections: Under what circumstances could you see yourself using the Red Clover Elixir in support of your work and personal process? If you had to describe the actions of this lunar elixir using one word, what would it be? What about using one sentence? What about using a whole paragraph? Again, be sure to journal everything.

Working: Journey Into the
Sacred Landscape of Blodeuwedd

Llyn Morwynion

Please perform the induction to travel over the Ninth Wave, as found on page 74, and then proceed with the working below. When you have completed it, be sure to return from across the Ninth Wave, using the visualization found on page 76.

Having crossed the Ninth Wave into the Otherworld, disembark and envision a silver tether that extends from the center of your torso to the vessel which bore you here; it is of endless length and will expand and retract as necessary as you explore this Realm Over Wave, while keeping you connected to the boat in order to facilitate your return.

Take three deep, anchoring breaths, and immerse yourself in the energies of this place. It is the reflection of the landscape between Mur Castell and Llyn Morwynion, here in the realm of the Mythic Otherworld.

The night is dark. You find yourself in a strange and hilly landscape. Patchy tendrils of mist rise from the earth and hang low to the ground. In the distance to your left is a figure holding aloft a torch walking quickly toward you with intense purpose. Their stride makes you feel fearful; turning away from them, you begin to run in the opposite direction.

The landscape is cruel. You stumble over mossy stones, slick and unyielding as they bruise your feet and send you tumbling to the ground. You struggle to right yourself and continue to flee, periodically glancing behind you to see if the lantern-bearing figure has closed any of the distance between you. You are still fairly far ahead but are unsure how long that lead will last, as the path begins to slope upward. Your now-frenzied footfalls appear to have found their echo...or is this something more? The multiple sounds propel your feet forward even as you look around you in the darkness, trying to identify the sounds and where they are coming from.

The sounds become louder and closer and more numerous, and you realize that you are no longer alone. Around you is a throng of women running beside you; what you are hearing is their voices and the sounds of their own panicked running. It is hard to see in the darkness but you've heard these voices before…and the snippets of what you can hear them saying are things that are very familiar to you. You look to your left, you look to your right. And with a flash of recognition you come to see that the women who are scrambling up the hill beside you, trying to get away from the lantern-carrying figure below, all look exactly like you. It is with this realization you know why you recognize the voice and the things they are saying: they are each speaking with your voice. They are speaking your pain. They are glancing behind themselves with your fears. And still the figure holding the lantern aloft follows…and begins to ascend the increasingly mist-enshrouded hill.

And so collectively, you look behind. And so collectively, you forge ahead. As you go and make your way as if in unison, listen. Listen to the words being spoken. Listen for the memories they are speaking. Take some time to be present in this moment and note what is being said…note everything that arises in answer within you at this moment as well. Take three deep, centering breaths…receive and remember.

When you are ready, you collectively press on with the ever-thickening fog rising to swirl around your feet. The darkness of the night and the mist-shrouded hill hides so much from your sight, making the ascent more and more difficult, causing greater and greater panic. You and the women around you stumble on the stones, trip over the tree limbs, and slip on the damp grass…always managing to right yourselves, and continue forward with even more fear, even more abandon, even more panic.

You look behind you once more to see that the figure with the lantern seems to have gotten even closer. Take a moment to reflect upon how this makes you feel. Who is the person following behind you? Why do they inspire such fear in you?

Suddenly, the night is split by a terrible scream, followed by a huge splash. And then a second scream … and then a third … and then a cacophony of frenzied splashing! Suddenly you hear a chorus of terrified screaming. As you glance around you, trying to understand what is happening, looking for the water that must be near but you cannot see, you realize that there are fewer and fewer of the accompanying women. And as they too begin to scream in horror at what they are hearing, they scramble ahead with renewed desperation; they too have noticed that the lantern-bearer is closing in and they cannot keep themselves from looking behind them.

You are surrounded by endless screaming and more frenzied splashing. Unsure of what to do next, you take a moment and come to a stop. Close your inner eye. Take three deep, centering breaths. When you are done, open your eye. Peering through the haze of the swirling mists around you, you realize you stopped just in time … for you are standing at the edge of a ridge and feel rather than see that the land ends and opens up into darkness … a deep fall through space. Terrified, you scramble back and away from the edge only to realize that the other women have not seen the danger because they are too focused on the lantern bearer behind them. You shout to them in warning, but they cannot or will not hear you—and so you watch with horror as their own feet carry them over the cliff and down into what must be a body of water below.

And then suddenly … it is over. You are surrounded only by silence and realize that of all the women who accompanied you up the hill, you are the only one remaining behind. Somehow, you feel lighter; something has changed. Take a moment in this space to take an inner inventory. Contemplate the women … those parts of you in this moment you recognize to be the fears you have carried in life that have fallen into the water. What now is missing? Who is the *you* who remains?

You are the only one left—and yet, you are not alone.

In this moment, the lantern bearer who had pursued you up the slope has now come into view. The lamp illuminates the space around you as they approach, and you lift up your hands to protect your eyes from the painful and increasingly bright light. Everywhere the light touches, it burns away the clinging mists. As if catalyzed by the bringing of the lantern to the top of the hill, the sky begins to lighten in the east as the sun begins to rise.

The hooded figure sets their lantern upon a stone beside them and extends a hand to you. For some reason, you no longer feel afraid and take a step toward them. As you take their hand, a gentle morning breeze springs to life around you. The first bird of the morning begins to sing, and you are enveloped by the heady scent of fragrant flowers. Take three deep, centering breaths … feel yourself fully in this moment. Feel the energy that rises within from where your hand is nestled in theirs. The breeze rises once again, stronger this time, with enough force to push back the hood of the person before you … revealing their face in the growing light of dawn.

You have no doubt who it is, with her long white fingers and her hair the gold of broom flowers.

It is Blodeuwedd.

She smiles serenely at you, and you realize you did not need to be overcome with fear or run from the truth of the light she carries nor the change it brings. Hand in hand, she leads you to a place where the hill slopes gently downward, skirting around the fatal drop. You follow her down the path, uplifted by the intoxicating scent of dewy heather until she brings you to the shore of the lake known as Llyn Morwynion—the Lake of the Maidens. As you survey the landscape, you notice that parts of the lake are surrounded by steep and rugged hills … while other approaches are flat and easy to navigate.

Blodeuwedd releases your hand and gestures for you to approach the water. She speaks:

"Look at who you are when you let go of what you fear."

You nod and follow her direction. Standing at the still and glassy water's edge, a dark pool of a perfect mirror, you kneel before the lake and seek your reflection upon its surface.

What is it you see? Take what time you need to see what Blodeuwedd has charged you to see...

You feel her hand upon your shoulder, and again she says, "Look at who you are when you let go of what you fear."

Almost immediately, a breeze ripples across the surface of the lake, blurring the place where you gaze upon the water, causing it to shift, impelling it to move. And as the waters become still once more, an image forms... and there in the brightening morning, as clearly as your own hand before you, you see a vision: the reflection of your purest and most authentic self, not held back by fear, not made small by pain. Who is this person? What do you need most to know about her? What does she know that you do not? How can you bridge the gap between where you are in the here and now, and where you are meant to be: fearless, centered, and sovereign?

Take what time you need to receive these answers and ask any other questions you may have.

When you are ready, thank your reflection for all the insights you have received. Ask for a symbol that you can work with to help you with your next step in this process; take what time you need to allow this symbol to reveal itself to you.

When at last you are done, stand and turn to Blodeuwedd. Thank her for her guidance and share an offering with her in gratitude.

She smiles and places her petal-soft fingers on your head, blessing you. Close your eyes and be fully present in this moment, breathing into it. You feel her fingers shift, and when you open your eyes, you find your head being brushed by the velvet-fringed feathers of a pure white owl. You step back, and she flaps in place before you, the large yellow moons of her eyes fixed upon yours, shining like jewels set into her heart-shaped face.

And then she takes off flying. You watch as she circles Llyn Morwynion three times before crossing the sky and heading west, away from the rising sun.

Take three deep, centering breaths. Remember all you have seen, received, and committed to in this moment. When you are ready, follow the thread connecting you to the vessel that took you to this Land Beyond Wave. Take your place in the boat once more to begin the journey over the Nine Waves to the place that is Here and the time that is Now.

Chapter 7

THE TIME OF RHIANNON

OF THE FIVE WELSH GODDESSES honored in the Avalonian Tradition, we have the most lore about Rhiannon. Appearing in both the First and Third Branches of *Y Mabinogi*, and with a brief mention in the Second Branch, she is generally accepted to have once been a Sovereignty goddess based upon the content of her tales, the meaning of her name ("Divine Queen"), and her frequent association with horses in her stories—a well-established symbol of Sovereignty for the Celts. She has analogues in the Gaulish horse goddess Epona, as well as the equine goddess Macha, who is a face of the triple-aspected Irish goddess, the Mórrígan. Rhiannon's name is etymologically connected both to the Mórrígan and to the Gallo-Brittonic goddess *Rīgantona, whose names share the meaning "Divine Queen" and who are both Sovereignty goddesses in their own right

While not conclusive proof that she is in fact herself a Sovereignty goddess, Rhiannon's association with horses in the narrative of the Four Branches appears to be deliberate as well as symbolic; when she arrives in the First Branch, we see her astride a magical white horse that even when walking could be overtaken by no other horse. Later, when her newborn son is spirited away by a monster, the child is found in a stall with a mare whose own foals disappear annually on the first of May, a significant feast day marking the beginning of summer. Falsely accused of having destroyed the missing baby, Rhiannon is sentenced by her husband the king to a bizarre punishment involving her sitting on a horse block outside of the castle for seven years. While there, she must recount the details of her predicament to strangers and offer to bear them on her back into the presence of the king. In the Third Branch, when she is imprisoned in an Otherworldly fortress with her son Pryderi, she is made to wear an ass's collar and is forced to carry hay.

The repetitive horse imagery may be significant in that it ties Rhiannon to the equine Sovereignty goddess with whom the king must mate to legitimize his kingship in Irish and other Indo-European traditions. "The worship of and connection between the horse and the fertility goddess, known among the continental Celts as Epona, has been documented as common practice in Europe."[16]

Sovereignty figures are an international folk motif found predominantly in the stories and legends from Celtic cultures. There are several variations on this theme, depending on the time period and culture in question, but in general, a goddess of Sovereignty (or a woman acting as her representative) tests the fitness of potential kings or chieftains, and if they are found worthy, enters into a sexual union with the king on behalf of the land. This sacred marriage ties the fate of the land to that of the ruler Sovereignty has thus empowered; as he prospers, so does the land. Should a king grow to be unrighteous, or else become infirm or maimed, the land is similarly afflicted and a new ruler must be found lest the country become a wasteland suffering from famine, disease, and war.

Another variant of the Sovereignty motif is one we have already examined in our discussion of Blodeuwedd. In this type, the conference of Sovereignty is tied into a period of time rather than rightness of rule. This kind of kingship typically takes one of two forms: it can

---

16. C. McKenna, "The Theme of Sovereignty in *Pwyll*," in C.W. Sullivan, ed., *The Mabinogi: A Book of Essays* (New York: Garland Publishing, Inc., 1996), 317.

be seasonal as illustrated by the "love triangle" in the Fourth Branch, or annual as is more commonly found in continental Europe with the phenomenon of the Year King, particularly in Mediterranean cultures.

By the time the story of the goddess we have come to know as Rhiannon was written down in the twelfth or thirteenth century, her tale had evolved over centuries of transmission in oral tradition to where both her divine and sovereign natures had become subtext rather than overt, although her role as one who tests the worthiness of kings is no less present.

In this work with the Moons of the Cycle of Revealing, we focus on the story of Rhiannon in the First Branch of *Y Mabinogi*, but she has a role in several other tales as well, both directly and indirectly. These mythic accounts are not unimportant in terms of study and greatly contribute to building a relationship with Rhiannon; a brief overview of these stories and some of their meanings is therefore included here.

The Second Branch recounts the tale of Branwen, Daughter of Llŷr and will be explored in greater depth here in chapter 8. Suffice it to say for the purpose of the present discussion that a brutal war is fought between Ireland and the hosts of the Island of the Mighty under the command of Bendigeidfran—Bran the Blessed, king of Britain and brother of Branwen. Only seven Britons survive the war, including Rhiannon's son Pryderi and Manawydan, son of Llŷr, brother to Bran and Branwen. Bendigeidfran is fatally wounded in the battle but before dying instructs his surviving men to remove his head and take it with them to his court at Harlech. There, Bran tells them, they would remain together for seven years, feasting and talking with his head as if he were not dead, and the Adar Rhiannon—the Birds of Rhiannon— would come to them. Doing as he instructed, everything Bran said came to pass:

> *As they began to eat and drink, three birds came and began*
> *singing some songs to them, and all the songs they had ever*

heard were coarse compared to that one. They were a distant vision seen above the waves, yet they were as clear to them as if they were together with them. And they were at that feast for seven years.[17]

We learn more about the Adar Rhiannon in the medieval Welsh romance, *Culhwch ac Olwen*. One of the tasks set before Culhwch in order to win the right to marry Olwen was to obtain Rhiannon's birds so that they might sing to Olwen's father, the giant Ysbadden who was fated to die the day she was wed on the night before her wedding. These birds, we are told in the tale, have the power to "wake the dead and lull the living to sleep."[18]

In the Third Branch, Pryderi and Manawydan return from their Otherworldly sojourns in Harlech and Gwales after burying the head of Bran at the White Tower in London to watch over the land. As brother to Bran, who had died without an heir, Manawydan was the next in line to ascend the throne as king of the Island of the Mighty. However, as time in the Otherworld runs differently than it does in this world, a period of eighty years had passed while the company had been feasting without memory of the great war in Ireland and its losses; during that time, Manawydan's nephew Caswallon had ascended the throne. Tired of war, Manawydan decides not to challenge the new king, and so was invited to live in Dyfed by Pryderi, who offers his friend the hand of his mother, the now-widowed Rhiannon, as well as stewardship over the seven cantrifs that had comprised Pwyll's lands. At the end of the First Branch, we are told almost parenthetically that Pywll, Rhiannon's husband, had died and Pryderi had mar-

17. Lady Charlotte Guest, *The Mabinogion* (London: Bernard Quaritch, 1877), 383–384.

18. Sioned Davies, trans., *The Mabinogion* (New York: Oxford University Press, 2007), 196.

ried a woman named Cigfa and had expanded his territory beyond the original borders of Dyfed he inherited from his father.

This may seem an odd thing, for a son to play matchmaker for his widowed mother, but it is an accurate reflection of the status of women in medieval Wales. Before marriage, a woman was under the legal authority of her father, after marriage that authority was passed to her husband. Should she outlive her husband, a woman's eldest son would become responsible for her. Now, even though Pryderi made the offer to Manawydan, who agreed to meet his mother to see if they were compatible, it was still completely Rhiannon's choice to enter into the marriage or not.

> *Then began Manawydan and Rhiannon to sit and to talk together, and from their discourse his mind and his thoughts became warmed toward her, and he thought in his heart he had never beheld any lady more fulfilled of grace and beauty than she. "Pryderi," said he, "I will that it be as thou didst say." "What saying was that?" asked Rhiannon. "Lady," said Pryderi, "I did offer thee as a wife to Manawydan the son of Llyr." "By that will I gladly abide," said Rhiannon. "Right glad am I also," said Manawydan; "may Heaven reward him who hath shown unto me friendship so perfect as this."[19]*

It is the gifting of lordship over the seven cantrifs of Dyfed that stands out as an oddity here, and its apparent bundling with the offer of marriage to Rhiannon may suggest that rulership over these lands is a consequence of receiving the blessing of the tutelary spirit of the land—by entering into a sacred marriage with the local Sovereignty goddess who is, in this case, Rhiannon.

Soon after the wedding, Rhiannon, Manawydan, Pryderi, and Cigfa visit the Gorsedd Arberth, the mound of wonders from the First Branch, which we will duscuss further later in this chapter. When they get to the

---

19. Guest, *The Mabinogion*, 398.

top of the hill, an enchantment falls over the land, and every human and domestic animal disappear. After spending time making their way in Dyfed by hunting the land, and then trying to practice various crafts in England in order to survive, the four companions return to Wales. One day while out hunting with their dogs, Pryderi and Manawydan discover a strange fortress on their land that had never been there before. Pryderi's dogs enter the fortress but never reemerge, so he goes in after them against Manawydan's advice. The fortress is empty save for a golden hanging bowl; when Pryderi tries to take it, he becomes frozen in place, unable to move or speak.

Manawydan waits for his friend to return, but after hours pass, he returns home without him. When Rhiannon hears what has transpired, she is angry with Manawydan for abandoning Pryderi, and goes off to find him herself. When she enters the fortress and sees her son stuck fast to the bowl, she tries to remove it from his hands, and in the process becomes stuck and paralyzed herself. With that, the entire fortress disappears from Dyfed, taking the imprisoned mother and son with it, leaving their partners behind. Eventually, Manawydan finds a way to lift the enchantment of Dyfed and secure the release of Rhiannon and Pryderi; they had been held captive in the Otherworld where they endured daily punishment as recompense for the abuse of Rhiannon's rejected suitor at the hands of Pwyll and his men in the First Branch, a matter discussed in full later in this chapter.

Moon 9
THE MOON OF DEDICATION

Moon Nine of the Avalonian Cycle of Revealing is called the Moon of Dedication, and is associated with the herb burdock (Arctium lappa). The lunar month begins on the first full moon when the sun is in Cancer; the full moon is in Capricorn. It is the first of four moons during the Time of Rhiannon.

Entering now into the Time of Rhiannon, we are presented with lessons relating to our inner Sovereignty, the ability to ask for that which we need, and the strength to endure any trial—especially those which challenge our personal truths. It is the nature of the universe to test our resolve in order to show us the places where we still have work to do, where our newly attained insights aren't as anchored as they could be, and where the changes we have made still hold the potential to slide back into old patterns. Remember that as we walk in Sovereignty, we are not obligated to respond to every inquiry, engage in every encounter, and partake of every opportunity that comes our way just because a door has been opened to us. It is important to clear away the debris on the road, and to avoid distractions which use up precious resources that will serve us better when used in other places. It is important for us to find ways we can lead by example, while holding space for others to come into their own wisdom without needing us to show it to them. As we seek empowerment, we must also remember to empower others. As we seek our own answers, we must remember that others have their answers inside them as well. As we walk in our truth in accordance with our will, we must also remember to give others the space to do the same. Walking the path in this way can catalyze healing and growth for everyone.

The Mythic Portion

Pwyll, prince of Dyfed, was visiting his chief court at Arberth. He had recently returned from spending a year in the Otherworld in the guise of Arawn, the King of Annwn. During the feast given in his honor, Pwyll and his retinue walked to the Gorsedd Arberth, a nearby hill with a particular quality: should a noble person sit upon the mound, they would come away either having suffered blows or having witnessed a marvel.

Hoping to see a marvel, Pwyll sat upon the Gorsedd Arberth. Almost immediately, a woman veiled in gold and riding a pure white horse appeared walking along the road before the mound at a steady pace. Sending one of his men to speak with the woman, first on foot and then on horseback, Pwyll was disappointed that neither of them could catch up with her even though she did not alter her slow pace. In fact, the quicker they pursued her, the farther away she seemed to be from them. The party departed the hill when the woman disappeared from sight. Returning the next day with the fastest horse in the land at the ready, Pwyll was thrilled to see the mysterious lady appear once again. The prince sent his rider forth, but she once again remained out of reach even though she did not quicken her pace.

Returning for a third day to the magical hill, the prince and his retinue awaited the woman, but this time it was Pwyll himself who sat astride the fastest horse in all of Dyfed. Once more, the woman in dazzling gold and white appeared and Pwyll gave chase, riding until his horse was almost spent. At last he called out to her, asking her in the name of the man she loved the best to stop for him. "Gladly," she replied, immediately drawing to a full stop, "but it would have been better for your horse if you had asked sooner." Drawing aside her golden veil, she told him her name was Rhiannon, daughter of Hyfaidd the Old, and that she was being married to a man against her will. She had come to Arberth seeking Pwyll because he was the only man she wanted to marry. Infused with love for her, Pwyll replied that there was no woman in the world he would prefer to marry over Rhiannon. The two arranged to meet again at the court of her father in a year, where she would have the marriage feast prepared.

The Work of the Moon of Dedication

The lessons of the Time of Rhiannon in general, and during the Moon of Dedication in particular, concern the ways in which we express our hard-won connections to Sovereignty in the outer world with all its attendant joys and challenges. Working on ways to make our inner understandings become manifest in ourselves and our lives is an enormous undertaking, and not one to be embarked upon lightly.

Just as Rhiannon rides forth from the Otherworld on her white horse of Sovereignty, so is the sovereign self we have cultivated—through reclaiming and transforming aspects of ourselves that have been lingering in shadow—ready to make its way out into the world. We are called to be like both Rhiannon and Pwyll: the rider who is focused and intent on going about their business to attain their goals, and the seeker who needs to learn how to ask for what they need as well as how to revise their plans when first attempts do not yield the desired results.

Change is hard; it requires persistent and disciplined dedication. With steady footfalls upon the ground of our inner lives, we slowly lay the path that takes us to our heart's desire. We may perceive that the going is slow and believe our goals remain elusive, but the inner changes resulting from our steadfast and deliberate action will ensure that we too will cross the threshold that transforms the potential that dwells within us into the reality that manifests around us—and we will be forever changed by this journey.

Others will take notice when we walk a path of personal Sovereignty powered by openness and authenticity. We may find that those who were actively engaged in challenging our choice to embark upon this pathway have already fallen away; it is hard for the shadows of others to keep up with an Otherworldly mount empowered by true will. There will be those, however, who see us for who we are, and in recognizing the path we are walking, will want to walk it too. They may try to ride along with us, but our saddles only hold one. They may seek to follow us, aggressively try to get our attention, or try to benefit from traveling in our wake.

We must not permit ourselves to be distracted or taken off course; it is not an unkind thing to recognize that everyone's path to self-actualization is their own, though it is a blessing to stop for those who truly wish to know how they can undertake their own journey. Asking for what we need is at the heart of Rhiannon's lesson for us, as is the ability to maintain our focus on who we are and what we are working to accomplish while still functioning in the physical world.

Some of Rhiannon's most meaningful teachings concern the power of our words and the transformational potency of our sovereign intentions. And what extraordinary lessons! When we ask for what we need, we will receive it. When we fearlessly formulate our intention, as Pwyll did, the Universe will respond in kind. When we hold on to our desire to attain our goals and put in the time and effort necessary to achieve them, we will be successful. There are many other instances where Rhiannon's stories illustrate the power of our words. She teaches us the importance of upholding the integrity of our promises, of following through on our commitments, of being truthful in our speech, and to maintain a high code of ethics even in the face of injustice.

Searching Deeper

While not identified as a divinity, Rhiannon was unquestionably depicted as an Otherworldly Maiden or Fairy Queen in the text and would have been readily recognized as such by the contemporary medieval audience of *Y Mabinogi*. Rhiannon emerges into the narrative of the First Branch as she rides along the road passing before the Gorsedd Arberth, a mound with magical properties that puts it solidly in the company of the famed hollow hills in Celtic myth which serve as portals to the Otherworld. These mounds are often neolithic burial chambers where the indigenous Britons visited their beloved dead and honored ancestors with offerings. It is possible that some of the lore and existent folk practices around the Otherfolk in the British Isles and Ireland may have their origins in pre-Christian ancestor veneration or worship, particularly when these practices are associated with chambered tombs and subterranean barrows.

The openings of these burial structures often had alignments with the rising or setting sun of the solstices or equinoxes such that a shaft of light would enter the barrow to illuminate the far chamber, sometimes featuring spiral carvings. This phenomenon is sometimes interpreted as an ancient belief in the rebirth of the dead, with the solar light revitalizing and perhaps impregnating the womb-tomb of the barrow with its life-giving energy. A threshold place between life and death, present and past, light and darkness, it makes sense that these mounds continued to be revered long past the time of those who had built them, entering into folklore as a doorway between this world and the Otherworld—one that opened in both directions.

When we meet Rhiannon, she is described as being garbed in gold brocade; perhaps the gold is symbolic of the sun that enters the burial mounds, for in the narrative she is said to draw level with the mound as she rode before it, a very evocative description that may indicate a solar association. It is more likely that her garments are the reddish gold often used to represent the red color of the Otherworld, as they are described in a similar fashion to the vestments worn by Arawn, king of Annwn, and his unnamed wife in the first part of the First Branch, when Pwyll takes Arawn's place in Annwn for a year. Further, when Rhiannon's newborn son is taken from her and is found in the threshold of the house of Tey-rnon, the baby is swaddled in the same golden brocade. Throughout the First Branch, it is only those characters with connections to the Other-world who are ever seen dressed in this rich golden fabric.

Another connection between Rhiannon and the Otherworld is the majestic white mare upon which she rides. The horse is a long-standing and cross-cultural symbol of Sovereignty in Celtic traditions, and the color white would have been instantly recognizable to the contempo-rary medieval audience as being associated with the Otherworld. Even without the stated color, the fact that Rhiannon's horse, even when walking at a slow pace is unable to be overtaken by even the swiftest of horses, marks it—and her—as an Otherworldly creature.

Folklore abounds with examples of the ways in which the influence of the Otherworld has the power to warp the reality of things in this world: for example, it affects the passage of time, such that someone can spend what feels like one night in a faery mound only to emerge and discover that a hundred years has passed; it has the ability to bridge great distances, such as hearing the song of the Adar Rhiannon as if they were in the same room, while in reality they are singing from the Otherworld, far across the water; it also has the ability to affect the speed of Rhiannon's mare in relation to those who approach it— the faster others ride to catch up with her, the further away Rhiannon's horse is, regardless of its apparent slow and steady pace. Rhiannon's association with the horse continues in both in the First and Third Branches of Y Mabinogi.

Seeking Sovereignty Within:
Journaling Prompts and Self-Reflective Questions

Moon Nine
The Moon of Dedication
The Time of Rhiannon

Mythic Focus: Rhiannon appears from the Otherworld on her white mare and is pursued by Pwyll, who is unable to catch up with her until he asks her to stop.

Personal Insights Around This Moon's Mythic Portion: *Meditate upon the portion of Rhiannon's story associated with this moon and reflect it within yourself. Her story is your story.*

The Focus of the Moon of Dedication by Phase

Seek the lessons of the Moon of Dedication at each moon phase by using the Stations of the monthly Cycle of Healing; be sure to journal all of the insights, symbols, and guidance you receive from each goddess at each moon phase. As you work with the information you receive between each phase, perhaps following the daily process outlined in chapter 3 of this book, and using tools such as trance postures and doorways as detailed in *Avalon Within*, be sure to record those insights in your journal as well.

Full Moon: Connect with Rhiannon at the full moon. Review the work of the previous month and the insights it brought to you, set up your work for the coming month, and ask for insights on the issue of focus which may have shifted or deepened due to the work you have done.

Third Quarter: Station of Descent in the cycle of the moon. Bring the issue of focus to Rhiannon to explore through the filters of the Station of Descent and the Moon of Dedication.

Dark Moon: Station of Confrontation in the cycle of the moon. Bring the issue of focus to Ceridwen to explore through the filters of the Station of Confrontation and the Moon of Dedication.

First Quarter: Station of Emergence in the cycle of the moon. Bring the issue of the focus to Blodeuwedd to explore through the filters of the Station of Emergence and the Moon of Dedication.

Night before the Full Moon: Station of Resolution in the cycle of the moon. Bring the issue of focus to Arianrhod to explore through the filters of the Station of Resolution and the Moon of Dedication.

At any point in the month, bring the issue of focus to Branwen to explore through the Station of Integration and the Moon of Dedication. Some women will do this on the night after the dark moon in counterpoint to working with Arianrhod on the night before the full moon.

Herbal Ally for the Moon of Dedication
Burdock (*Arctium lappa*)

Creating the Mother Elixir: On the night of the full moon, create your Burdock Lunar Elixir using the directions found on page 105 of chapter 4. Be sure to label and date the bottle you are using to store the Mother Elixir. Journal any of your experiences around the creation of the Burdock Elixir.

Prepare the Daughter Elixir: After you have made the Mother Elixir, use the directions found on page 107 of chapter 4 to prepare a dosage bottle for use in the daily experience of this elixir throughout the month. Remember to use a blue or amber dropper bottle for this purpose, and to clearly label your Daughter Elixir.

Daily Work with the Burdock Elixir: As discussed in chapter 4, begin your daily exploration of the burdock elixir. Be sure to journal everything you can about how the elixir makes you feel, what you think it its energetic actions are, where it sits in your energy body, and any and all impressions, insights, symbols, visions, and memories it presents to you:

WEEK ONE OF MOON NINE: Immerse yourself in the lunar elixir by taking it every day, reflecting upon how it makes you feel, and journaling all of the insights that come to you when you meditate upon the energies of the elixir.

WEEK TWO OF MOON NINE: Continue to take the lunar elixir daily, but this week spend time experiencing and comparing the energetic impact of burdock as an essence, and burdock as a magical herb that you burn, as detailed in chapter 4. Again, reflect upon how each makes you feel, and journal all of the insights that come to you when you meditate upon the energies of the elixir and the energies of the herb itself.

WEEK THREE OF MOON NINE: Continue to take the lunar elixir daily, but this week spend time researching the medicinal, folkloric, and magical uses of burdock, beginning with the information provided in Part Three of this book. Compare your findings this week with your direct experiences, being sure to journal all of the insights and connections you've made.

WEEK FOUR OF MOON NINE: Continue to take the lunar elixir daily, but this week meditate upon the mythic portion of the month and reflect upon the ways in which the energies of burdock are related to the present portion of Rhiannon's tale, and how it helps you to build a relationship with Rhiannon herself.

End of Moon Reflections: Under what circumstances could you see yourself using the Burdock Elixir in support of your work and personal process? If you had to describe the actions of this lunar elixir using one word, what would it be? What about using one sentence? What about using a whole paragraph? Again, be sure to journal everything.

Moon 10
THE MOON OF CONSUMMATION

Moon Ten of the Avalonian Cycle of Revealing is called the Moon of Consummation, and is associated with the herb dandelion (Taraxacum officinalis). The lunar month begins on the first full moon when the sun is in Leo; the full moon is in Aquarius. It is the second of four moons during the Time of Rhiannon. The full moon corresponds with the Station of Resolution in the Avalonian Cycle of Healing, and it is t. day of Gwyl Awst.

Whether we are entering into a partnership with a lover, a friend, a colleague, or ourselves, it is important that we do so with our eyes wide open, while also being centered in our hearts. This is because the true nature of partnership is that it creates something new. There is a Celtic triad that says: "Three parts to everything: He One, She One, They One in the Third." Similar to the Lovers card of the tarot, the esoteric meaning of this kind of unity speaks of the transformation of the soul that occurs when consciousness is in clear partnership with the unconscious and when Self is in clear partnership with Source. We become someone different: we have a sense of who we can be when we are complete unto ourselves and are living our lives in alignment with our true will. This is a time of heightened creativity and a celebration of the goals achieved that have grown out of this partnership. Embrace and celebrate the blessings of life … right here, right now.

The Mythic Portion

At the appointed time, Pwyll and his retinue traveled to the court of Rhiannon's father where a grand wedding feast awaited him. Sitting happily side by side in the place of honor, Rhiannon and Pwyll were approached by richly attired man who asked for a boon. Without hesitation, Pwyll promises to grant him anything in his power to give. Rhiannon was dismayed that he should answer so, especially in front of the noble guests, for the petitioner is Gwawl, Rhiannon's rejected suitor. Gwawl asked Pwyll for the wedding feast and for Rhiannon's hand; as the couple had not yet slept together, their marriage was not yet consummated. Rhiannon tells Pwyll to agree to give her to Gwawl lest he be dishonored, so the disheartened Pwyll does as she suggests. Rhiannon informs Gwawl that it is not within Pwyll's power to grant him the feast because she had already given it to the men of Dyfed but tells him to return in a year's time when she would have a new feast prepared for him and the two will be married. Satisfied, Gwawl departs.

Giving Pwyll a magic bag with instructions on how to use it, Rhiannon tells Pwyll to return in a year as well, this time disguised as a beggar. Humbled, Pwyll does as Rhiannon directs, and after the year has passed, he returns to the feasting hall, and approaches Gwawl, who is sitting in the place of honor with Rhiannon, to ask for a boon. Gwawl does not recognize him but prudently replies that he is happy to grant any reasonable request. Pwyll asks simply for the bag that he is carrying to be filled with food; Gwawl good-naturedly complies, having servants put a few dishes full of food in the bag, yet it was still not full. Trays of food are emptied into the satchel, but it is still no fuller than before. As more and more of the feast disappears into the bag, Gwawl becomes nervous and asks the disguised Pwyll if his bag will ever be filled. Pwyll replies that when a high-born man puts his two feet in it and proclaims the bag filled, it will be so. With Rhiannon's encouragement, Gwawl quickly rounds the table to do so, and when both of his feet are in the bag, Pwyll pulls it up over Gwawl's head and ties it so that he cannot escape.

Pwyll blows a horn and rips off his disguise as his companions descend upon the hall, taking Gwawl's men prisoner. The men from Dyfed then kick the bag containing Gwawl and make a sport of abusing him until an upset Rhiannon puts a stop to the dishonorable behavior. With Rhiannon's council, Pwyll and Gwawl make assurances to each other concerning his release, his forfeiture of any claim on Rhiannon, and promises that no vengeance will be sought between them. When all parties are satisfied at last, Gwawl takes his leave, and a new feast is set before Pwyll and Rhiannon; they sleep together that night, and the next day begin the journey back to Dyfed as husband and wife.

The Work of the Moon of Consummation

When the energies of intention become manifest in the physical plane … when the sparks of Awen are kindled to a glowing that illuminates our creative path and permits us to express ourselves … when the circumstances of our lives have come into alignment with our sacred intention … when we are in clear communication with all parts of the Self and can hear the voices of our guides and the goddess from a place of greater clarity and discernment … when we find ourselves in a place of true contentment, having learned how to put down the baggage of the past in order to journey without hindrance into the future … then step back. Breathe into this place of harvest and accomplishment. Take advantage of the expanded perspective that comes with being at the apex of the cycle to celebrate our accomplishments, and to commit to continue to do the hard work; the light half is only halfway over at this juncture, and there's certainly more to do.

But today? Here? Now?

We must strive to bless and celebrate ourselves … both our shadow and our Sovereignty. We must acknowledge what we have accomplished, respect ourselves for doing what it takes to get here, and take note of where our harvest may yet be a bit thin but to not walk away from this part of ourselves. Instead, we must strive to love ourselves as fully and completely as we can.

Remember too that the path within must be reflected in that which is without. The spiritual journey is not meant to take place on the subtler realms alone—it should find its partner in the physical plane as well. It may be difficult to connect with or understand those who have not had the same experiences, but it is not our duty to judge … it is better to teach by example. We must have patience with ourselves as well; just as we may falter, so too must we forgive ourselves to learn from our mistakes and honor our responsibilities.

Searching Deeper

Medieval Welsh society featured a very formal social structure, especially where nobility was concerned. *Cyfraith Hwyel Dda* or *The Laws of Hwyel the Good*—a tenth-century prince who unified Wales and was believed to have codified Welsh law—proscribed a very specific hierarchy of worth for every member of a prince's court, which included the amount due to them or their families as compensation for their injury or death, their *galanas* or blood price. Additionally, the law code outlined the responsibilities and obligations of every member of the court and even specified where each was to sit during feasts. Likewise, there was a particular code of ethics in place, and standards of behaviors expected of nobility was clear. The power of one's word was binding; it was critical to honor oaths and meet obligations in order to uphold one's responsibilities and remain in good social and political standing.

The magical, Otherworldly origins of Rhiannon—perhaps remnants of her former divinity—might have been enough to have her stand out in the Four Branches, but her actions are themselves remarkable even if she were but a mortal queen of her time. It may well be that her boldness and autonomy are a memory of a former social paradigm where women held more power.

If she herself comes from a metaphorical "Otherworld" of a past or fading culture, the power shift in her personal autonomy where it comes to marriage and childbirth might be symbolic of what happens when women are absorbed into the new order—one of patriarchal constraint and societal limitation for women. Yet, "while Rhiannon is evidently aware of the inequalities of contemporary society, she has not embarked upon a struggle against it so much as within it. This is a crucial distinction since unlike Arianrhod, who refuses to accept social patterns, Rhiannon seeks to improve her lot by working with the system. Thus Rhiannon does not flee from the obligation to marry but simply chooses a type of man to suit her best."[20]

In the First Branch, when Pwyll finally asks Rhiannon to stop because no other horse or rider can overtake her horse, she does so and tells him nature of her business:

"I am Rhiannon, the daughter of Hyfaidd Hen, and they sought to give me to a husband against my will. But no husband would I have, and that because of my love for thee, neither will I yet have one unless thou reject me. And hither have I come to hear thy answer."[21]

At their marriage feast, Pwyll makes a foolish promise in front of all assembled to give Gwawl, Rhiannon's disguised former suitor, anything he desires. Rhiannon at first takes Pwyll to task for his impulsiveness, saying:

"'Be silent for as long as you like,' said Rhiannon. 'Never has a man been more stupid than you have been.'"[22]

20. Fiona Winward, "The Women in the Four Branches," *Cambrian Medieval Studies* 34 (1997): 85.

21. Guest, *The Mabinogion*, 347.

22. Davies, *The Mabinogion*, 12.

Yet Rhiannon guides Pwyll to a solution to this situation that will both keep his honor intact as well as secure Rhiannon as his wife. She deftly navigates the difficulties of Gwawl having asked for her hand as well as the marriage feast by exploiting the loopholes of what Pwyll has unwittingly agreed to—it was she who set out the feast; it was not Pwyll's to give, although she promises another feast to Gwawl in one year—and with the aid of a magic bag and her cleverness, she was eventually able to win out the day and marry the man she chose.

However, it is the same Rhiannon who, years later, having been falsely accused of a crime she did not commit, cannot convince those who spoke against her to tell the truth. And so, resigned to her fate, Rhiannon chooses to work within the social construct and accept her punishment, proving herself to be a great and noble lady whose perseverance is rewarded when her innocence is at last proven. As a wife and mother, Rhiannon is no longer the autonomous woman of her maidenhood, and now demonstrates by example the behavior expected of the medieval Welsh woman. "The virtues to be fostered are patience, modesty, wisdom, chastity, loyalty—these are the virtues that will ultimately win the day."[23]

---

23. Winward, "Women in the Four Branches," 102.

Seeking Sovereignty Within:
Journaling Prompts and Self-Reflective Questions

Moon Ten
The Moon of Consummation
The Time of Rhiannon

Mythic Focus: After several challenges overcome by her cleverness and quick wit, Rhiannon marries Pwyll, her choice of husband.

Personal Insights Around This Moon's Mythic Portion: *Meditate upon the portion of Rhiannon's story associated with this moon, and reflect it within yourself. Her story is your story.*

The Focus of the Moon of Consummation by Phase

Seek the lessons of the Moon of Consummation at each moon phase by using the Stations of the monthly Cycle of Healing; be sure to journal all of the insights, symbols, and guidance you receive from each goddess at each moon phase. As you work with the information you receive between each phase, perhaps following the daily process outlined in chapter 3 of this book, and using tools such as trance postures and doorways as detailed in *Avalon Within*, be sure to record those insights in your journal as well.

Full Moon: Connect with Rhiannon at the full moon to set up your work for the month and to receive insight on the issue of focus. This is also the **Station of Resolution** in the cycle of the sun, marked by the holy day of **Gwyl Awst**, so will acknowledge the harvest revealed in the height of the light half.

Third Quarter: Station of Descent in the cycle of the moon. Bring the issue of focus to Rhiannon to explore through the filters of the Station of Descent and the Moon of Consummation.

Dark Moon: Station of Confrontation in the cycle of the moon. Bring the issue of focus to Ceridwen to explore through the filters of the Station of Confrontation and the Moon of Consummation.

First Quarter: Station of Emergence in the cycle of the moon. Bring the issue of the focus to Blodeuwedd to explore through the filters of the Station of Emergence and the Moon of Consummation.

Night before the Full Moon: Station of Resolution in the cycle of the moon. Bring the issue of focus to Arianrhod to explore through the filters of the Station of Resolution and the Moon of Consummation.

At any point in the month, bring the issue of focus to Branwen to explore through the Station of Integration and the Moon of Consummation. Some women will do this on the night after the dark moon in counterpoint to working with Arianrhod on the night before the full moon.

Herbal Ally for the Moon of Consummation
Dandelion (*Taraxacum officinalis*)

Creating the Mother Elixir: On the night of the full moon, create your Dandelion Lunar Elixir using the directions found on page 105 of chapter 4. Be sure to label and date the bottle you are using to store the Mother Elixir. Journal any of your experiences around the creation of the Dandelion Elixir.

Prepare the Daughter Elixir: After you have made the Mother Elixir, use the directions found on page 107 of chapter 4 to prepare a dosage bottle for use in the daily experience of this elixir throughout the month. Remember to use a blue or amber dropper bottle for this purpose, and to clearly label your Daughter Elixir.

Daily Work with the Dandelion Elixir: As discussed in chapter 4, begin your daily exploration of the Dandelion Elixir. Be sure to journal everything you can about how the elixir makes you feel, what you think its energetic actions are, where it sits in your energy body, and any and all impressions, insights, symbols, visions, and memories it presents to you:

Week One of Moon Ten: Immerse yourself in the lunar elixir by taking it every day, reflecting upon how it makes you feel, and journaling all of the insights that come to you when you meditate upon the energies of the elixir.

Week Two of Moon Ten: Continue to take the lunar elixir daily, but this week spend time experiencing and comparing the energetic impact of dandelion as an essence, and dandelion as a magical herb that you burn, as detailed in chapter 4. Again, reflect upon how each makes you feel, and journal all of the insights that come to you when you meditate upon the energies of the elixir and the energies of the herb itself.

Week Three of Moon Ten: Continue to take the lunar elixir daily, but this week spend time researching the medicinal, folkloric, and magical uses of dandelion, beginning with the information provided in Part Three of this book. Compare your findings this week with your direct experiences, being sure to journal all of the insights and connections you've made.

Week Four of Moon Ten: Continue to take the lunar elixir daily, but this week meditate upon the mythic portion of the month and reflect upon the ways in which the energies of dandelion are related to the present portion of Rhiannon's tale, and how it helps you to build a relationship with Rhiannon herself.

End of Moon Reflections: Under what circumstances could you see yourself using the dandelion elixir in support of your work and personal process? If you had to describe the actions of this lunar elixir using one word, what would it be? What about using one sentence? What about using a whole paragraph? Again, be sure to journal everything.

Moon 11

THE MOON OF PURIFICATION

Moon Eleven of the Avalonian Cycle of Revealing is called the Moon of Purification, and is associated with the herb wild thyme (Thymus serpyllum) and the lunar month begins on the first full moon when the sun is in Virgo; the full moon is in Pisces. It is the third of four moons during the Time of Rhiannon.

As the cycle turns downward again, our commitment to our growth is challenged—difficulties arise to push our limitations and stretch our understanding. Painful lessons can yield great harvest if they are shouldered with patience, peace and understanding. It is easy to give in to what is not true—but perseverance and dedication to right action in the face of difficulty gives us the strength to see it through.

The Mythic Portion

After their marriage, Rhiannon and Pwyll take up residence at Pwyll's court in Arberth where Rhiannon builds a reputation as a good and generous queen. After three years without an heir, however, Pwyll's advisors suggest he put Rhiannon aside, but he refuses, confident that they will have a child. And indeed, within a year, Rhiannon gives birth to a son. Six nurses are assigned to the care of the newborn and his mother, but they all fall asleep and wake the next morning to find the child gone. Panicked, they conceive a plan to save themselves, killing a puppy and spreading its blood and bones all over the sleeping Rhiannon. When she awakens and asks for her son, the nurses tell her that she destroyed the child in the night, and though they tried to stop her, she was too strong for them to subdue. Rhiannon pleads with them to tell the truth, but they refuse to change their story. Thus accused, Rhiannon is brought before the court, and Pywll lays a punishment upon her, and she agrees to comply: for seven years, she is to sit on the mounting block outside of the gates of Arberth. While there, she is to tell everyone who passes how she destroyed her newborn child and then offer to carry them to the court on her back.

The Work of the Moon of Purification

Rhiannon's grief is the grief of all mothers sending their children out into the world. Whether we birth children or ideas, art or music, programs or processes, or commit ourselves to living a life in alignment with who we are and what we wish to be in the world, there is a degree of risk involved. We are forced to acknowledge our vulnerability, process our lack of the support we hoped to have, and face our fear that we will fail. From the moment we are born, we begin the process of separating from our mother, from our origins, from our Source. So much of our inner pain is generated by this disconnection—the sense of feeling lost, unworthy, unlovable, and unloved. This separation of the son from the mother in particular represents a primal wound so strong that it is embedded in our cultural and mythic memory. But what is it that makes this mytheme so poignant? Why is it something that transcends space and time, to evolve and shift, and yet to remain so enculturated? Who is the Stolen Child ... this Divine Prisoner?

The answer is not hard: The Divine Prisoner is each of us.

He is that part of ourselves that has been parted from our Divine Mother. We are imprisoned by this disconnection in so very many ways: whether the literal removal of the Female Divine by the predominant monotheisms of our time or the patriarchal damage that oppresses women, devalues women's work, and punishes any behaviors in men that are considered "feminine"; or our culture's overarching value of what is logical and empirical over what is emotional and intuitive; or our subjugation of this planet and reducing all who dwell upon it or within it as resources to be exploited. Anywhere the metaphor takes you represents what is true, for it is the magic of myth that is universal enough for everyone to see themselves in it, yet personal enough that we can use it to better understand ourselves and our struggles.

It is not only the son who is separated from the mother; women also suffer from being imprisoned. We are taught to distrust other women, compete with them, and judge them just as Rhiannon's nurses do in the tale. Consumed with their own self-preservation, the frightened women bonded together in a lie rather than uniting in a truth. No matter how Rhiannon begged them to say what really happened, no matter that she promised she would protect them from any potential harm, the nurses knew that their several voices would hold more weight than Rhiannon's singular voice, and they simply did not trust that their queen, this grieving new mother who had just lost her child hours after birth, would support them. How much suffering could have been averted had these women spoken the truth which would have seen the grieving parents rally their resources to find their missing babe, instead of accepting that he was gone, and never even knowing to look for him? It is tragic indeed.

There is no denying, on the other hand, that in a very literal sense our primal separation is that of the child from the mother. We are transitioned from a place of safety, warmth, and comfort into a new world where even in the gentlest of circumstances, shock and confusion result from the sudden separation and distinction; we are set adrift in a sea of experience for which we lack the neural connections to process or understand. As we grow and adapt to life in this world, our conscious, intellectual selves constantly seek to make sense of our environment;

for many of us, this is the part that has learned that we are separate, we are alone, and we are left to fend for ourselves.

The bootstrap mentality permeates Western culture and forces each successive generation and even individuals to make it on their own without the ethic that we should be lifting each other up. We have accepted the lie that we must be independent rather than interdependent. We live in a society that values logic over emotion, knowledge over wisdom, judgment over empathy, and individuality over collectivity rather than seeking the balance of both. This is not to say we should not be our own person; rather, we must learn to both honor our inner Sovereignty while also acknowledging that it is in the collective good to honor the Sovereignty of others as well. We are in a prison of our own making culturally, psychologically, and spiritually. We need to reunite with the mother ... to develop emotional maturity, and cultivate a sense of the circle, from the most literal to the most metaphorical of senses.

For it is we who hold the key to our personal prisons, with its bars formed out of fear, out of the belief that we are unworthy of love, or of honor, or of respect. We have accepted that our needs are irrelevant, our intuitive selves are too woo-woo, and our instincts are wrong. And as much as we seek to be upheld, loved, heard, witnessed, and cared for—we need to consider the mother who also suffers from our separation ... she who holds our unmet needs, unvoiced questions, unresolved emotions, disconnect from our inner power.

At this time of turmoil, we are called to reassess our priorities and because of this, the wisdom of the mothers is returning. By learning to honor the emotional self, striving to heed our instincts, seeking to take personal responsibility for our lives, building a sense of trust in the village, consciously forging bonds of community, and embracing a sense of living in respectful balance with the Earth, we help to facilitate that most beautiful of reunions: The Divine Mother, in joy, once more holds her Divine Child ... and we become a humanity that is whole once more.

Searching Deeper

The mytheme of a child being stolen from the mother is a powerful one that connects to the international folk motif of the Divine Prisoner seen elsewhere in Celtic British legend. In the Welsh tale *Culhwch ac Olwen*, one of the stories usually collected along with *The Four Branches of the Mabinogi*, we learn that Mabon ("Divine Son") was taken from his mother Modron ("Divine Mother") when he was only three days old. The child is hidden and imprisoned, only to be freed after King Arthur's men undertake a journey that leads them to consult with each of the Oldest Animals in turn before discovering and freeing boy who later joined their war band.

Mabon's imprisonment is also mentioned in the Welsh Triads:

> *Triad 52—Three Exalted Prisoners of the Island of Britain: Llŷr Half-Speech, and Mabon son of Modron, and Gwair son of Geirioedd.*[24]

Like Rhiannon, Modron is a goddess of Sovereignty, and she is believed to be a cognate deity (a term used in the study of comparative mythology to indicate connections between divinities from different cultures based upon the shared etymological meaning of their names) of the Gaulish mother goddess Matrona, as their names both mean "Divine Mother." In the same way, Mabon is a cognate deity of Matrona's son, Maponos (another "Divine Son"). In Welsh myth, Modron is named the daughter of Avallach, identified in some tales as the King of Avalon who dwelt on Glastonbury Tor. She is mentioned in Triad 70 of *Trioedd Ynys Prydein*, which enumerates the Three Fair Womb-Burdens of the Island of Britain; the second of which is:

---

24. Bromwich, *Trioedd Ynys Prydein*, 424.

Owain, son of Urien and Morfudd his sister who were carried together in the womb of Modron, daughter of Afallach.[25]

The father of the twins mentioned in the above triad is Urien Rheged, a sixth-century semi-historic warrior-king who ruled the early northern British kingdom of Rheged. This is the same Urien at whose court the historical bard Taliesin is said to have served and for whom we have several praise poems collected in *Llyfr Taliesin*. Modron herself may have connections with the character of Morgan le Fay, as Arthurian tales call Morgan the wife of Uriens of Gorre and the mother of the hero Owain. It is likely not a coincidence that the husband and son of Modron and Morgan le Fay have the same names.

A theory forwarded by Welsh scholar W. J. Gruffudd suggested that the *Four Branches of the Mabinogi* are a mythic cycle which originally recounted the life of the hero Pryderi; he is the only character that appears in all four of the Branches: he is born in the First Branch, serves as a warrior in the Second Branch, comes into his own as a ruler in the Third Branch, and is killed in single combat with Gwydion in the Fourth Branch. If this is the case, and the most accepted meaning of the word *Mabinogi* is "tales of the youth," with the root word *mab* meaning "youth" or "son," perhaps Pryderi is a reflex (a term used in the study of comparative mythology to describe a relationship between two different deities who are not cognate to each other but who exhibit similar attributes and/or mythic stories) of Mabon, and these are the stories of the Divine Son—and his Divine Mother.

---

25. Bromwich, *Trioedd Ynys Prydein*, 449.

Seeking Sovereignty Within:
Journaling Prompts and Self-Reflective Questions

Moon Eleven
The Moon of Purification
The Time of Rhiannon

Mythic Focus: Rhiannon's newborn son goes missing. She is falsely accused by his nurses of having destroyed him and is punished unjustly for a crime she didn't commit.

Personal Insights Around This Moon's Mythic Portion: *Meditate upon the portion of Rhiannon's story associated with this moon and reflect it within yourself. Her story is your story.*

The Focus of the Moon of Purification by Phase

Seek the lessons of the Moon of Purification at each moon phase by using the Stations of the monthly Cycle of Healing; be sure to journal all of the insights, symbols, and guidance you receive from each goddess at each moon phase. As you work with the information you receive between each phase, perhaps following the daily process outlined in chapter 3 of this book, and using tools such as trance postures and doorways as detailed in *Avalon Within*, be sure to record those insights in your journal as well.

Full Moon: Connect with Rhiannon at the full moon to set up your work for the month and to receive insight on the issue of focus. Review the work of the previous month and the insights it brought to you, set up your work for the coming month, and ask for insights on the issue of focus which may have shifted or deepened due to the work you have done.

Third Quarter: Station of Descent in the cycle of the moon. Bring the issue of focus to Rhiannon to explore through the filters of the Station of Descent and the Moon of Purification.

Dark Moon: Station of Confrontation in the cycle of the moon. Bring the issue of focus to Ceridwen to explore through the filters of the Station of Confrontation and the Moon of Purification.

First Quarter: Station of Emergence in the cycle of the moon. Bring the issue of the focus to Blodeuwedd to explore through the filters of the Station of Emergence and the Moon of Purification.

Night before the Full Moon: Station of Resolution in the cycle of the moon. Bring the issue of focus to Arianrhod to explore through the filters of the Station of Resolution and the Moon of Purification.

At any point in the month, bring the issue of focus to Branwen to explore through the Station of Integration and the Moon of Purification. Some women will do this on the night after the dark moon in counterpoint to working with Arianrhod on the night before the full moon.

Herbal Ally for the Moon of Purification
Wild Thyme (*Taraxacum officinalis*)

Creating the Mother Elixir: On the night of the full moon, create your Wild Thyme Lunar Elixir using the directions found on page 105 of chapter 4. Be sure to label and date the bottle you are using to store the Mother Elixir. Journal any of your experiences around the creation of the Wild Thyme Elixir.

Prepare the Daughter Elixir: After you have made the Mother Elixir, use the directions found on page 107 of chapter 4 to prepare a dosage bottle for use in the daily experience of this elixir throughout the month. Remember to use a blue or amber dropper bottle for this purpose, and to clearly label your Daughter Elixir.

Daily Work with the Wild Thyme Elixir: As discussed in chapter 4, begin your daily exploration of the Wild Thyme Elixir. Be sure to journal everything you can about how the elixir makes you feel, what you think it its energetic actions are, where it sits in your energy body, and any and all impressions, insights, symbols, visions, and memories it presents to you:

WEEK ONE OF MOON ELEVEN: Immerse yourself in the lunar elixir by taking it every day, reflecting upon how it makes you feel, and journaling all of the insights that come to you when you meditate upon the energies of the elixir.

WEEK TWO OF MOON ELEVEN: Continue to take the lunar elixir daily, but this week spend time experiencing and comparing the energetic impact of wild thyme as an essence, and wild thyme as a magical herb that you burn, as detailed in chapter 4. Again, reflect upon how each makes you feel, and journal all of the insights that come to you when you meditate upon the energies of the elixir and the energies of the herb itself.

WEEK THREE OF MOON ELEVEN: Continue to take the lunar elixir daily, but this week spend time researching the medicinal, folkloric, and magical uses of wild thyme, beginning with the information provided in Part Three of this book. Compare your findings this week with your direct experiences, being sure to journal all of the insights and connections you've made.

WEEK FOUR OF MOON ELEVEN: Continue to take the lunar elixir daily, but this week meditate upon the mythic portion of the month and reflect upon the ways in which the energies of wild thyme are related to the present portion of Rhiannon's tale, and how it helps you to build a relationship with Rhiannon herself.

End of Moon Reflections: Under what circumstances could you see yourself using the wild thyme elixir in support of your work and personal process? If you had to describe the actions of this lunar elixir using one word, what would it be? What about using one sentence? What about using a whole paragraph? Again, be sure to journal everything.

Moon 12

THE MOON OF RECONCILIATION

Moon Twelve of the Avalonian Cycle of Revealing is called the Moon of Reconciliation and is associated with the herb mother-wort (Leonurus cardiaca). The lunar month begins on the first full moon when the sun is in Scorpio; the full moon is in Taurus. It is the last of four moons during the Time of Rhiannon.

As with all things, the cycle turns again to return to where it began. How we enter into the next cycle has everything to do with the ways in which we have embraced the lessons of what came before. Releasing our attachment to situations and people who have harmed us permits us to be in a place of greater Sovereignty. Forgiving ourselves for the things that we have done which have not been in support of our sovereign selves helps us to be more open to receiving the gifts of healing arising from our perseverance in the face of situations outside our control. This helps free us from anxiety and readies us to enter the Cauldron of Transformation anew. There's no end, but there is more room to grow.

The Mythic Portion

Around the same time that Rhiannon was accused and punished for having destroyed her son, the lord of Gwent-Ys-Coed in southeastern Wales, named Teyrnon Twryf Liant, owned the most beautiful mare in all of the land. Each year on May Eve, the mare would give birth, but the foals always disappeared without a trace that same night. On this occasion, Teyrnon was determined to unravel the mystery. Armed with weapons, he brought the foaling mare into his house in order to keep watch over her. After night fell, a strong and sturdy foal was born. As Teyrnon was admiring the newborn, he heard a terrible commotion—an enormous clawed arm reached through the window to steal the foal. Grabbing a sword, he saved the foal by cutting off the creature's arm, who screamed and ran off into the darkness with Teyrnon in close pursuit.

As he followed the creature's trail, Teyrnon remembered that he left the door of the house open. He raced home to secure the horses and arrived to find a richly swaddled infant child laying in the doorway. Straight away, he brought the baby to his wife who had never borne a child, and they decided to raise it as their own, although they recognized that the baby was likely the offspring of nobility. They named the child Gwri Golden-Hair, and he grew at such an astounding rate that after only four years he was the size and maturity of a child twice his age. Gwri's foster mother gave him the colt who had been born on the day he was found as his own.

Around this time, Teyrnon and his wife began to hear stories of Rhiannon's penance. Looking at the quickly-growing Gwri, they both realized that he bore a striking resemblance to Pwyll, at whose court Teyrnon had once served. They determined that Gwri was likely the son of Pwyll and Rhiannon, and decided it was the right thing to return the boy to his parents so that Rhiannon's unjust punishment could finally end. They rode to Arberth where Rhiannon met them at the gate and offered to carry them to the court, but they refused. After feasting with Pwyll and Rhiannon with Teyrnon seated between them, the lord of Gwent-Ys-Coed revealed how the boy had come to be in his care and stated that no one could look upon him and not acknowledge that he was the son of Pwyll; Rhiannon had clearly been unjustly accused.

Rhiannon replied, "Oh, if only this was true! Then I would be delivered of my anxiety!" And it is thus that the boy who had been called Gwri was named by his true mother, based on the first thing she said upon learning he had survived; he was called Pryderi ap Pwyll Pen Annwfyn, which means Anxiety, son of Wisdom, the Head of Annwn. Rhiannon was exonerated of all wrong-doing, and Pryderi was raised to be the most noble of men. After Pwyll's death, Pryderi became lord over all of Dyfed, and later unified the kingdoms of southern Wales under his just rule.

The Work of the Moon of Reconciliation

In the end, it is Rhiannon's graceful endurance, her commitment to her truth, and her refusal to be moved from the knowledge of who she is even in the face of injustice that ultimately bring her vindication: her child restored to her and all imbalances are set to right. Rhiannon teaches through example how we can fortify ourselves as we move through the challenges of our own lives. She inspires us with the hope that when we endure while centered in ourselves, not only will we make it through any trials before us, we will be transformed in the process.

The experiences that life brings us are not always under our control. No one invites tragedy, loss, illness, financial struggle, or abuse into their lives. Sometimes we are caught in cycles of poverty or domestic abuse from which it is difficult to rise up. Some of us live in places that have been devastated by natural disasters, ravished by war, or know intense oppression. The challenges of our day to day lives can include struggles with chronic pain, mental illness, pervasive loneliness and neglect, and intense fatigue from doing all the things needed to function in this world and have what is needed to survive. Single parents working multiple jobs to make ends meet for themselves and their children do not typically have the luxury of time to pursue daily spiritual practices or the resources needed in order to live the life they envision for themselves. Those who have physical disabilities are challenged at every turn with issues of accessibility, and those with chronic illness often struggle to have the energy needed to engage in the work they long to be doing.

Rhiannon's example teaches us that we need not allow the present or permanent circumstances of our lives to be what defines us. If anything, it is during her punishment that she finds and expresses the most primal and pure manifestation of her Sovereignty, embracing her equine aspect in a clear and powerful way. We are called, then, to find and embrace our inner Sovereignty during our times of greatest travail; to bring our focus within when the circumstances around us do not support the truth of who we know ourselves to be; to fortify ourselves from within—that place where we have all that we need, where nothing can be taken away from us, and where the truth of who we are is not dependent upon whatever is around us.

By looking at the trials of our lives—where we are suffering, where we know lack, where we feel loss—as portals into recognition of our inner strength and inherent power, we are able to affect a deep and lasting shift in our perspective and in how we approach our challenges. Rhiannon calls us to transform the mounting block into a throne, to seek and maintain our Sovereignty no matter the circumstances of our lives. When we look at our challenges as opportunities for growth rather than punishment or the manifestation of some cruel mechanism of fate, we find that they can be deep teachers that catalyze change and show us the wisdom of letting go.

So, let us let go of our expectations of how we thought things would be, in order to allow ourselves the gift of presence in how things are.

Let us let go of our disappointment in situations that didn't unfold the way we hoped they would, so we can learn what we must from them as we gather the courage and resources we need in order to try again.

Let us release self-recrimination, something that only serves to further obscure the truth and bind us to a past we cannot alter.

Let us release the need for perfection, so that we may instead celebrate what is present and permit ourselves the vulnerability that comes with declaring something to be, at last, complete.

We must let go of blame, so that we can take responsibility for our healing and commit ourselves to change.

We must let go of fear so that love can enter.

When we are on the other side of these limiting beliefs—when we have made it through the darkness and the trauma, through the disappointment and the pain, through the trial and the challenge—we must also gift ourselves with the ability to set our burdens down, and free ourselves from anxiety. We must ensure that we only allow the strength and wisdom that arises from our challenges to move forward with us.

At its deepest level, reconciliation can be approached as a powerful inner accounting; a balancing of our energetic books which allows us to assess our strengths and weaknesses in order to identify the places where we have successfully affected positive change alongside those parts of our spiritual gardens still in need of tending. Acknowledging these parts of ourselves is not intended to bring us shame, cause us to feel unworthy, or think we have not done enough work. Rather it is an opportunity for self-acceptance and forgiveness that allows us to put down the burdens we need no longer carry so we may move forward with joy and clarity to the next round of cycle.

Searching Deeper

It is at this point that Rhiannon's story becomes deeply complex. Early Celticists theorized that there were at least two versions of this tale that split off from the original while it was yet part of an oral tradition, and that the medieval redactor struggled to put the pieces back together.[26] More recent theories suggest that the story was constructed in this way deliberately, even if we do not fully understand the meaning.[27]

To begin, the parallel storyline between Rhiannon's loss of her newborn and Teyrnon's mare's annual loss of her foal cannot be overlooked. There are Otherworldly happenings afoot, not in the least because this takes place on Calan Haf (the threshold day between winter and summer) that the infant is found on Teyrnon's threshold to underscore this point. The foal is born the same night as Rhiannon's son, and as punishment for allegedly having destroyed her child, Rhiannon is forced to act like a horse at the gates of the town.

Teyrnon himself is an interesting character. In the same way that Rhiannon's name derives from *Rīgantona*, an Old Celtic name meaning "Divine Queen," Teyrnon's name is believed to be the Welsh form of the Old Celtic *Tigernonos*, which means "Divine or Great Lord." His full name in the First Branch is given as Teyrnon Twryf Liant, which means "Divine Lord of the Thundering Waters."[28] While we simply do not have enough information to form any solid conclusions about any of this (Pwyll is quite clearly given as Pryderi's father here in the First Branch as well as elsewhere in Welsh literature including the mythological poems of Taliesin), it is intriguing to wonder what it means that the names of Pryderi's mother and foster father are mirror images of each other.

There may also be some significance in the fact that horses and the ocean are connected in the mythology of many cultures. For example, in Irish tradition Manannán mac Lir is a god of the sea, and his watery chariot is pulled by a horse that could traverse both land and water. In-

---

26. W. J. Gruffydd, *Rhiannon: Inquiry into the First and Third Branches of the Mabinogion*, (Cardiff: University of Wales Press, 1953).

27. Ford, *The Mabinogi*, 110.

28. Davies, *The Mabinogion*, 231.

deed, the waves of the sea themselves were sometimes called "the horses of Manannán." Interestingly, Rhiannon weds Manawydan fab Llŷr in the Third Branch of *Y Mabinogi*, who is clearly a cognate divinity to Manannán mac Lir, although he does not display any association with the sea in the Welsh tale.

Because Teyrnon, whose full name also reflects a connection with water, was successful in saving his foal from the monster (which ostensibly dropped the newborn it had stolen from Rhiannon when its arm was cut off) he was able to save Pryderi as well. Years later, Teyrnon saved Rhiannon from her unjust punishment when he did the right thing and brought the boy he had raised as his own back to his family:

> *Teyrnon turned to Rhiannon and said, "This is your son, my lady. And whoever told lies against you are wrong." Rhiannon replied. "What a relief from my anxiety if that were true!" and it is from this utterance that Pryderi, from the word pryder, meaning "anxiety," received his name from Rhiannon.*[29]

The family is thus reunited, and Rhiannon regains her rightful place as queen.

---

29. Davies, *The Mabinogion*, 20.

Seeking Sovereignty Within:
Journaling Prompts and Self-Reflective Questions

Moon Twelve
The Moon of Reconciliation
The Time of Rhiannon

Mythic Focus: Rhiannon is reunited with her lost son, rejoins her husband, and is restored to her queenship.

Personal Insights Around This Moon's Mythic Portion: *Meditate upon the portion of Rhiannon's story associated with this moon, and reflect it within yourself. Her story is your story.*

The Focus of the Moon of Reconciliation by Phase

Seek the lessons of the Moon of Reconciliation at each moon phase by using the Stations of the monthly Cycle of Healing; be sure to journal all of the insights, symbols, and guidance you receive from each goddess at each moon phase. As you work with the information you receive between each phase, perhaps following the daily process outlined in chapter 3 of this book, and using tools such as trance postures and doorways as detailed in *Avalon Within*, be sure to record those insights in your journal as well.

Full Moon: Connect with Rhiannon at the full moon to set up your work for the month and to receive insight on the issue of focus. Review the work of the previous month and the insights it brought to you, set up your work for the coming month, and ask for insights on the issue of focus which may have shifted or deepened due to the work you have done.

Third Quarter: Station of Descent in the cycle of the moon. Bring the issue of focus to Rhiannon to explore through the filters of the Station of Descent and the Moon of Reconciliation.

Dark Moon: Station of Confrontation in the cycle of the moon. Bring the issue of focus to Ceridwen to explore through the filters of the Station of Confrontation and the Moon of Reconciliation.

First Quarter: Station of Emergence in the cycle of the moon. Bring the issue of the focus to Blodeuwedd to explore through the filters of the Station of Emergence and the Moon of Reconciliation.

Night before the Full Moon: Station of Resolution in the cycle of the moon. Bring the issue of focus to Arianrhod to explore through the filters of the Station of Resolution and the Moon of Reconciliation.

At any point in the month, bring the issue of focus to Branwen to explore through the Station of Integration and the Moon of Reconciliation. Some women will do this on the night after the dark moon in counterpoint to working with Arianrhod on the night before the full moon.

Herbal Ally for the Moon of Reconciliation
Motherwort (*Leonurus cardiaca*)

Creating the Mother Elixir: On the night of the full moon, create your Motherwort Lunar Elixir using the directions found on page 105 of chapter 4. Be sure to label and date the bottle you are using to store the Mother Elixir. Journal any of your experiences around the creation of the Motherwort Elixir.

Prepare the Daughter Elixir: After you have made the Mother Elixir, use the directions found on page 107 of chapter 4 to prepare a dosage bottle for use in the daily experience of this elixir throughout the month. Remember to use a blue or amber dropper bottle for this purpose, and to clearly label your Daughter Elixir.

Daily Work with the Motherwort Elixir: As discussed in chapter 4, begin your daily exploration of the Motherwort Elixir. Be sure to journal everything you can about how the elixir makes you feel, what you think its energetic actions are, where it sits in your energy body, and any and all impressions, insights, symbols, visions, and memories it presents to you:

WEEK ONE OF MOON TWELVE: Immerse yourself in the lunar elixir by taking it every day, reflecting upon how it makes you feel, and journaling all of the insights that come to you when you meditate upon the energies of the elixir.

WEEK TWO OF MOON TWELVE: Continue to take the lunar elixir daily, but this week spend time experiencing and comparing the energetic impact of motherwort as an essence, and motherwort as a magical herb that you burn, as detailed in chapter 4. Again, reflect upon how each makes you feel, and journal all of the insights that come to you when you meditate upon the energies of the elixir and the energies of the herb itself.

WEEK THREE OF MOON TWELVE: Continue to take the lunar elixir daily, but this week spend time researching the medicinal, folkloric, and magical uses of motherwort, beginning with the information provided in Part Three of this book. Compare your findings this week with your direct experiences, being sure to journal all of the insights and connections you've made.

WEEK FOUR OF MOON TWELVE: Continue to take the lunar elixir daily, but this week meditate upon the mythic portion of the month and reflect upon the ways in which the energies of motherwort are related to the present portion of Rhiannon's tale, and how it helps you to build a relationship with Rhiannon herself.

End of Moon Reflections: Under what circumstances could you see yourself using the Motherwort Elixir in support of your work and personal process? If you had to describe the actions of this lunar elixir using one word, what would it be? What about using one sentence? What about using a whole paragraph? Again, be sure to journal everything.

Working: Journey Into the
Sacred Landscape of Rhiannon

Gorsedd Arberth

Please perform the induction to travel over the Ninth Wave, as found on page 74, and then proceed with the working below. When you have completed it, be sure to return from across the Ninth Wave, using the visualization found on page 76.

Having crossed the Ninth Wave into the Otherworld, disembark and envision a silver tether that extends from the center of your torso to the vessel which bore you here; it is of endless length and will expand and retract as necessary as you explore this Realm Over Wave, while keeping you connected to the boat in order to facilitate your return.

Take three deep, anchoring breaths, and immerse yourself in the energies of this place. It is the reflection of the Gorsedd Arberth here in the realm of the Mythic Otherworld. Stand now at the foot of this round and pregnant hill of magic. It is surrounded by a hedge of hawthorn, following the perimeter of the ancient bank and ditch enclosure that once marked this as a sacred space. Walk along the path hugging the foundation of this holy hill, seeking and finding the break in the hedgerow—the place where you can pass between. Stand before this open space and connect with your intention as a seeker who wishes to sit upon the Gorsedd Arberth to receive wisdom and support from the Otherworld. Feel yourself fully present in this moment. When you are ready, take a deep breath in, hold it as you step through the threshold, and when both of your feet are firmly planted on the other side, exhale.

Become aware of the path that winds around and up the hillside, and with intention, begin to walk toward the top. With each step, you move higher up the hill, while simultaneously feeling yourself seeking deeper into your self. With each step, all energies of resistance, all ties of attachment fall away and your find yourself centered, fully grounded, and fully present. To sit upon the Gorsedd Arberth is to risk becoming assailed with many blows and wounds—or else one will see a wonder. It is the degree of one's own Sovereignty that determines which of the two you will encounter.

Find the very center of the hill, and there, at its apex, you see a bowl filled with sweet honey mead. Take it into your hands and fill it with your gratitude for the work you have come to do in this space. Charge it with your intention to gift it to honor the ancestors, the spirits of place, and all who dwell upon the land. When you are ready, pour it out with reverence and watch as the liquid is absorbed into the earth and is received. Become aware of how the energies of your intention sink down into the hill and through it spreads out into the landscape, illuminating the lines of energy arching across the land.

Feeling welcome in this space, find a place to sit crossed-legged on the top of the hill. Close your eyes and connect with your breathing, relaxing into a natural and rhythmic pattern as you clear your mind from all distractions. When you feel centered and ready to receive, take nine deep and intentional breaths. With each inhalation, the veil between the worlds becomes thinner. With each exhalation, attachment to this world falls away. In and out. In and out. With the ninth and final breath, open your eyes and find yourself sitting on the shore of a small island, surrounded by ocean as far as the eye can see.

Stand and plant your feet firmly on the beach of the island. Take three deep centering breaths. As you anchor your focus, it comes to you that you have journeyed to Gwales, an Otherworldly island off the shore of Dyfed. Observe everything you can about the landscape of this place. Its dominating geographical feature is the elevated area in the center of the island. Upon it is built a sturdy fortress; even from where you stand, you notice that it possesses many windows and many doors. Follow the path that leads you away from the shore, bringing you up and up and up the sloping hillside until you are standing in front of the fortress' main entrance. It is opened to you.

Take a moment as you stand before this doorway and become aware of your breath. Feel it rise and fall in unison with the ocean waves that crash and recede on the shores of the island all around you. With your inner eye, follow your breath down into the hidden core of the self, moving deeper and deeper into the fabric of your personal history with each cycle of breath. With focused intention, connect with those parts of yourself that hold your deepest pain, the wounds or memories that fill you with sorrow or regret, the fears that keep you stuck and imprisoned. You don't need to become overwhelmed with the energies of these shadow aspects of self—simply become aware of them, consciously acknowledge them, and bless their presence in your life.

Ask if there are any particular shadow aspects that you are most in need of examining today. Allow the awareness of this part of yourself to rise to the surface of your consciousness, bringing with it anv at tendant emotional experiences. Take some time to really   and experience these emotions, honoring them as the bearers of information they are. When you are ready, ask this painful part of yourself to reveal itself to you in the form of a symbol. When you have received it, acknowledge and remember everything you can about it.

Keeping this image in the forefront of your consciousness, look to the fortress in front of you. When you are ready and with focused intention, pass through the open doorway and enter. Find yourself in a great feasting hall that is richly appointed with beautiful tapestries and artwork. At the center of the hall is a grand table burdened with every kind of food and drink. Become aware of the tantalizing smells of the delicious food. As you move closer to the table, you find that you can hear the rise and fall of the soft laughter of many people surrounding you, although you can see no one else in the hall.

Still, you feel comfortable in this space and survey the enormous table until you find the place you know has been lain for you. Sit before your place setting, and notice when you look down that the plate itself is a very reflective golden color—you can make out your own features in its mirrored surface. Hungry, you reach for a platter of some of the rich food before you but no matter what you do, you find that anything you try to take hold of is just out of reach. Thirsty, you reach for a carafe of wine, but in the same way, there are none you can pick up to pour into your empty cup. You feel frustrated and take three deep breaths. As you do so, you ask what it is that keeps you from participating in the feast around you. Keep yourself open to receive the answer: perhaps it will be in the form of a symbol, a voice you hear, a memory you experience, or a scene that plays out in front of your eyes. Allow the answer to unfold in the way you most need to experience, and be sure to commit to memory what you have seen.

Take three deep, centering breaths. As you integrate this insight, you become aware that the laughter has died down into silence; arising from the silence you hear the most heartbreakingly beautiful birdsong you have ever known. Really listen to this incredible music and take note of how hearing it makes you feel in body, mind, and spirit. Although you cannot see them, you know without a shadow of doubt there are three birds singing that seem to be simultaneously a great distance away but sound as though they are right there in the hall with you. Spend some time experiencing their complexly textured song and know that you are being visited by the Adar Rhiannon—the Birds of Rhiannon.

Still listening, bring the image of the symbol of focus you received outside before you entered the fortress—the one that represents the shadow aspect you need most to work with at this point in your journey. When that image becomes clear in your mind's eye, focus your attention on the melody of the first bird, the one singing with the voice of the past. Experience this tune growing louder and more distinct. It has a message for you about the origins of the pain you are focusing on. Journey along with the notes of the tune and look into the mirrored plate before you until you see another symbol form on its surface representing the origin of this pain. Listen and remember.

When you are ready, shift your attention to the melody of the second bird. It sings with the voice of the present and has a message for you about the ways in which this sorrow manifests and affects your life in the here and the now. Journey along with the notes of the tune and look into the mirrored plate before you until you see yet another symbol form on its surface—this one represents the manifestation of this pain. Listen and remember.

When you are ready, shift your attention once more to become aware of the melody of the third bird. It sings with the voice of the future and has a message for you about what you can do to release the pain of this wound so that it no longer affects your life. Journey along with the notes of the tune and look into the mirrored plate before you until you see yet another symbol form on its surface—this one represents the release of this pain. Listen and remember.

Take three deep, anchoring breaths with gratitude for the symbols you have received as well as to reweave the three strains of the birds' song back into one grand and harmonized piece. When you have done so, the three birds suddenly appear in the hall with you, singing together as they fly in a circle around your head three times. As they do so, you feel yourself becoming lighter, you feel your burdens fading, and experience your heart becoming filled with a deep and abiding joy—all pain disappears, all sorrow forgotten.

Remember how it feels to be thus released of your cares. Look at yourself on surface of the golden plate once more. See the person you can be when you release that which holds you back, whatever keeps you stagnant and living in fear. See the person you will become when you heal this wounded aspect of yourself. Take three deep and centering breaths. See. Listen. Remember.

Become aware of the sounds of laughter once more and realize that it is bubbling up from within you. Finally, you can fully participate in the feast before you, but you are so full of joy that the laden tables hold no further interest. Take note, however, of what you see and hear and experience.

When you are ready, rise from the table, and stand before the only closed door in the hall. With your breath and intention, open the door and look through it out over the sea, where you can make out the shoreline of Cornwall. The enchantment is broken, and it is time for you to return home, bringing with you the memory of all you have seen and experienced. When you are ready, step through the door…and find yourself back on the Gorsedd Arberth, sitting in the sunlight…grateful for having seen a wonder.

When you are ready, take three deep centering breaths. Remember all you have seen, received, and committed to in this moment. Follow the thread that connects you to the vessel that took you to this Land Beyond Wave. Take your place in the boat once more to begin the journey back over the Nine Waves to the place that is Here and the time that is Now.

Chapter 8

THE TIME OF BRANWEN

Branwen, whose name means "white raven," is featured in the eponymous tale "Branwen, Daughter of Llŷr," the Second Branch of *Y Mabinogi*. It is tempting to read something into the fact that the Second Branch is the only one named for a woman, signifying the great importance of Branwen ferch Llŷr. However, this naming convention does not appear in the original manuscript; it was Lady Charlotte Guest who adopted the standard of naming the Four Branches after characters in the narrative when she translated the work into English.

Nevertheless, Branwen emerges from the narrative of the Second Branch bearing some of the hallmarks of a goddess of Sovereignty. She is the sister of Bendigeidfran (Bran the Blessed), the king of Britain, and she is called one of three Chief Maidens of the Isle of the Mighty. When Branwen consents to wed Matholwch, the king of Ireland who comes to Bran's court seeking her hand, she enters into a sacred marriage with the Irish king while also taking on the role of the Peace Weaver, one who lays down her body to serve as a bridge that unites two nations. During the wedding feast, Branwen's half-brother Efnysien mutilates the horses of the Irish contingent in anger because he hadn't been consulted about the marriage. This was an enormous insult to Matholwch, as the horse is a symbol of Sovereignty in Celtic tradition. As part of the compensation for Efnysien's actions, Bran gifts

Matholwch with the Cauldron of Regeneration, a magical vessel that could bring back to life any dead warrior placed within it.

Of all the figures from Welsh myth that have been covered, Branwen most exemplifies the proper behavior of a woman within the medieval Welsh social order. She is depicted as the perfect wife and queen in every way—gracious, noble, compliant, and beautiful. At the beginning of the Second Branch, Branwen is only talked about; we do not see or hear from her until later in the narrative. Unlike Rhiannon's direct involvement in her marriage and wedding feast, Branwen's formulaic acceptance of her betrothal to Matholwch and subsequent marriage to him happen off-stage. It is not until she becomes an estranged wife that Branwen begins to emerge as a character in her own right.

Herself a paragon of right action, fulfilling her duty as wife and queen, and bearing Matholwch a son, Branwen is made to suffer unjustly after several years have passed in their marriage. Although she obeys her husband and follows his directive with characteristic grace, Branwen takes action to redress the wrong and dishonor being done to her. Here it is Matholwch who has failed in his duty to protect his wife, and so the responsibility reverts back to Bran, her brother. Branwen has regained her personal power because she has effectively become a single woman once more. Content to work within the social paradigm expected of her, Branwen expects the same of those around her; when wronged, we see her ingenuity come to the fore.

Branwen further illustrates her wisdom as she correctly interprets for Matholwch the vision of the scout who describes the coming of Bran and his armies to Ireland, and it is she who brokers the peace between Britain and Ireland by suggesting that Gwern, her young son, be made king—a proposal accepted by both sides of the conflict in the interest of peace. Perhaps hinting once more at her underlying importance beyond that of fulfilling the role of the tragic peace weaver motif, it is Branwen more than any other woman in the Four Branches who becomes most directly involved in creating political policy.

Branwen's status as a goddess has been renewed in modern Pagan practice, where she is honored by those whose spiritual paths are inspired by Celtic British or Brythonic traditions. Since her legend was not written down by those who worshiped her as a goddess, we do not have a traditional depiction of Branwen as a fully realized deity. Instead, the rawness of her story makes Branwen an emotionally accessible goddess; because she has experienced suffering, she is an overflowing vessel of compassion for those who have been unjustly punished, have lived through domestic violence, and who have endured enormous loss. Branwen's story teaches us that we have the power to remain sovereign within ourselves no matter what may be going on around us. By listening to our inner needs and using it to set change in motion outside of us, the universe will answer our call. Rather than a tale of a tragic woman abandoned to the cruelties of fate, Branwen's myth teaches that the path to divinity can be found when we seek harmony between the shadow and sovereign aspects of the self. When we learn to bridge what is with what we desire—even if a part of us must die—we find the path that leads us back to Source.

Moon 13
THE MOON OF REFLECTION

Moon Thirteen of the Avalonian Cycle of Revealing is called the Moon of Reflection, and is associated with the herb woad (Isatis tinctoria). The lunar month begins on the true Blue Moon, traditionally consider to be the second full moon in any given sun sign, which happens every two and a half to three years, making it truly rare. It is the sole moon that makes up the Time of Branwen. This full moon corresponds with the Station of Integration in the Avalonian Cycle of Healing.

The Moon of Reflection brings with it the blessings of expanded sight; it takes us out of the details of the daily weave and shifts our perspective so that we may see the whole of the tapestry. The opportunity to pause and realign allows us to recognize where we have come from, and permits us to visualize where we seek to go; it is a powerful practice, indeed. How do we build the bridge that brings us back to Source? By taking stock of all that has changed, acknowledging the ways we have grown, forgiving ourselves for the work yet left undone, and bringing all those energies back to our center. Looking behind at what was, and looking ahead at what could be, the Moon of Reflection calls us to reclaim the whole of who we are in the here and now.

The Myth

Branwen is sister of Bendigeidfran (Bran the Blessed), the king of the Island of the Mighty, a poetic name for Britain. Matholwch, the king of Ireland, approaches Bran to seek the hand of Branwen in marriage. A council is convened, and it is decided with Branwen's consent that she would be married to the Irish king. One of her stepbrothers, Efnysien, angry at not having been consulted on the matter of the marriage, mutilates the horses of the Irish visitors during the marriage feast, bringing dishonor upon Bendigeidfran and insulting Matholwch greatly. Bran makes amends with Matholwch by replacing his horses, compensating him with gold and silver, and gifting him with the Cauldron of Rebirth, a wondrous vessel with the power to bring dead warriors back to life. Thus appeased, Matholwch returns to Ireland with Branwen, who is warmly welcomed and becomes known for her grace, honor, and generosity.

The first year of their marriage goes well, and Branwen bears a son named Gwern. However, in the second year, Matholwch's advisors begin speaking against the foreign-born queen, recalling the dishonor their king suffered at the wedding feast. In the end, they compel Matholwch to put Branwen aside, and he sends her to work in the kitchens where she is beaten every day by a butcher with bloodied hands. Branwen suffers her unjust punishment with grace and dignity for three years, all the while raising a starling and teaching it to speak. She describes Bran to the bird so it will recognize her brother and attaches a note to its wing telling of her dishonor and mistreatment.

The starling flies out and delivers her message to Bran, who amasses an invasion force to rescue his sister. As Bran is a giant, no boat can hold him, so he accompanies his fleet by wading across the waters to Ireland. The resulting vision is so perplexing to the Irish that Matholwch seeks the counsel of Branwen to interpret the messenger's description of the invading Britons. Where they saw a forest on the ocean, she recognizes the masts of the ships sailing to her rescue. Where they saw a moving mountain with two huge lakes surrounding a ridge, she recognizes the face of her brother looking towards Ireland. In an effort to slow the advance of the Britons, the Irish destroy the bridge over the river Llinon; the riverbed was filled with lodestones that prevented the passage of any vessel, but Bran stretches his body across the water, serving as a bridge for his men.

At Branwen's behest and on her counsel, the kings of the two islands sit down to forge a peace in a house specially built by the Irish for Bran, who was so big that no building could ever contain him. To appease Bran, Branwen's son Gwern is named by Matholwch as the new king of Ireland. But, alas, there is treachery afoot; Irish warriors lay in wait around the massive house, hidden in bags of flour hanging from hooks on the walls, in order to ambush the Britons. Efnysien discovers and kills the soldiers one by one, and then enters the counsel hall where he takes up his nephew Gwern, and throws him into the fire. Branwen tries to leap after her son, but Bran restrains her and grabs his shield as the chaos of war erupts around them. The Irish light a fire under the Cauldron of Rebirth, and begin to place their dead warriors within. Finally feeling some remorse for all that he has done, Efnysien hides himself among the Irish corpses so that he is thrown into the cauldron; when he is within, he stretches himself out until the cauldron breaks into four pieces, and he himself dies, along with any hope of the dead returning to life.

Although the men of the Island of the Mighty are victorious, the war was an enormous tragedy for both sides; only seven Britons returned from Ireland, which suffered a loss of life so great that only five pregnant women remained, hidden in a cave in the wilderness. The sons of these women divided the island between them, giving rise to the five provinces of Ireland. Bran was wounded in his thigh with a poisoned spear, and directed his men to take his head with them to Harlech, where it would talk and feast with them for seven years as if he were still alive, and where the birds of Rhiannon would sing to them, making them forget their troubles. Then they would go to the

Island of Gwales, where the company would remain for eighty years until a door facing Cornwall was opened; from there, his men were charged with burying his head in the White Hill in London, where he would protect the Island of Britain from invasion for as long as his head remained buried there.

After giving this instruction, Bran died, and his men took his head, along with the grieving Branwen, across the waters to Anglesey. Once there, Branwen looked back upon the coast of Ireland, and ahead toward the mainland of Britain; thinking about the death and destruction which had occurred in both lands, she died of a broken heart. She was buried there in a four cornered tomb on the banks of the River Alaw.

The Work of the Moon of Reflection

Looking at Branwen's story in the Second Branch, it is possible for us to see her move through the Stations of the Avalonian Cycle of Healing as her tale unfolds, mirroring her correspondence with the energies of Integration.

Descent—Branwen Crosses the Sea to Begin Life in Ireland
Inner Reflection: Entering the inner cauldron to undertake the work of the shadow requires us to overcome our fear so that we may journey into the unknown lands within us. We may see the beginnings of what we will face as we begin to dive deep, but we must continue forward, and trust in our inner process.

Confrontation—Branwen is Punished and Abused
Inner Reflection: Experiencing wounding will cause our inner Sovereignty to become imprisoned and isolated. We fixate on situations that have caused us pain and then (consciously or unconsciously) make choices as a result of that pain which are not in our best interest, and cause us to further isolate ourselves—both from others, and from the truth.

Emergence—Branwen Sends Message to Bran
Inner Reflection: The path to reclaiming our Sovereignty requires us to find our voice, to hear the inner and unconscious self speak to the outer, conscious self, and to externally communicate the inner need so that it may become actualized. When all parts of the self are in clear communication, we are empowered to set external changes into motion based upon our internal needs.

Resolution—Branwen Returns to Her Land
Inner Reflection: Changes in our lives and profound spiritual transformations can make our lives feel so radically different, we may no longer recognize ourselves and we may need time to process the ways in which the world—our world—has changed. The heart breaks open in order to return it to a place of deep and lasting connection with Source.

———————

Reflecting upon the tragic story of Branwen, we can gain some insights around how to attain a place of balance within ourselves. Just as Bran responded to Branwen's call, when we have sufficiently cleared the bridge that connects our conscious mind to Source, we are able to hear and act upon the messages that come to us through our receptive and intuitive selves, rising to the surface of our knowing from the shadow lands of the unconscious.

When we are able to hear from the places where we are suffering, and from the places where we are held prisoner, our conscious mind can act upon these inner messages and work to free us from our distress and inner bondage. Similarly, just as Branwen was the only one who could interpret the strange sighting off the coast of Ireland, is it up to us to be able to receive and understand the symbols all around us, whether through the recognition of patterns in our lives, or from unexpected messages from Source.

While others may not be able to see the patterns that we can see, and they may not be able to understand the signs that come to us from the world around us, Branwen teaches us to trust who we are and what we know, even if our vision is not shared by others. For when our bridge is built and sufficiently clear, the resulting confidence in our ability to see things for what they are will in turn allow us to allocate our external resources in response to our inner needs. And what a beautiful place of balance we will have reached when we can both discern our true needs as well as have the wherewithal to meet those needs for ourselves. This bridge between the Conscious and the Unconscious allows us to see the big picture of our lives, helps us integrate new perspectives with old experiences, and shows us how to remain anchored in the timeless Now as we come into alignment with our Sacred Center.

Connecting with Branwen at the Blue Moon and immersing ourselves in the energies of Integration at least once a month provides us with enough perspective to see the big picture of our growth path— where we have come from, and where we are going—to understand the past and to envision the future. As Lady of Two Islands, Branwen represents the archetype of the Peace Weaver, acting as a bridge between two nations. In the same way, she teaches us how to create a bridge between two states of being, unifying both who we were and are, as well as the Self in the now and the potential we have yet to realize.

Searching Deeper

Branwen is an example of a woman who takes on the role of the Peace Weaver, from the Old English word *freoduwebb*. More than a literary motif, real life noble women would lie their bodies down to form a bridge between nations, unifying warring factions through marriage and by producing an heir of both bloodlines with the idea that both sides would be hesitant to attack someone of their own blood and lineage. It was an honorable duty, but it was not without danger as the Second Branch clearly illustrates. While Branwen is able to forge peace several times—first through her marriage to the king of Ireland and second through negotiating a truce between the Britons and the Irish by having her son named king of Ireland—her story is a tragedy all around.

Matholwch's punishment of Branwen for the insult committed by her kinsmen is unjustified because he accepted the generous compensation offered to him by Bran. This choice sets off a chain of destructive events which serve as a powerful illustration of what happens when a king is unjust and enters into a state of imbalance with the goddess of sovereignty: war, death, and destruction make a Wasteland of Ireland because of this injustice. And what becomes of Sovereignty herself? She and her power return to the land, withdrawing her heart and safeguarding the sacred center that she herself embodies. Branwen was queen of two islands, the bridge that linked them both. Likewise, Sovereignty is a threshold figure; she facilitates the passage from one state of being to the next. When balance is restored, the Wasteland becomes fertile again, the postulant becomes king, and the hag regains her youth and beauty.

There is a Bronze Age burial ring cairn called Bedd Branwen (Branwen's Grave) on Anglesey located near Llanddeusant that is very close to the River Alaw. Although dating back to pre-Celtic Britain, the site could potentially have been known to the redactors of the tale of Branwen, but we do not know if the site was associated with Branwen before the writing of the Second Branch. The visual focus of Bedd Branwen is a central megalith that features a deep vertical fissure that gives the stone the appearance of having been cleaved in two—a poetic symbol, perhaps, for Branwen's broken heart, which may be the entire reason the site was connected to her. The possibility that the site may have been associated with Branwen far back into the time when the story was part of oral tradition, could suggest that the tale retains a folk memory of the site as a cult center, further supporting the idea of

Branwen of having been a sovereignty or land divinity in pre-Christian times. Further, her connection to the Cauldron of Regeneration and her namesake raven—a messenger bird associated with death and battle—may indicate that she may have once held a more chthonic function as well.

There are several dualities at work in the text of Branwen, which is fitting in many respects given her embodiment of the Peace Weaver motif, which also informs her position at the center of the Avalonian Cycle of Healing, holding the Station of Integration. She facilitates the ultimate reconciliation of opposites to form a complete and assimilated whole.

First is the connection between Branwen and her brother Bran. As mentioned earlier, Branwen's name is usually glossed to mean "White Raven," but it can also just as easily mean "Holy Raven," as the *-wen* suffix means "white, shining, or holy." In linguistics, such a suffix is an example of something called a *terminal deific*, where a portion of a name appended to the name word's root indicates the divine status of the person who bears it. It is this linguistic characteristic of the Welsh language that permits us to interpret characters from early vernacular tradition as having been reverse-euhemerized divinities; that is, they had once been gods, but over time had decreased in stature, often to become not-quite-human characters like giants, fairy queens, witches, and magicians. Another common terminal deific in Welsh with roots in Old Celtic, is the *-on* or *-ona* suffix as seen in the names of characters including: Rhiannon, Mabon, Modron, Gwydion, Epona, Rīgantona, Nemetona, Matrona, and so on.[30] It is particularly important to keep these linguistic features in mind when reading Welsh legends as mythological texts, as nowhere are these characters explicitly identified as divinities.

---

30. Edward Hamp, "Mabinogi and Archaism," *Celtica* 23, (1999): 96–110.

If we were to translate Branwen's name to mean "Holy Raven," it sets up an interesting contrast with her brother's name. In most translations of *Y Mabinogi*, his name is given as *Bendigeidfran* which means "Bran the Blessed." Now, as *Bran* itself means "raven," it would appear that both siblings have essentially the same name: Holy Raven and Blessed Raven. The raven is a powerfully symbolic animal in Celtic traditions. Sometimes conflated with its very close corvid cousin, the crow, they are considered Otherworldly messengers; in their function as carrion birds, they are associated with death and especially with war.

In Irish tradition the Mórrigan ("Great Queen") is a threefold goddess primarily associated with battle and prophecy; as her name suggests, she also embodies the Sovereignty of the land. She is made up of a collective of three sisters, and while there are variations on the goddesses who comprise the Mórrigan (their areas of divine influence overlap with each other), the most well known grouping is made up of Mórrigu ("Great Queen"); Babd or Babd Catha ("Battle Crow"); and Macha ("Of the Plain"). Further, a dedicatory stele found in France features a Gaulish war goddess named Cathubodua ("Battle Crow").

In light of this insight into the Mórrigan and their name meanings, it is interesting to consider that both Irish and Gaulish Celts had goddesses of war named for and connected with crows, while the closest equivalent survival of the Celtic Britons appear to be Bran and Branwen. Bran is clearly a warrior-king; not only does he lead his war band in attacking Ireland to rescue Branwen, but he also features on the frontline of the mystical battle described in the Welsh poem "Cad Goddeu" ("The Battle of the Trees"). Branwen, on the other hand, is a Peace Weaver, working to unite two countries by bridging them through her person and bearing a child descended from each nation. And yet, there is some role-reversal at play between the siblings as well. For it is Branwen who initiates the war between Britain and Ireland when she sends a message to her brother about the abuse she is suffering at the hands of Matholwch. And later, it is during the invasion of

Ireland that Bran literally becomes a bridge over an impassable river, laying his giant body across the waters to allowing his men to reach the other side. In their own ways, then, both Bran and Branwen embody the famous Welsh proverb: *A fo ben, bid bont*—"If you want to be a leader, be a bridge."

Ultimately, both Bran and Branwen perish at the end of the war which ravaged Ireland and decimated the armies of Britain. Bran, who is the likely precursor of the Fisher King in the Grail mythos whose secret name is Bron, is pierced through the thigh, albeit in this tale, with a poisoned spear. Branwen, the object of Bran's quest and subtextual guardian of the Cauldron of Regeneration—an almost direct precursor to the grail which can heal the wounded king—that accompanies her to Ireland, dies of a broken heart and is buried on the holy island of Ynys Môn (Anglesey).

Although it is not stated that the siblings are twins, there is a literary motif known as "twinning," a common element in mythic language. The motif is used to explore the nature of duality both as a way express symmetry as well as to set up a means of comparison between two opposing value systems.[31] Their complementary roles, almost identical names, totemic correspondences, and inability to survive one without the other, make the connection between Bran and Branwen of potentially greater significance than may initially be apparent.

This is further underscored when we consider the half-siblings of Bran and Branwen, Nysien and Efnysien, with whom they share their mother, Penarddun ("Chief Beauty"). Now, Penarddun was the wife of Llŷr Llediath ("Llŷr Half-speech"), who was the father of Bran, Branwen, and Manawydan, and most certainly a cognate deity of the Irish sea God, Lir. In *Trioedd Ynys Prydein*, Triad 52 names Llŷr as

---

31. U. Bianchi, "Twins: An Overview" in L. Jones (ed.), *Encyclopedia of Religion* (2nd ed., vol. 14, 9411–9419). (Detroit: Macmillan Reference USA, 2005), 9412.

one of Three Exalted Prisoners of the Island of Britain, and says that he was imprisoned by Euroswydd.[32] There appears to be a lost story here, as it is this same Euroswydd who is the father of Nysien and Efnysien with Penarddun; there is no way of knowing if Euroswydd imprisoned Llŷr in order to carry off Penarddun, or if Penarddun ran away with him willingly, and Llŷr was made a prisoner so the lovers could be together.

Either way, Nysien ("Peaceful") and Efnysien ("Unpeaceful") were full brothers to each other. While the Second Branch does not mention whether the brothers were twins, the two were so opposite that even their names were antithetical, although they are appropriately descriptive of their natures.[33] Of the brothers, the Second Branch says:

"And one of these youths was a good youth and of gentle nature, and would make peace between his kindred, and cause his family to be friends when their wrath was at the highest; and this one was Nissyen; but the other would cause strife between his two brothers when they were most at peace."[34]

True to his name, it is Efnysien who instigates and continues to inflame the hostility between Ireland and Britain throughout the narrative, and his actions have been interpreted both as being the work of an unmoored psychopath and the desperate attempts of a tribal warrior of the traditional Celtic type to defend his nation's Sovereignty, seeing Branwen's marriage into a foreign country as a threat to his people's safety and autonomy. Either way, he is at turns destructive—maiming the Irish horses to circumvent the wedding, throwing his young nephew Gwern into the fire to avoid peace between Ireland and Britain—and heroic—finding and destroying the hiding Irish warriors seeking to

---

32. Bromwich, *Trioedd Ynys Prydein*, 146.

33. J. MacKillop, "Efnysien" in *A Dictionary of Celtic Mythology*. (Oxford: Oxford University Press, 2004), 173.

34. Guest, *The Mabinogion*, 369.

ambush Bran and his men, sacrificing his own life to destroy the Cauldron of Regeneration so that the slain warriors of the Irish would remain dead and not continue to pose a threat to his countrymen.

Nysien doesn't play much of a role in the narrative, other than to present as a foil to his brother; he appears to have accompanied Bran's war band to Ireland, but as he is not named as one of the seven survivors, we can assume that like Efnysien, he lost his life in the battle—another example of twinning as a motif that expresses both symmetry and dichotomy.

Astrological Significance of the Moon of Reflection

The Time of Branwen is the true Blue Moon: instead of the erroneous definition of a Blue Moon being the second full moon in a month (something that appeared in an issue of *Sky and Telescope* magazine in 1946 that has since taken root in popular culture), it is properly defined as the second full moon in a sun sign; for example, when there are two full moons when the sun is in the sign of Scorpio, the Blue Moon is the second of the two). Alternatively, the Blue Moon can also be defined as the fourth full moon in a season that has four rather than the usual three, e.g., when there are four full moons occuring during the three months that comprise the season of autumn. Whether by sun sign or by season, either reckoning will refer to the same moon. As the oft-quoted saying "once in a Blue Moon" suggests, this lunar phenomenon is indeed quite rare, occurring once every two and a half to three years.

Connecting with Branwen at the Blue Moon, the full moon of Reflection, is an excellent opportunity for us to review our life path and personal progress since the time of the last Blue Moon: the goals attained, the changes made, the lessons learned, the shadow tendencies healed. We can reflect as well upon the work yet to be done: Shadow patterns still present, wounds yet unhealed, shifts yet unmade, limitations yet unchallenged, and all that does not serve us which still needs releasing. After this review of where we have come from, we work to set our focus on where we are going; this is accomplished by seeking out that which we most need to know in order to set up our work for the next three years: from the present moment until the Blue Moon comes again.

Seeking Sovereignty Within:
Journaling Prompts and Self-Reflective Questions

Moon Thirteen
The Moon of Reflection
The Time of Branwen

Mythic Focus: Branwen marries the King of Ireland, who mistreats her and banishes her to the kitchens to avenge an insult made to him by Branwen's half-brother. In servitude, she trains a starling to speak and sends a message to her brother Bran, King of Britain, asking for help. A terrible battle results between Ireland and Britain, and many lives are lost. Branwen dies of a broken heart.

Personal Insights Around This Moon's Mythic Portion: *Meditate upon Branwen's story and reflect it within yourself. Her story is your story.*

The Focus of the Moon of Reflection by Phase

Seek the lessons of the Moon of Reflection at each moon phase by using the Stations of the monthly Cycle of Healing; be sure to journal all of the insights, symbols, and guidance you receive from each goddess at each moon phase. As you work with the information you receive between each phase, perhaps following the daily process outlined in chapter 3 of this book and using tools such as trance postures and doorways as detailed in *Avalon Within*, be sure to record those insights in your journal as well.

Full Moon: Connect with Branwen at the full moon to set up your work for the month and to receive insight on the issue of focus. This is also the **Station of Integration** in the cycle of the sun.

Third Quarter: Station of Descent in the cycle of the moon. Bring the issue of focus to Rhiannon to explore through the filters of the Station of Descent and the Moon of Reflection.

Dark Moon: Station of Confrontation in the cycle of the moon. Bring the issue of focus to Ceridwen to explore through the filters of the Station of Confrontation and the Moon of Reflection.

First Quarter: Station of Emergence in the cycle of the moon. Bring the issue of the focus to Blodeuwedd to explore through the filters of the Station of Emergence and the Moon of Reflection.

Night before the Full Moon: Station of Resolution in the cycle of the moon. Bring the issue of focus to Arianrhod to explore through the filters of the Station of Resolution and the Moon of Reflection.

At any point in the month, bring the issue of focus to Branwen to explore through the Station of Integration and the Moon of Reflection. Some women will do this on the night after the dark moon in counterpoint to working with Arianrhod on the night before the full moon.

Herbal Ally for the Moon of Reflection
Woad (*Isatis tinctoria*)

Creating the Mother Elixir: On the night of the full moon, create your Woad Lunar Elixir using the directions found on page 105 of chapter 4. Be sure to label and date the bottle you are using to store the Mother Elixir. Journal any of your experiences around the creation of the Woad Elixir.

Prepare the Daughter Elixir: After you have made the Mother Elixir, use the directions found on page 107 of chapter 4 to prepare a dosage bottle for use in the daily experience of this elixir throughout the month. Remember to use a blue or amber dropper bottle for this purpose, and to clearly label your Daughter Elixir.

Daily Work with the Woad Elixir: As discussed in chapter 4, begin your daily exploration of the Woad Elixir. Be sure to journal everything you can about how the elixir makes you feel, what you think it its energetic actions are, where it sits in your energy body, and any and all impressions, insights, symbols, visions, and memories it presents to you.

Week One of Moon Thirteen: Immerse yourself in the lunar elixir by taking it every day, reflecting upon how it makes you feel, and journaling all of the insights that come to you when you meditate upon the energies of the elixir.

Week Two of Moon Thirteen: Continue to take the lunar elixir daily, but this week spend time experiencing and comparing the energetic impact of woad as an essence, and woad as a magical herb that you burn, as detailed in chapter 4. Again, reflect upon how each makes you feel, and journal all of the insights that come to you when you meditate upon the energies of the elixir and the energies of the herb itself.

Week Three of Moon Thirteen: Continue to take the lunar elixir daily, but this week spend time researching the medicinal, folkloric, and magical uses of woad, beginning with the information provided in Part Three of this book. Compare your findings this week with your direct experiences, being sure to journal all of the insights and connections you've made.

Week Four of Moon Thirteen: Continue to take the lunar elixir daily, but this week meditate upon the mythic portion of the month and reflect upon the ways in which the energies of woad are related to the present portion of Branwen's tale, and how it helps you to build a relationship with Branwen herself.

End of Moon Reflections: Under what circumstances could you see yourself using the Woad Elixir in support of your work and personal process? If you had to describe the actions of this lunar elixir using one word, what would it be? What about using one sentence? What about using a whole paragraph? Again, be sure to journal everything.

Working: Journey Into the
Sacred Landscape of Branwen

Bedd Branwen

Please perform the induction to travel over the Ninth Wave, as found on page 74, and then proceed with the working below. When you have completed it, be sure to return from across the Ninth Wave, using the visualization found on page 76.

Having crossed the Ninth Wave into the Otherworld, disembark and envision a silver tether that extends from the center of your torso to the vessel which bore you here; it is of endless length and will expand and retract as necessary as you explore this Realm Over Wave, while keeping you connected to the boat in order to facilitate your return.

Take three deep, anchoring breaths, and immerse yourself in the energies of this place. It is the reflection of Ynys Môn, the Island of Anglesey, here in the realm of the Mythic Otherworld. It is to this island between islands—existing in the physical world in the Irish Sea, just off the coast of Wales and close to the eastern shore of Ireland—that Branwen and the seven British survivors of the war between the Island of the Mighty and Ireland make landfall, leaving the carnage of death and destruction behind them. Here in the Otherworld using Otherworldly sight, you stand in a place which allows you to see both the distant shore of Ireland when you look to your left, as well as the mainland of Wales over the waters of the Menai Strait when you look to your right. Feel yourself fully in this place between, a sacred island and safe haven—a place of clarity and far vision.

Become aware of the sounds of a running river; walk toward it, using the sound to guide you, and find yourself standing beside the waters of the Afon Alaw. Walk along the bank against the river's flow and follow the undulating pathway cut into the landscape by the course of the river until it dips around to pass near to an earthwork of exceedingly ancient origin. The place pulses with energy, and feeling a powerful draw to approach, you walk toward it and away from the riverbank.

Before you, a ring of kerb stones creates a low perimeter around a barrow (a raised earthen mound that covers ancient urn burials) that is crowned by a large central stone. On the ground just outside of the stone ring, you see an earthenware cup inscribed with uniquely patterned markings. You feel drawn to pick it up; when you do, you notice it is filled with a sweetly scented liquid—a fine honey mead. With your breath and intention, hold the cup between your hands and charge its contents with deep gratitude. When the mead feels completely charged, take a moment to connect with your intention to honor this hallowed ancestral ground, the spirits and guardians of place, and the essence of all who were buried here. When you are ready, take three deep and centering breaths and with intent, pour out your libation, feeling the energies of your intention as they are absorbed into the ground along with the mead. Your offering has been received.

An energy of welcome settles around you and you feel ready. Next, step gently between the stones that define the circle. Take note of what it feels like to be in this space between the worlds, where the living and the dead connect in remembrance during the in-between times. You are in one of the liminal places and spaces where connections with the Otherworld are as close as the pause between breaths and as easy as stepping with purpose over a threshold.

Turn your attention now to the center stone, which feels as if it has somehow been activated by your presence and intentionality in this space. Move to stand a respectful distance in front of it. Do not touch it; instead, take note of how this sacred place makes you feel. What is it like to stand on this hallowed ground, the place where a myth has come to reside which is so powerful that it has helped to keep the memory of this place alive thousands of years after its creation. It begins to glow with powerful earthen energies so bright that the light almost obscures the details of its form, but you can tell that it is a large, rounded, flat-topped stone standing low to the ground at about hip height. The energy which emanates from it pulses like a heartbeat whose source is deep within the Earth. Take a moment and breathe this energy into your own being. With each cycle of breath, feel your own heartbeat synchronize with that of the stone. Breathe in each pulse, and exhale into each silence. When you are ready, step forward and merge with the center stone, becoming one with it.

Push yourself to experience what it feels like to embody this stone, the central stone of Bedd Branwen, the Grave of Branwen. Take what time you need to feel fully immersed, fully at one. Inhabit every square inch of the stone; bring your attention to the part that sits heavily on the earth, capping the cyst tomb that lies below—containing urns and offerings to the beloved dead. Sense what you can of what lies buried in the ground below, that which is hidden yet not forgotten. Bring your attention now to the very top of the stone, the part that faces the sky, the part that has absorbed thousands of nights of moonlight and experienced hundreds of thousands of days of sunlight warming its surface.

Like this ancient stone connecting the world below and the world above, feel what it is like to be a bridge—to embrace a stance that unifies that which has been divided, to come to a place of integration between opposing states of being. Like Branwen who laid her body down in more than one way to be a Peace Weaver, stretch yourself to experience what it is to be truly liminal, to straddle the in-between places in a quest to birth healing and reconciliation.

Bring your awareness now to the deep crack that bisects the stone, a dark and angry gouge that creates a vertical equator in the stone, cleaving it in two as it runs downward, tracing a central perpendicular to the ground. Move yourself into this broken place, and allow yourself to experience what it is like to embody this deep and ancient wound. Be open to the images, feelings, thoughts, and memories that may arise from you as you pour yourself into the cracked open space that in many ways defines this most iconic stone—this stone of Bedd Branwen.

Where are the places that you have been broken? What parts of you cry out in pain unsalved, in injuries unhealed, in fears unspoken? Imagine that this deep fissure that splits your embodied stone nearly in two is not a flaw that mars its wholeness or perfection but is instead a sacred opening... a mouth poised in eternal readiness, awaiting an opportunity to share its deepest secrets, to express its greatest truths, and to ask for that which it most needs. What would it say? As you embody this stone—now holding the center of your being, the navel of your world, the vessel of your truth—what message comes through from the deepest shadow of yourself? What do you hear from the height of your most sovereign self? Speak, feel, and listen.

Spend as much time as you need in this place of centered embodiment, allowing your truths to come forth in all of their joy and all their sorrow.

With gentleness and the intention to bring with you the conscious understanding of all that you have seen, spoken, and experienced, slowly withdraw your consciousness from the stone. Envision yourself standing next to it once more, and feel yourself returning to your body.

When you feel yourself completely present in your physical form and leaving nothing behind in the stone, look down at the place where you stand. See yourself as you truly are right now at this very moment. Consider your life as it is at this very present moment. Where are you in your journey? Who are the people in your life? On what do you spend your daily energy? How do you feel about where you are, who you are with, and what you are doing with your life? What are the things that are present that bring you joy? What brings you sorrow? What aspects of yourself have you been able to bring into the light of Sovereignty? What aspects of yourself are still challenged by the limitations of shadow? If this were the end of your life's journey, how would you feel about the place to which you have come?

Look now to the left toward what is behind you. Ask to be shown the path you have walked that has brought you to where you are in this moment. What are the three experiences that have most affected your journey to where you stand in the here and now. What lessons do these experiences bring with them for you? Which lessons have you integrated? Which lessons are yet in need of integration?

Look now to the right, toward what is before you. Ask to be shown a vision of your best self, the most sovereign version of yourself that you can conceive. What is the progression of how your life will unfold if it continues to follow the path which has brought you to the here and the now? How does this make you feel? What are the three challenges you will face on the next portion of your journey if all things continue as they are? What tools do you have to meet them? Where will this portion of the journey yet to come bring you? Do you like what you see and feel? If you do, how can you best support where you are going? If you do not, what can you do differently to change your course?

Take three deep and centering breaths. Remember all that you have seen, and received, and committed to in this moment. Take a moment to once again thank the ancestors in whose sacred space you stand, the spirits of place who guard and keep the land, and Queen Branwen, the Peace Weaver and Bridge Between the Worlds, for permitting you to share in the living essence of this sacred land.

When you are ready, step out of the circle once more, and follow the thread that connects you to the vessel which took you to this Land Beyond Wave, taking your place in the boat once more, to begin the journey back over the Nine Waves, to the place that is Here, and the time that is Now.

Chapter 9
THE TIME OF ARIANRHOD

O F ALL OF THE FEMALE characters in the Four Branches, it is only Arianrhod who maintains her personal power and autonomy throughout the narrative; indeed, if there are remnants of past social orders to be found in the tales of *Y Mabinogi*, it is most strongly evidenced in the Fourth Branch, especially as it concerns Arianrhod in whom we see a woman in complete control over her life and her destiny.

Dwelling on an island fortress set apart from the rest of Gwynedd, she is ruler of her own court and lives by her own rules. Not only do we s⸱e Arianrhod buck convention with her rejection of the role of motherhood, but we see her go unpunished for her unorthodox behavior. According to scholars, it is this rejection of the roles of wife and mother that allow Arianrhod to continue to operate with the power and privileges of a single woman.[35] We see her competently performing the duties of a lord: she is concerned with the well-being of her people, is well-versed in courtly behavior, and is clearly well-educated. When Gwydion and Lleu visit her realm in disguise, she is shown receiving them warmly, telling stories and conversing easily with Gwydion, her brother, who is oft-praised for the excellence of his bardic abilities. "This may be the most attractive vision we have of the stubborn daughter of

---

35. Winward, "Women in the Four Branches," 89.

Don: the welcoming hostess who attracts the interest of her male guests with *ymdidan* (conversation) about their favorite subjects."[36]

These circumstances would have been unusual for medieval Welsh women and may have been a narrative survival from a different time, perhaps originating in pre-Christian Celtic Britain and preserved in orality before being written down. It is a general contrivance of myth and legend that they tend to reflect the sociocultural context which birthed the tale, and when it does not, it may reflect on an older order. We do know that pre-Christian Celtic women enjoyed more autonomy, rights, and privileges than their medieval peers, so—as with the matrilineal inheritance paradigm which seems to feature in the Fourth Branch—a woman who rules in her own right and appears to answer to no man may be a reflection of that earlier cultural norm, and may have been preserved and included in the Fourth Branch as part of depicting Arianrhod as Other.

Arianrhod's Otherworldly status is not explicit in the narrative, aside from her heritage as the daughter of Dôn, the Divine Ancestress of a powerful lineage—a lineage which includes Arianrhod's magicusing uncle Math and brother Gwydion. It is worthy of note that the land Arianrhod rules over is named after her, a convention which scholars associate with "powerful goddesses who give their names to the lands with which they are connected."[37] Perhaps then, this, more than anything, marks Arianrhod as a representative of Sovereignty as often these are tutelary divinities, like Eriu, goddess of Ireland.

Most directly, Arianrhod's claiming of Mother Right, and the struggle of Gwydion against it, is an extension of the subversion we've seen throughout the Fourth Branch. It is also significant to note that, regardless of Math's kingship and the magical abilities possessed by both

---

36. Roberta Louise Valente, "Gwydion and Arianrhod: Crossing the Boarders of Gender in Math," *Bulletin of the Board of Celtic Studies* 35 (1988).

37. Valente, "Gwydion and Arianrhod," 9.

he and Gwydion, they are powerless to break the destinies lain by Arianrhod upon her son. The most these powerful men can do is to find a way around Arianrhod's pronouncements.

Symbolically, Arianrhod may be seen as an initiator, the Terrible Mother archetype who sets up challenges before her son, the Solar Hero, through which he earns his manhood/kingship and/or comes to actualize his godhood. As the daughter of Dôn and Beli, both of whom have analogues in Irish myth as the divinities Danu and Bel, it is likely that Arianrhod was also originally divine. Her name means "Silver Wheel," which is very suggestive of the moon and its phases. This lunar motif, coupled with a wheel's symbolic connection to the turning seasons, as well as Arianrhod's laying of destinies throughout the Fourth Branch, makes a strong argument for considering her a personification of fate. Furthermore, this kind of testing of a potential king is a classic hallmark of a sovereignty goddess.

Moon 14
THE MOON OF CYCLE

Moon Fourteen of the Avalonian Cycle of Revealing is called the Moon of Cycle and is associated with the herb Queen Anne's lace (Daucus carota). The lunar month begins on the full moon when a total lunar eclipse occurs, which is the full moon of the Time of Arianrhod. It is possible for there to be more than one Moon of Cycle in a given year or none may occur in a year at all.

The time of the lesson bringer can seem unyielding in its insistence that we grow, but it is only by recognizing the greater pattern that we are able to find the missed stitches, mend the torn fabric, and set the weaving right once more. Once we embrace the power of the Moon of Cycle as the opportunity it is to follow the thread of the current as it moves from a place of light into darkness and back into the light once more, it gifts us with the power to ride the wheel of becoming in a way that more effectively keeps us on the path that helps us birth our destiny.

The Mythic Portion

Arianrhod is the lady of her own court, Caer Arianrhod, and she dwells on an island off the coast of northwest Wales. She is invited by her brother Gwydion to come to the court of their uncle Math, the king of Gwynedd, who is in need of a maiden to serve as his foot holder. When she arrives at court, Math asks her if she is a virgin. Arianrhod responds, "I know only that I am." To test the truth of her statement, Math bends his magic rod and instructs her to step over it. As she does so, a blond infant boy falls from her with a cry. Horrified and shamed, Arianrhod runs from the court; as she departs, a "small thing" falls from her which Gwydion immediately scoops up and wraps in a piece of silk; he brings it to his chamber and places it in a chest at the foot of his bed. Math names the blond infant Dylan and has him baptized; after receiving his name, the child immediately makes for the sea, whereupon he takes on its aspect as he enters the water. He proves that he is able to swim as well as any fish and for this reason is come to be called Dylan eil Ton ("Dylan, Son of the Wave"). It is said that no wave ever broke beneath him.

Some time later, Gwydion is awakened by a noise coming from the chest by his bed. He opens it and discovers the "small thing" is now a fully-grown infant emerging from the silk within. Gwydion calls for a wet nurse for the child and notices the boy grow and thrive—at twice the rate of any other child! The child is raised at court for four years, where he is acknowledged and mentored by Gwydion, whom he comes to love greatly. One day, Gwydion brings the boy to Arianrhod, who becomes angry at her brother for this reminder of her shame. She lays a *tynged* or destiny upon him: the boy will have no name save the one she gives to him. Angry, Gwydion storms off with the child.

Gwydion returns to Caer Arianrhod by boat soon after, conjuring a ship out of seaweed. Using his powers to disguise himself and the boy, he pretended to be a craftsman able to make the most wondrous golden leather shoes. When Arianrhod hears of the shoemaker in her harbor, she sends him the measurements of her feet so that a pair can be made for her. The first pair he makes is too big, the second too small; at his suggestion to get the proper measurement, Arianrhod goes personally down to the ship. While the disguised pair set to work upon her shoes—Gwydion cutting the leather and the boy stitching—a small wren alights upon the mast of the ship. The boy takes up a stone and casts it at the bird, hitting it with an impressively precise aim. Delighted at his skill, Arianrhod exclaims, "The fair one has a skillful hand!" Immediately, the glamour of Gwydion's magic falls away, and everyone is revealed as who they are. Gwydion proclaims that the boy has now been named, from Arianrhod's proclamation: Lleu Llaw Gyffes—"the fair one of the skillful hand."

Angry at being thus deceived, Arianrhod lays a second tynged upon her son: he shall bear no arms save those she gives to him. Calling her a wicked woman, Gwydion departs with the boy once more. Several years pass, and Lleu grows into a strong youth of great skill but clearly suffers without the ability to train with weapons. Gwydion calls Lleu to him, and the pair depart for Caer Arianrhod once more, this time disguised as a pair of bards. They are welcomed and spend the evening with Arianrhod and her court in feasting and storytelling before retiring for the night as her guests.

Waking early the next morning, Gwydion uses his enchantment to conjure up the illusion of a fleet of invading ships bearing down upon the island. As everything erupts in a din of preparation for the coming battle, Arianrhod and one of her maidens come to the chamber of the bards to tell them what is happening. The disguised Gwydion pledges that they will assist in defense of the island but will need to be armed to do so. Grateful for their assistance, Arianrhod has weapons and armor brought to them. Upon Gwydion's request, she unwittingly helps Lleu get into his armor while her maidens assist Gwydion. Once Arianrhod fastens the last buckle and has girded Lleu with a sword for the coming battle, Gwydion declared that the weapons were no longer needed and lets his enchantment drop. Immediately, the invading fleet disappears, and he and Lleu are revealed for who they truly are. Deeply angered at Gwydion's trickery—both personally and for the undoing of her tynged as well as for the potential for loss of life that could have arisen from her people's panicked scrambling to prepare for war—

Arianrhod condemns him for his recklessness and lays a third and final tynged upon Lleu: "He shall never have a wife of the race that now inhabits this earth."

"Verily," said he, "thou wast ever a malicious woman, and no one ought to support thee. A wife shall he have notwithstanding."[38]

And with that, the two depart. Gwydion begins to conceive a plan to overcome this last destiny placed upon Lleu by his mother—a plan that would require great magics ... and the assistance of Math.

The Work of the Moon of Cycle

Although the story of the Fourth Branch seems to go to great pains to depict Arianrhod as an irrational, unreasonable, and unnatural woman, something quite different emerges when we look below this surface characterization. Arianrhod begins her tale in mastery and ends her tale in mastery; she is Lady of Caer Arianrhod from beginning to end. Her status in the story does not change, although her actions set a great deal of change in motion around her. In this, Arianrhod teaches us how to be centered in who we are regardless of the events around us in the world. Unlike Rhiannon, who teaches us to endure in the face of hardship and hold fast to our truths with the knowledge that we will eventually be vindicated, Arianrhod takes outward action, setting others on a course to meet her where she is instead of the other way around. And also unlike the ever-patient Branwen or Blodeuwedd before she discovers her own agency, Arianrhod is not content to do what is expected of her. No matter how Gwydion tries to shame her or how often he scolds her, she refuses to do what he wants because it wasn't what *she* wants.

In the Avalonian Tradition, we speak of the light half of the year as being represented by the Torc of Sovereignty, symbolizing the shining

---

38. Guest, *The Mabinogion*, 426.

path to authenticity that we weave while walking it. The dark half of the year is represented by the Cauldron of Transformation, which is entered to engage in the inner alchemy that is shadow work. Both of these energies are well represented in the tale and person of Arianrhod.

In the Fourth Branch, Caer Arianrhod is on an island off the coast of Gwynedd where Arianrhod dwells as its lady. No island presently exists in that place, and local lore suggests that the island had been claimed by the sea—but if one were to look out over the waters during the neap tide, the highest points of the island can yet be glimpsed. Caer Arianrhod is also the name given in Welsh lore to the constellation more commonly called the *Corona Borealis*—the Northern Crown. The Corona Borealis looks very much like a torc, a neck ring with a closed round back and open front, a mark of high status in Celtic cultures. This starry glyph, set into the Realm of Sky, is a celestial double of the submerged island fortress of Caer Arianrhod that now exists in the Realm of Sea, joining other mystic islands of the Otherworld. The Realm of Sea is the domain of the Cauldron of Regeneration, and is the resting place of the ancestors and the souls of all who await rebirth. It is empowering to consider that a place of strength and sovereignty— the fortress over which Arianrhod holds dominion—can be found submerged in the waters of the unconscious, our personal connection to the energies of the Realm of Sea.

All that we aspire to become, and the lessons life brings us to help us achieve our goals, can be said to be part of a cosmological paradigm that is mirrored within us. The strength needed to realize our potential in order to achieve our destiny (metaphorically "written in the stars" of the Realm of Sky) lies within our unconscious self (the Realm of Sea) where it is waiting for us to acknowledge it, claim it, and manifest it in this world—the Realm of Land. Arianrhod guides us in this process, and can be considered the Great Teacher in Welsh tradition. She sets challenges before us that may seem cruel and unreasonable at the outset, but they act to catalyze our growth in ways we never dreamed possible.

Searching Deeper

One of the more peculiar characteristics of Math, King of Gwynedd, is that he must have his feet in the lap of a maiden at all times—save while at war—lest he die. While the office of the king's foot holder is described in the *Laws of Hywel Dda*, this duty appears to have been only performed by men, and the words used in the original Welsh of the Fourth Branch seem to suggest that Math's feet were required to be in "the fold of a maiden's womb," evoking sexual connotations not apparent in the English translation:[39]

> … [T]his passage describes the position of Math's feet, which are *ymlyc croth morwyn* (literally "in the fold of the womb of a virgin"). The noun *croth*, often translated as "lap," has the base meaning "womb," "uterus," or "belly." The phrase *ymlyc croth morwyn* connotes varying degrees of intimate contact with the *morwyn* (virgin), from the more innocent "in the fold/curve of a virgin's belly" or "in the lap of a vir-gin" to the decidedly risqué "in the groin" or "pubic hair of a virgin" or even "within the womb of a virgin" whose hymen remains magically intact.[40]

This passage, and the requirement itself, is a source of puzzlement for scholars, but what if it could be interpreted as a rather pointed symbol of Math's kingship being dependent on having the feminine principle—in this case, the representative of Sovereignty—as its foun-dation? Indeed, after Gwydion's trickery sends Math off to a false, manufactured war so that his uncle's foot holder, Goewin, could be left behind—thus creating an opportunity for his brother Gilfaethwy to

---

39. *The Laws of Hywel Dda* (Continued), *The Cambro-Briton*, Vol. 2, No. 21 (May, 1821), 395.

40. Sarah Sheehan, "Matrilineal Subjects: Ambiguity, Bodies, and Metamorpho-sis in the Fourth Branch of the Mabinogi," *Signs* 34 (2): (2009), 322.

rape her in Math's own bed—when Math returns to discover what his nephews have done, he responds by telling Goewin: "'...I will take you as my wife,' he said, 'and give you authority over my kingdom.'"[41]

This marriage transforms the power dynamic between the two, making it more of a partnership, whereas before the representative of sovereignty was being held in a subordinate position under Math's feet. It has been proposed that Math's strange requirement for a virgin foot-holder suggests that he is impotent, much like the Fisher King, and that he gets around his inability to join with sovereignty directly by subjugating her representative, thereby maintaining this feminine force as the almost literal foundation for his rule.[42] Math can also be seen as a mediating personage, bridging the matrilineal paradigm of inheritance, as seen with his sister's sons acting as his heirs, with that of the new patrilineal paradigm, the foundation of the struggle between Gwydion and Arianrhod that unfolds in the Fourth Branch. (See pages 174–175 for more information.)

Arianrhod enters the narrative after Math punishes his nephews, who not only raped his virgin foot-holder and put his life in danger, but also started a war with Dyfed through Gwydion's magical trickery which caused the deaths of many warriors, including Rhiannon's son Pryderi, the lord of Dyfed. Using his own magic, Math causes the brothers to spend the next three years in the form of three different pairs of wild beasts—successively deer, then wild boar, then wolves— and, trading off genders each year, they bore each other sons whom Math restored to human forms. Once the brothers have completed their punishment, they return to their positions at Math's court. Gwydion is set to the task of finding a replacement for Goewin; the text

---

41. Davies, *The Mabinogion*, 52.

42. Jean Markale, *Women of the Celts* (Rochester, VT: Inner Traditions, 1986), 132.

does not explain what the lord of Gwynedd did for the three years he was without a foot holder.

Arianrhod's declaration that she is a maiden, followed by her giving birth when subjecting herself to Math's "test," has several possible meanings. First, her understanding of what constitutes a maiden may be anchored in a definition which meant that she was "complete unto herself" and "beholden to no man." This definition is certainly supported by her solo rule of Caer Arianrhod where she is under the authority of no man. In this case, maidenhood or virginity have to do with personal authority—Sovereignty—rather than a physiological state; a woman could have sexual partners and yet still maintain her virginity in lieu of a husband. Therefore, although she may not have been visibly pregnant, she may have been with child; Math's test accelerated the gestation of her firstborn, Dylan, although some authors question if the wand caused her to abort the fetus that became Lleu.

The second option is a bit darker. There is an inherently sexual nature to Math's maidenhood test that required Arianrhod to open her legs to step over his bent rod, a rather obvious phallic symbol. It may be possible to interpret this act as a coded (and compelled) sexual act with Math. If Arianrhod was indeed a maiden and was impregnated by Math's wand, this may have been a case of rape. Some scholars believe that Arianrhod was the original raped foot holder and that for some reason, the redactor substituted Goewin for Arianrhod.[43] Whether impregnated by magic or by intercourse, the nonconsensual nature of the pregnancy and birth of Dylan and Lleu is deeply troubling. Arianrhod's subsequent rejection of taking on the mother role for these children born by rape or compulsion appears to be much more understandable in this context.

---

43. W. J. Gruffydd, *Math Vab Mathonwy, An Inquiry into the Origins and Development of the Fourth Branch of the Mabinogi, with the Text and a Translation* (Cardiff: University of Wales Press Board, 1928).

A third interpretation is that Arianrhod was simply lying about her status to protect her honor, and that the father of her children was none other than her brother, Gwydion. Subtextual clues exist in the original Welsh where in speaking about her yet-unnamed son with Gwydion, she refers to the child as "your son/boy," although this could just as easily be a reference to Gwydion's role as a surrogate mother and foster father to the boy.[44] This theory does not address, however, why Gwydion would have suggested Arianrhod for the position of Math's foot holder, a role that required the woman be a virgin when he knew firsthand she was not.

Whether because it was rape or simply because of her public shaming, Arianrhod's rejection of motherhood was certainly considered unnatural—authorial disapproval certainly comes through in the narrative. Gwydion constantly derides her as wicked and actively works against her wishes when it comes to his foster (or otherwise) son. Clearly, the audience is meant to feel the same about this awful, unnatural woman who abandons her son and actively seeks to keep him from fully participating in adult and courtly life. Here again we have to consider Arianrhod's actions as possibly reflecting a past cultural paradigm.

When Arianrhod lays down the three *tynghedau* (destinies) on Lleu, they are binding; neither Gwydion nor Math, with all of their magic, could make them go away. They could only find ways to trick Arianrhod into fulfilling the terms of her prohibitions for two of the three tynghedau; with the last, they were forced to meet Arianrhod's requirement and find a wife not of the race of women on Earth. The fact that she had this degree of power over Lleu, even as a mother who has rejected her son, speaks to the power of Mother Right. Although this is not explicit in the narrative, we see examples of mothers exercising these powers both in the Four Branches and elsewhere in Celtic legend. The three tynghedau can be seen as reflections of the Celtic practice of

---

44. Davies, *The Mabinogion*, 55.

matrilineal inheritance: family names were passed down through the mother, women were involved in the training of warriors, and had a say in the forming of marriage alliances.

Astrological Significance of the Moon of Cycle

The Time of Arianrhod is heralded by the total lunar eclipse. By definition, a lunar eclipse occurs when the full moon passes into the Earth's shadow fully or partially. This event only occurs a few times a year because the orbit of the moon around the earth is tilted five degrees off the earth's ecliptic, or our planet's orbital plane around the sun. As the moon orbits the Earth, it passes through the plane of the ecliptic twice a month; these points of intersection are called lunar nodes. The ascending node is the point of intersection as the moon moves from south to north in its orbit, and the descending node is the point of intersection as the moon moves north to south. When a full or dark moon occurs concurrent with or close to one or the other of these lunar nodes, an eclipse occurs. Otherwise, the five-degree tilt of the moon's orbit is sufficient for the sun to completely illuminate the Earth-facing side of the moon, even as it travels "behind" the Earth during the full moon phase, as well as for the moon not to occlude the sun as it travels "between" it and the Earth during the dark moon phase.

Just as lunar eclipses can only occur during the full moon phase, solar eclipses can only occur during the dark moon phase. We can think about it this way: on the night of the full moon, the moon rises as the sun sets and the moon sets as the sun rises. They are opposite each other in the night sky, making a 180-degree angle relative to Earth in an alignment called an opposition. When the moon is dark, however, we cannot see it because in addition to the side of the moon being illuminated by the sun facing away from earth during this phase, the dark moon is rising and setting at the same time as the sun. This alignment is called a conjunction; the moon and the sun are on the same side of the sky, and the angle the moon makes with the sun relative to the Earth is 0 degrees.

There are three main types of lunar eclipses, each describing how much of the moon falls within the Earth's shadow: total, where the entire moon passes through the Earth's shadow; partial, where only a portion of the moon has the Earth's shadow cast upon it; and penumbral, which can be difficult to notice if you aren't looking for it, as the moon falls within the outermost shadow of the planet with very subtle effects. It is only the total lunar eclipse that is considered the Moon of Cycle in the Avalonian Cycle of Revealing; these tend to occur at least once every two and a half years.

Total lunar eclipses hold very particular energies which have strong resonance with Arianrhod in several ways. The meaning of her name, "Silver Wheel," seems to suggest that she has lunar associations but not in any static sense; a wheel suggests movement in the same way that the seasonal round is referred to as the Wheel of the Year. From a lunar perspective this could refer to the phases of the moon as well as a total eclipse, as during such an event the moon appears to move through all of its phases in one night. Further, as the eclipse moves into the Earth's shadow, its color begins to shift from silver white, to earthshine black, and then to red during the period of the eclipse's totality, before reversing back again. The grouping together of white, black, and red has many esoteric correspondences, including being the colors of the stones produced during the alchemical process as well as representing the Celtic cosmological realms of Sky, Land, and Sea. Arianrhod, then, seems to have a very specific, cosmic resonance with time.

From both an energetic and metaphorical perspective, this makes a total lunar eclipse a powerful time to look at the deeply ingrained patterns of our lives, especially those which are connected to the unconscious aspects of the self, the inner reflections which hold resonance with the energies of the moon. Whether these are shadow tendencies that challenge us over and over again, or seeds of Sovereignty that will spring forth from the personal growth that arises from knowing ourselves as best as we can, identifying the nature and manifestation of patterns which no longer serve us empowers us to make conscious choices that can transform our lives.

In the Fourth Branch of *Y Mabinogi*, Arianrhod lays three tynghedau (fates or destinies) upon her son; because of this, some modern devotees of Arianrhod see her as a goddess of fate, a weaver and spinner of destinies similar to the Germanic Norns or the Greek Moirai. Her association with spinning may have to do with the wheel as her symbol, although the spinning wheel is believed to have been invented in India and did not reach Europe until the thirteenth century CE, so this may have been a medieval correspondence.

Arianrhod has an interesting connection with Ariadne, the Greek mistress of the labyrinth whose clew or ball of yarn allowed Theseus to navigate the maze safely. While their names appear similar, they have different etymological roots; Ariadne means "Most Pure" or "Very Holy." However, what these two figures have in common is that they both have associations with cyclic energies—whether the spinning of yarn, the threading of a labyrinth, or the twists and turns of fate—and they both share a connection with the constellation otherwise known as the Corona Borealis, the Northern Crown. In Greece, this crown is said to belong to Ariadne, given to her by the god Dionysus whom she eventually came to marry. The Welsh, however, called this same constellation *Caer Arianrhod*, the Fortress or Castle of Arianrhod; as previously discussed on page 287.

Astrologically speaking, Arianrhod has a lot of resonance with Saturn, the planet named after the Roman god of time, who rules restriction, discipline, and karmic lessons. Through her lunar association, Arianrhod too has a connection to time; as we have already discussed, the moon likely formed early humans' first connection to the concept of time. Furthering her resonance with Saturn, Arianrhod's placing of tynghedau on her son show her in the role of the Great Teacher who challenges us to overcome obstacles in order to grow and fulfill our destiny.

Another connection with soul lessons and fate has to do with the ascending and descending nodes of the moon, which we discussed earlier in this section; they are the points where the moon intersects the Earth's ecliptic. When this intersection occurs during a full moon, a lunar eclipse occurs. These same points are called the north and south nodes in astrology, and they represent a person's karmic pathway in this lifetime. Some believe that these are lessons held over from our past lives which we are meant to resolve in our present incarnation. These nodes are always in opposite signs from each other, and together they chart a pathway of growth into wholeness. The south node represents the energies from the past that we need to overcome and move away from, while the north node indicates the direction of growth; these are the core life lessons that we are here to learn, and the energies we are moving toward embracing. The nature of these lessons is reflected both by the signs that the nodes themselves are in, as well as the houses these nodes fall in on our natal chart.

Now, the total lunar eclipse is the Moon of Cycle in the Avalonian Cycle of Revealing, and can occur multiple times in a year, or not at all. Unlike the Moon of Reflection (Moon Thirteen—the Blue Moon) which adds a moon to the yearly cycle once every two and a half to three years (see chapter 8), the Moon of Cycle instead *overlays* its energies onto one of the other moons in the Cycle of Revealing. It can be considered an energetic modifier, bringing karmic or life lesson awareness to the patterns of our lives related to the energetic lessons that moon already holds on its own. For example, should a total lunar eclipse take place during the Moon of Transformation (Moon Three), several things occur:

1. This moon, one of the four moons that comprise Ceridwen's Time, is now overlain with the energies of the Moon of Cycle, and so the month becomes centered on Arianrhod instead of Ceridwen, although the latter is still present albeit in more of a background role.

2. Because of this overlay, we go to Arianrhod at the full moon during the eclipse, rather than Ceridwen. We will be able to get Ceridwen's insight later on in the month when we connect with her during the dark moon for the work of the Station of Confrontation.

3. The Moon of Cycle can be conceived as being a lunar equivalent of a Saturn return in one's natal chart. It can be a challenging period, where uncomfortable truths are brought to our attention in ways that we cannot ignore—especially if we have been successful in ignoring them in the past. This is an opportunity to settle some unfinished business, and really get to the bottom of some long-standing challenges—those that keep us at the mercy of our shadow, as well as those that prevent us from fully reclaiming our Sovereignty in certain aspects of our lives.

4. The lessons of the Moon of Transformation have to do with rooting out the ways in which particular aspects of shadow manifest in every level of being (physical, emotional, mental, and spiritual), and determining the changes we need to make in order to meet those challenges, even if outmoded aspects of the self need to fall away so that we can be reborn through the integration of these new understandings. When the Moon of Cycle overlays the Moon of Transformation, we are called to look at the patterns of shadow behaviors as they manifest through the layers of being from a karmic or life lesson perspective. These are core challenges that when met, contribute to the overall transformation of the self that is our life's work. There are bigger energies at work here

than would normally be present, so the tenor of the lessons the present moon would normally bring is augmented by the Moon of Cycle; likewise the effects of the Moon of Cycle is directed by the energies of the moon it overlays.

Seeking Sovereignty Within:
Journaling Prompts and Self-Reflective Questions

Total Lunar Eclipse
The Moon of Cycle
The Time of Arianrhod

Mythic Focus: Arianrhod journeys to Math's court and is asked to prove her virginity in order to serve as his footholder. She steps over his magic rod and immediately give birth to a son, Dylan, who crawls off to the sea. As she runs from the court, a small thing falls from her, which Gwydion takes and incubates in a chest until a baby emerges. He brings the boy to Arianrhod, who lays three tynghedau upon him; Gwydion uses his magic to trick her into naming and arming the boy, but her last tynged prevents the boy—Lleu—from taking a wife from the women of the race of Earth. This leads to Gwydion and Math's creation of Blodeuwedd.

Personal Insights Around This Moon's Mythic Portion: *Meditate upon Arianrhod's story and reflect it within yourself. Her story is your story.*

The Focus of the Moon of Cycle by Phase

Seek the lessons of the Moon of Cycle at each moon phase by using the Stations of the monthly Cycle of Healing; be sure to journal all of the insights, symbols, and guidance you receive from each goddess at each moon phase. As you work with the information you receive between each phase, perhaps following the daily process outlined in chapter 3 of this book, and using tools such as trance postures and doorways as detailed in *Avalon Within*, be sure to record those insights in your journal as well.

Full Moon: Connect with Arianrhod on the night of the full moon that is also the total lunar eclipse. Review the work of the previous month and the insights it brought to you, set up your work for the coming month, and ask for insights on the issue of focus which may have shifted or deepened due to the work you have done.

Third Quarter: Station of Descent in the cycle of the moon. Bring the issue of focus to Rhiannon to explore through the filters of the Station of Descent and the Moon of Cycle.

Dark Moon: Station of Confrontation in the cycle of the moon. Bring the issue of focus to Ceridwen to explore through the filters of the Station of Confrontation and the Moon of Cycle.

First Quarter: Station of Emergence in the cycle of the moon. Bring the issue of the focus to Blodeuwedd to explore through the filters of the Station of Emergence and the Moon of Cycle.

Night before the Full Moon: Station of Resolution in the cycle of the moon. Bring the issue of focus to Arianrhod to explore through the filters of the Station of Resolution and the Moon of Cycle.

At any point in the month, bring the issue of focus to Branwen to explore through the Station of Integration and the Moon of Cycle. Some women will do this on the night after the dark moon in counterpoint to working with Arianrhod on the night before the full moon.

Herbal Ally for the Moon of Cycle
Queen Anne's Lace (*Daucus carota*)

Creating the Mother Elixir: On the night of the full moon, create your Queen Anne's Lace Lunar Elixir using the directions found on page 105 of chapter 4. Be sure to label and date the bottle you are using to store the Mother Elixir. Journal any of your experiences around the creation of the Queen Anne's Lace Elixir. Additionally, make the Lunar Elixir of the natural herb for this month, the one that the Moon of Cycle overlays. More information about this can be found on page 105.

Prepare the Daughter Elixir: After you have made the Mother Elixir, use the directions found on page 107 of chapter 4 to prepare a dosage bottle for use in the daily experience of this elixir throughout the month. Remember to use a blue or amber dropper bottle for this purpose, and to clearly label your Daughter Elixir.

Daily Work with the Queen Anne's Lace Elixir: As discussed in chapter 4, begin your daily exploration of the Queen Anne's Lace Elixir. Be sure to journal everything you can about how the elixir makes you feel, what you think it its energetic actions are, where it sits in your energy body, and any and all impressions, insights, symbols, visions, and memories it presents to you:

WEEK ONE OF THE MOON OF CYCLE: Immerse yourself in the lunar elixir by taking it every day, reflecting upon how it makes you feel, and journaling all of the insights that come to you when you meditate upon the energies of the elixir.

WEEK TWO OF THE MOON OF CYCLE: Continue to take the lunar elixir daily, but this week spend time experiencing and comparing the energetic impact of Queen Anne's lace as an essence, and Queen Anne's lace as a magical herb that you burn, as detailed in chapter 4. Again, reflect upon how each makes you feel, and journal all of the insights that come to you when you meditate upon the energies of the elixir and the energies of the herb itself.

WEEK THREE OF THE MOON OF CYCLE: Continue to take the lunar elixir daily, but this week spend time researching the medicinal, folkloric, and magical uses of Queen Anne's lace, beginning with the information provided in part three of this book. Compare your findings this week with your direct experiences, being sure to journal all of the insights and connections you've made.

WEEK FOUR OF THE MOON CYCLE: Continue to take the lunar elixir daily, but this week meditate upon the mythic portion of the month and reflect upon the ways in which the energies of Queen Anne's lace are related to the present portion of Arianrhod's tale, and how it helps you to build a relationship with Arianrhod herself.

End of Moon Reflections: Under what circumstances could you see yourself using the Queen Anne's Lace Elixir in support of your work and personal process? If you had to describe the actions of this lunar elixir using one word, what would it be? What about using one sentence? What about using a whole paragraph? Again, be sure to journal everything.

Working: Journey into the
Sacred Landscape of Arianrhod

Caer Arianrhod

Please perform the induction to travel over the Ninth Wave, as found on page 74, and then proceed with the working below. When you have completed it, be sure to return from across the Ninth Wave, using the visualization found on page 76.

Having crossed the Ninth Wave into the Otherworld, disembark and envision a silver tether that extends from the center of your torso to the vessel that bore you here; it is of endless length and will expand and retract as necessary as you explore this Realm Over Wave, while keeping you connected to the boat in order to facilitate your return.

Disembark and find yourself on the shore of another sea, waves advancing and receding here in this timeless, mythic Otherworld. Take three deep, anchoring breaths, and immerse yourself in the energies of this place. It is night and the stars shine high above you, set like diamonds in the velvet night. The moon is almost full and hangs bright and low in the sky. The crashing of the waves fills your ears as you look out over the tumultuous ocean. The tide is receding, drawing the ocean back away from the beach, which is comprised of many water-rounded stones … white and grey, smooth and pitted, large and small. You walk across the expanse of glistening rocks, drawing as close as you can to the edge of the water.

High upon a promontory overlooking the sea, you discern the ramparts of a protected hill fort to your left. In front of you stretching into the ocean, you can see the outline of a small island. The moon is bright enough to illuminate a gleaming spiral tower, shining as if it were somehow made of glass, rising up from the center of the island. It comes to you that the island is one of legend—it is called Caer Arianrhod.

Spend some time here looking out toward the west, matching the ebb and flow of your own breath with the rhythm of the tides. As you inhale, the waters draw back, collecting their energy for the exhale, when the waves surge forward to crash upon the shore around your feet. Take nine cycles of breath, keeping your eyes fixed on the moon. With each successive breath, the moon sinks lower and lower in the sky until the ninth breath, when the bottom curve of the moon seems to contact the distant line of the horizon and casts a long path of light over the wave-rippled surface of the ocean. The path grows longer and longer until it ends at the edge of the water where the sea meets the shore … directly in front of your feet.

Time seems to freeze, and the journey of the moon halts with it, although the waves continue to be the breath of the ocean. The wind has died down, no longer whipping through your hair … no longer filling your ears with its clamor—only the sound of the crashing waves remains. You look out toward the horizon, marveling at the enormously bright and shining moon, when your eyes detect faint movement. Straining to see with clarity, you begin to recognize a form differentiating itself from the disk of the moon, moving toward you and drawing closer and closer to the shore. Suddenly you realize you are looking at the form of a woman stepping gracefully, effortlessly along the silver road of light that bisects the darkness of the ocean. As she draws closer and closer, you see that she is a tall, strong woman with pale skin contrasting with shadow-dark hair, black as the night sky. She is literally garbed in light that shifts and pulses along with the rhythm of the tides. The light surrounds her form with energetic scintillations.

In the span of three heartbeats, she stands before you, this bright Lady of the Moon. Her large dark eyes take your measure, sparkling as if with starlight. Her essence and brightness are almost too much for you to bear. You bow your head as much to honor this great lady before you as to escape the intensity of her gaze and the brightness of her visage. She reaches out to you and lifts your chin to face her fully, fixing her eyes upon your own with a strength that keeps you from looking away once more.

There is no doubt who she is—Arianrhod, the Silver Wheel.

With her dark and starry eyes unwavering, she speaks with the voice of the ocean ... the sound reverberating as if through time and through space, rattling your very bones, and yet you feel as if every neuron in your brain is firing all at once. Your inner eye is bright and illuminated.

"Are you whole?" she asks you. "Are you ever-virgin? Complete unto yourself?"

Answer her aloud. Speak your response and take note of her reply.

"Where are you incomplete? Where are you attached to what has already passed, the memory of what has come before, the calling of the Realm of Sea? Where are you attached to what has not yet come to be, the unformed thing that is the future, the whispers of the Realm of Sky?"

Again, answer her aloud. Take what time you need to speak your responses and take note of her reply.

"I am here to set the weavings of your destiny in motion. There are three things you must do," she says to you.

"First, you must Name it. What is your destiny? As best as you know it, speak it here and now."

Again, answer her aloud. Speak your response and take note of her reply.

She plucks at the air around her, and drawing from the moonlight, a sliver thread appears between her foam-white fingers. She hands one end of it to you. Take it. Make note of its energy and how it makes you feel.

She speaks again:

"Second, you must Empower it. How will you accomplish this destiny? What tools do you bring to bear? As best as you know it, speak it here and now."

Speak your response aloud and take note of her reply.

Again she plucks at the air around her. Drawing from the moonlight, a sliver thread appears between her foam-white fingers. She hands one end of it to you. Take it. Make note of its energy and how it makes you feel. How does it feel to hold both threads? How are they similar? How are they different?

She speaks again:

"Third, you must Partner with it. How will your life be changed by this destiny? What new thing will this bring into the world? As best as you know it, speak it here and now."

Speak your response aloud and take note of her reply.

Once more she plucks at the air around her, and drawing from the moonlight, a sliver thread appears between her foam-white fingers. She hands one end of it to you. Take it. Make note of its energy and how it makes you feel. How does it feel to hold all three of these threads? How are they similar? How are they different?

Arianrhod takes up the other end of the threads you hold. With fingers deftly moving, she plaits the three of them into one interwoven strand. After tying off the end, she takes the whole of it from you and holds it above her head. You see there the shining of a constellation, a series of stars forming a torc-shaped crescent known as Caer Arianrhod, the Fortress of Arianrhod. With a flash of silvery light, woven moonlight in her hands emulates the shape of the constellation above her. When the light fades, she draws her hands down and holds them out before her in a gesture of offering.

You look down at her hands and see they hold a silver torc—a symbol of Sovereignty.

She speaks once more:

"I offer this to take and wear if you choose. I do not lay any destiny upon you that you do not yourself choose to pursue. What you see in the here and now may lead you to a different vision in the cycles to come, so do not fear knowing the whole of the tapestry's expanse in this place and at this time. If you take this torc and wear it as a symbol of your self-dedication, know that you will come to know the pattern by the weave. You will feel the rhythm by the weft. The fullness of your destiny will reveal itself to you in time. The choice, as it ever should be, is yours—this is the nature of Sovereignty."

Take a moment to consider her words. Do not choose lightly.

Take three deep, centering breaths, and let your decision rise to the surface. Center it within yourself.

When you are ready and have made your choice, speak it to her. If you decline, let it be known. If you accept, take the torc she offers you, and place it around your neck. In either case, take some time and breathe into the moment. Feel how things shift. Feel how things remain the same. Allow yourself to integrate the revelations of this exchange.

When you are ready, thank the Lady Arianrhod in a way that feels right to you. Give her an offering of some sort, and spend some time in her presence, asking what you will, hearing her words, receiving what guidance she chooses to share.

At last, she makes a gesture of blessing. Just as time and the motion of the moon and the sound of the winds halted suddenly before, they now begin once more. The moon continues to sink below the horizon, bringing the path of light down with it. As this pathway recedes from view, so too does Arianrhod's energy dissipate until she also fades from your sight.

Take three deep, centering breaths. Remember all you have seen, received, and committed to in this moment. When you are ready, follow the thread that connects you to the vessel that took you to this Land Beyond Wave. Take your place in the boat once more for the journey back over the Nine Waves, to the place that is Here and the time that is Now.

Part Three

CULTIVATION

Chapter 10

THE PHYSICIANS OF MYDDFAI AND THE LADY OF THE LAKE

EDIEVAL WALES WAS FAMED FOR the herbal tradition of the
Meddygon Myddfai—the Physicians of Myddfai. A parish in
Carmarthenshire, Myddfai became known from the thirteenth century
onward as the home of a lineage of court physicians, as well as for an
area called *Pant y Meddygon* (the Valley of the Physicians), which was
rich in medicinal plants. It was not unusual for professions to be hered-
itary in medieval Wales, with training passed through apprenticeship
from parent to child. We see this really clearly in Middle-Age Welsh
law manuscripts, which are plentiful and generational.

The family first gained prominence when Rhiwallon Feddyg of
Myddfai became the court physician of Lord Rhys Gryg, son of the famous prince of South Wales, Rhys ap Gruffydd. Under the patronage
of Rhys Gryg, Rhiawallon and his sons collected medicinal formulae,
diagnostic methods, and treatment practices of their profession into a
manuscript. A copy of this text was included in the compilation of medieval Welsh writings called *The Red Book of Hergest* (*Llyfr Coch Hergest*), an important source of early Welsh materials including poetry, history, and especially the stories of *Y Mabinogi*. Although the manuscript

itself dates back to the late fourteenth century, it is believed that some of the recipes and healing charms preserved therein date back much farther, perhaps even to the sixth century, representing the first time some of the traditional healing practices of Wales were committed to writing. The collection itself is not typical of similar medieval medical manuscripts from Europe, as the Meddygon Myddfai included detailed instructions both on how to prepare herbal remedies as well as dosage information and length of treatment.

In 1861, the Welsh MMS Society included these materials in a book called *The Physicians of Myddfai: Or, the Medical Practice of the Celebrated Rhiwallon and His Sons, of Myddfai, in Carmarthenshire*. It was edited by the Welsh scholar Rev. John Williams ab Ithel, and translated into English by John Pughe, himself a physician. Pughe also wrote the preface, which gives a brief overview of Welsh medicine, a history of the Meddygon Myddfai, as well as some of their medical maxims. This is followed with "The Legend of Llyn y Fan, or The Lady of the Lake," compiled from several sources in 1841. This popular Welsh folktale, which has several known variations, established a supernatural lineage for the Physicians of Myddfai, who were said to be the children of a lake fairy and a mortal man. The legend said it was their mother, the Lady of the Lake, who taught them the use of herbs for healing.

The rest of the text is comprised of lists of medicinal recipes and remedies, most of which are strictly comprised of herbs, though there are some which also include components derived from animals. In addition to these formulae that treat symptoms and heal disease processes, the Myddfai collection includes information on anatomy, basic types of surgery, classifications of diseases, dietary warnings and advice, and even a few prayers and charms that are supposed to affect healing as well as some that could be used to assist in reaching a diagnosis.[45]

---

45. Morfydd Owen, "Meddygon Myddfai: A Preliminary Survey of some Medieval Medical Writing in Welsh" *Studia Celtica* 10 (Jan. 1, 1975), 210.

The last known physician of this lineage was John Jones, who died in 1789; his gravestone can be seen to this day at St. Michael's Church in Myddfai.

There are several threads of knowledge evidenced in these healing practices and remedies. As with most medical literature from medieval Europe, much derived from classical Greek and Roman sources that likely first came to the British Isles during the Roman period. An additional influence comes from Greek writings rediscovered in the eleventh century which triggered a revival and expansion of study in the twelfth and thirteenth centuries. This revival explains the presence of the humoral philosophy of Hippocrates and Galen in the Welsh medical literature, and indeed some of the collection can be traced to original Latin materials; those that cannot may reflect a more native Welsh healing tradition. This is especially true where the writing resembles the mnemonic styles known from Welsh literature as reflecting oral transmission before things began to be redacted in the medieval period. It has been suggested that it is the collecting of these previously oral teachings into writing that may form the basis of the fame of the Physicians of Myddfai.

Tl e writings of the physicians reflect a few other cultural pieces as well. Several herbs that were known to be very commonly used, like meadowsweet, are only mentioned once or twice in the collection. It is thought that this is a result of the herb having been in such common usage that to include it in the formulary would have been considered redundant. We can also deduce the ways in which the medical community of the time approached women's health care as much by looking at what information isn't included in these writings as by what is. While there are several herbal formulae addressing female-specific ailments such as those treating disease of the breast, herbs to aid fertility, and a charm to assist in childbirth, there is still an information gap about women's herbal healthcare. Perhaps we may cautiously consider that the deeper herbal knowledge of women's issues were not a part of professional medical training and were instead found in the realms of folk practice, midwifery, and village wise women.

As the middle ages were not the safest of times for women herbalists and midwifes, it is likely that the knowledge around these remained in oral tradition, safely couched in the language of folk practice. Our knowledge is quite limited when it comes to the specifics of what was used and when, but a study of the archaeological record both as it concerns paleobotany and grave goods (for example, meadowsweet flowers have been found in Bronze Age burials in Wales)—along with collected folk practice and lore around particular herbs in the modern era—helps us fill in some of the pieces.

The town of Myddfai today has established itself as a learning center for traditional Welsh herbal practices, and local herbalists have conscientiously gone out into the countryside to interview community elders in an effort to collect folk remedies and herbal healing methods which have been in active use and passed down from generation to generation. Studying the Physicians of Myddfai manuscript and formulary, as well as making a visit to Myddfai and to the site of Llyn y Fan Fach, are both highly recommended for those interested in Welsh ethnobotany and making a connection with the local traditions of the Lady of the Lake.

Llyn y Fan Fach and the Lady of the Lake

In the story of the Lady of Llyn y Fan Fach, a shepherd (in some sources he is named Gwyn) pastures his widowed mother's cattle on the nearby slopes of the Black Mountain near Llyn y Fan Fach—the Lake of the Small Hill. One day, he encounters a lake fairy lounging upon the surface of the water, combing her long hair. Filled with love for her, he approaches the maiden and wordlessly offers her the bread he has brought with him for his meal. She rejects it, saying, "Hard baked is thy bread; I am not easy to catch!" before disappearing below the water. The next day he returns. On the advice of his mother, this time he brings raw dough as an offering for the lake fairy. When she appears again, he speaks his love for her, and she says, "Unbaked is thy bread! I will not have thee." She dives into the lake once more, but her smile encourages him to return again, this time with half-baked bread. The shepherd waits all day on the shore of the lake, and when the fairy finally appears, she accepts his offering and takes his hand. He proposes marriage to her, and she disappears below the water once more.

Forlorn, the youth tries to follow her into the lake even though it could mean his demise, but suddenly his beloved reappears, now accompanied by a white-haired man of strong and noble bearing as well as another maiden who is identical to her in every way. The man tells Gwyn that he is the father of these two maidens and will permit his daughter to marry him if he is able to identify which of the two was the woman he loved. Panic-stricken, the youth desperately looks for s   g to distinguish his beloved from her identical twin, fearing he will lose her forever. Just as he is about the give up hope, one of the maidens subtly points her toe toward him, moving just enough for Gwyn to notice. He immediately steps forward and takes her by the hand.

Having chosen correctly, the father of his beloved says to him, "I charge you to be a good and gentle husband to my daughter, and as a dowry, I will give her as many heads of cattle, sheep, goats, and horses that she can count of each without losing her breath. Should you treat her poorly and strike her with three blows without cause, she and all the livestock I have gifted her will return to our home beneath the lake." Gwyn agrees to these terms and gives his assurances that he would never harm the woman he loves. Then, counting by fives, the maiden secures an enormous amount of animals for her dowry, which her father called out of the lake as a gift to the young couple. They were soon married and went to live on a farm not far from the town of Myddfai. The lady took the name Nelferch and bore three sons to Gwyn; the loving family lived together in joy and prosperity for many years.

Alas, as with most prohibitions, Gwyn did eventually break his contract with Nelferch's father. He struck the first causeless blow when he playfully swatted her with his gloves as he asked her to fetch their horse so they could get to a christening she was delaying attending. Years later, Nelferch began to weep inconsolably at a wedding in the face of everyone else's joy. Gwyn tapped her on the shoulder to ask why she was crying and she replied that she foresaw a troubled future for the couple, and informed Gwyn that he had now struck the second blow. Vowing to be more mindful, it was many years later that Gwyn and Nelferch were attending a funeral where she was laughing joyfully in contrast to everyone else's sorrow. Gwyn touched Nelferch on the arm, imploring her to stop laughing. She explained that she was happy because when people die, they leave the pain and the sorrow of the world behind them. "And now," she said, "I must also leave you behind, my husband. You have struck the final causeless blow, and our marriage is over."

With that, she turned away from him and headed back to their farm where she called to all of her cattle and oxen, and to her horses, goats and sheep. They left the fields they had been plowing, the pastures they had been grazing, and even the slaughtered calf hanging on a hook came back to life and joined the procession of animals which followed the lady back to Llyn y Fan Fach to return with her under the waters.

The devastated and inconsolable Gwyn was never to see his beloved again, no matter how much time he spent calling to her and seeking her out on the banks of the lake. However, her sons would often wander in search of her and one day she appeared before her eldest son, Rhiwallon. She revealed to him that his destiny was to become one of the greatest healers the world had ever seen; he would serve humanity by restoring them to health and providing relief from pain and suffering. Nelferch gave to him a bag filled with prescriptions and formulary for the restoration and preservation of health, explaining that if he and his family studied these deeply, they would gain renown for centuries as the most skillful physicians in Wales. Before disappearing once more, she promised her son that she would come to him whenever he had need of her counsel. Wisely, the sons committed the whole of their knowledge to writing so that their art would never be lost and would always be available in service to humanity.

Lake Fairies and Their Origin

Scholars believe the tale as we have it today is a confluence of several stories that were connected to the land. The Fairy Bride as a folk motif is very popular in Welsh literary tradition, and several such tales are known particularly as associated with the lakes in and around Myddfai. A study of early Welsh literature shows that it was not uncommon for noble Welsh families to trace their lineage back to famous historical personages or characters from legend, so it is not surprising that the famous healers of Myddfai who served generations of Welsh nobility would have such a story attached to their family history. While descending from such a notable personage would serve to increase the prestige of the physicians, it may also represent a trace echo of something deeper.

As in other Celtic lands, Wales has a rich corpus of folklore and traditional stories about fairies. Modern folklorists identify five different general categories of fairies in Welsh tradition: *Ellyllon*, fairies of the valleys and groves bearing similarities to elves; *Coblynau*, fairies of the mines that are very like dwarves or gnomes; *Bwbachod*, fairies of the household similar to brownies or goblins; *Gwyllion*, fairies of the mountains who are hag-like and dangerous; and *Gwragedd Annwn*, the fairies of lakes and streams. These Otherworldly beings are collectively called *Y Tylwyth Teg*, "the fair folk."[46]

---

46. Wirt Sikes, *British Goblins: Welsh Folk-lore, Fairy Mythology, Legends and traditions* (London: Willian Clowes and Sons, 1880), 55.

Some of these beings are inherently good and helpful, such as the *Gwragedd Annwn* ("Wives of the Lower World"), while others like the Gwyllion are known to be generally dangerous; however most of the fair folk are depicted as having both beneficent and malevolent aspects. Sometimes this is dependent upon how these fairies are treated by the humans who interact with them, while in other tales we see subclasses of these beings exhibiting temperaments associated with the type of fairy they are. It is because of their potentially dangerous nature that in some parts of Wales, these beings are instead called *Bendith y Mamau*, the "Blessings of the Mothers"—a euphemism used to avoid speaking the name of the fair folk directly, which could attract their sometimes-negative attention.[47]

A theory about the origin of fairies in Celtic traditions is that they were once ancient divinities whose stories were kept alive in oral tradition; through the gradual process known as reverse euhemerization, they were reduced in status and stature to become supernatural creatures such as giants, witches, enchanters, and fairies. Perhaps, then, lake fairies may once have been local goddesses of the land whose worship centered on the bodies of water or other landscape features associated with them. Or perhaps the lake fairies were never diminished goddesses at all but were simply nature spirits or the anthropomorphized essence of the lakes themselves, a type of genus loci, or spirit of the land. According to Welsh folk belief, fairies were thought to be the souls of virtuous druids; they were considered to be too good for hell but since they weren't Christian, they couldn't enter heaven. Instead, they returned to the lands where they once lived; they were believed to be immortal and possess the power to make themselves invisible.

The Lake Maiden is a particularly Welsh iteration of the Fairy Bride motif, and there are many tales about them. The Otherworldly home of the Gwragedd Annwn is a place that existed very closely to our own

---

47. Sikes, *British Goblins*, 56.

world and could be accessed (in either direction) at threshold times and places, especially through bodies of water, near rivers, or under lakes. The Lady of the Lake of Llyn y Fan Fach is particularly evocative in that it suggests there is an entire separate community or country beneath the waters populated by Otherworldly beings that look like humans (or can take on human form) and who posses great beauty and magic. While legends show that lake fairies can marry and have children with human men, they also appear to have had a very distinctive culture with their own rules and social conventions and display the kinds of supernatural characteristics that we have come to associate with the indigenous Otherworld of Britain.

For example, the normal rules of time and space do not necessarily apply to the Otherworld and its denizens, which is why even the slaughtered animals came back to life and returned under the waves when the Lady of the Lake called them back to her. Magical prohibitions against certain behaviors is a common element in the Lake Maiden tales, and in the tale of the Lady of Llyn y Fan Fach, the three unjust blows, and even the social mores and philosophical perspectives of the Otherworldly characters, are clearly coded in the tale as Other. This is particularly evidenced by the behavior of the Lady of the Lake when she is shown laughing at a funeral, crying at a wedding, and avoiding attending a christening.

Hidden History?

Transformational cultural shifts and the history of social change are hidden layers of information often unconsciously encoded and transmitted subtextually through the medium of myth. Sometimes these can be found in a category of myth called onomastic tales, which are retroactive explanations for mysterious cultural practices or peculiar landscape features. When these tales are passed along in oral tradition, they tend to shift and change over time such that the original meanings may be lost but the symbolic residue remains. Knowing that the ono-mastic tale is an established mechanism that is a consequence of oral tradition, we can engage in a kind of mythic archaeology to uncover potential meanings and histories that have been unknowingly embed-ded in these stories.

Perhaps then, the part of the story that describes Rhiwallon receiv-ing healing knowledge from his mother may be a folkloric resonance that preserves the memory of that time in history when the ability to practice the healing arts was taken from the hands of women—mid-wives, priestesses, wise women—to become the sole provenance of men. If we look at the tale of the Lady of Llyn y Fan Fach as carrying within it this sort of mythic memory, perhaps then the lineage of the Physicians of Myddfai may have its origins in that older order and lat-ter part of the tale is subtextually commemorating that cultural shift.

Alternatively, in the way that folk traditions often preserve long-forgotten histories, perhaps there had once been a shrine or cult center at Llyn y Fan Fach dedicated to a goddess of healing. While there is no evidence of such a religious center at Llyn y Fan Fach, it is asso-ciated with an interesting piece of folk tradition. Gwyl Awst, the first of August and the height of summer, is one of the four British Celtic holy days and has resonance with the Irish feast of Lughnasadh. It is said that if you go to Llyn y Fan Fach on Gwyl Awst, you may be able to catch a glimpse of the Lady of the Lake and she may elect to speak with you.

It's not hard to find examples of lake fairies as healers in Welsh leg-end, and perhaps this is a vestige of the lore of the Ninefold Sister-hoods who always had heading as one of their skills. A connection may therefore be made between the Lady of the Lake of Avalon in Arthu-rian tradition and the Lady of the Lake of Myddfai; in both situations, the Otherworldly lake-dwelling women are healers, and herbalism plays a big role in their healing arts.

Reflecting the Tale Within

Aside from the mythic meaning as reflected in a culture's history and lore, we can seek out the lessons of the story by embodying it and reflecting its symbolic meaning into our lives. With broad strokes, some of the teachings which can be extracted from the story of the Lady of Llyn y Fan Fach are these:

In addition to being a portal to the Otherworld as many bodies of water in Celtic myth and legend are, the lake in this tale also can represent the unconscious mind, the spiritual realm, and that which lies within us. The Lady of the Lake is an avatar of the inner self—the higher self in women or the anima in men. She plays the role of guide, a goddess, or a messenger from the Otherworld. She holds knowledge of the inner landscape and possesses the tools necessary to affect deep and lasting healing. Gwyn, the young man whose name means "white, shining, holy" and is often a theonym in Welsh mythos (indicating that the character was once divine) represents the conscious mind that seeks beyond what is in front of him. He finds wisdom and spirit in everyday life and learns that nothing is mundane.

When the conscious mind looks within for meaning and truth, it makes space for guidance to rise to the surface from the depths of the unconscious mind. A deep and lasting connection is not easy to make, and often requires persistence and a sacrifice of some sort to be successful. What may arise from the profound and divinely inspired insights can cause a crisis of identity—here represented by the sisters' challenge—and we are faced with a choice between truth and illusion, between Sovereignty and shadow. However, if we are authentic and dedicated in our seeking, the universe will often lend a hand to help us make the right choices, and the resulting union of the conscious and the unconscious selves brings love, prosperity, and abundance, as represented in the tale as the union of the two lovers, the dowry gifts of cattle, and a home filled with children.

And yet, we must work to maintain the changes we have made in our lives, and to not take for granted the responsibilities that come with the insights that bring wisdom and growth. In order to remain in right relationship in our conscious partnership with Self, there are new perspectives we are expected to maintain and new standards for behavior required of us. External situations that challenge the clarity of our connection to our Sovereignty and threaten to cross our inner boundaries are presented as opportunities to grow and heal, indicating the degree of integration we have obtained. The prohibition against three unjust blows presented in the tale challenge us in three ways: how to respond to experiences of grief which are concurrent with joy, how to be centered and content even in situations of challenge, and how to choose our higher calling even in the face of convention and others' expectations.

While the three blows in the tale were unjust, they were also unthinking; we are thus cautioned that when we slip into unconscious behaviors—that is, when we react from a place of shadow, rather than respond from the perspective of Sovereignty—we are in danger of being at the mercy once more of our inner illusions. When activated, shadow impulses can overwhelm whatever wisdom we have obtained, returning it to the realm of the unconscious, and leaving us pining for a balanced relationship with Sovereignty once more.

However, the Universe is not cruel; the Lady of the Lake returned to visit with her children and gift them with the healing wisdom that founded the lineage of the Myddfai physicians. In the same way, we can work to affect lasting healing when we are willing to continue our growth and return once more with a child's trust and openness to seek out the healing wisdoms dwelling within the depths of our shadow. We can then take these hard-won lessons and share them with others, deliberately as teachers, or indirectly through the example of our lives.

Chapter 11

ĀN ĀVĀLONIĀN
MĀTERIĀ MEDICĀ

*The information provided in this chapter is intended to assist you in begin-
ning your research into the folkloric and medicinal properties of the herbal
allies associated with each of the Lunar Keys of the Avalonian Cycle of Revealing. In support of the intention to build discernment and foster trust
in your inner wisdom, it is recommended that you engage in the intuitive
exploration of these herbal energies—as outlined in chapter 4, and reflected
in the Seeking Sovereignty Within: Journaling Prompts and Self-Reflective
Questions sections that accompany each moon in part two of this book—
before reading this chapter.*

HERBAL ALLIES OF THE TIME OF CERIDWEN

Moon 1

THE MOON OF INITIATION

Herbal Ally: Mugwort

Botanical Name: *Artemisia vulgaris*

Welsh Name(s): Y Ganwraidd Lwydd, Canwraidd Iwyd, Llys Ibuan, Llwydlys, Llys Ifan, Beidiog Lwyd

Other Common Names: Cronewort, muggons, chrysanthemum weed, common mug, felon herb, old man's plant, St. John's plant, Old Uncle Henry, sailor's tobacco, wild wormwood, herba matrum, mater herbarum, she-vervain

———————

Mugwort (*Artemisia vulgaris*) is a powerful herbal ally for women, both as a regulator of the menstrual cycle and as a spiritual doorway into the Mysteries of the Divine Feminine. Its common name is thought to derive from its use in brewing as a beer flavoring, but its botanical name expresses mugwort's association with energies of the moon and the goddess Artemis, who was particularly concerned with the protection of women, especially those in childbirth. Mugwort is a moon-loving plant that turns its leaves upside down at night, revealing their silvery-gray undersides that seem to drink in the shimmering moonlight.

A widely used and respected herb particularly for women's issues, mugwort nevertheless found itself unrecorded in many of the herbariums and formal collections of herbal remedies in the British Isles and Europe, including the formulary of the Physicians of Myddfai. It has been postulated that this is either because mugwort was in such common usage that including it in these collections would have been redundant, or its abortifacent properties made midwives hesitant to mention its use (or if they did, the certainly male writers and compilers may have censored the herb for reasons of morality).

Medicinally, mugwort acts as a nervine to soothe anxiety, lessen PMS symptoms, and also bring on menstrual flow both as an emmenagogue and an abortifacient. Be careful not to use this herb while pregnant, as it was also used in traditional medicine to induce labor when a woman had reached full-term. It can aid in digestion, bring on detoxifying or fever-reducing sweating as a diaphoretic, and bring relief to those suffering with fibromyalgia and irritable bowel syndrome. It is an important herb in Traditional Chinese Medicine, where it is burned on or near acupuncture points in a process called moxibustion that helps facilitate healing.

A sacred herb in many cultures, mugwort was once known as *Mater Herbarium*, "Mother of Herbs"; its widespread usage as both a medicinal and magical herb certainly lend itself to the theory that it may be one of humanity's oldest known herbal allies.[48] Mugwort was believed to have protective powers and was thus worn by travelers and hung over the doorway of homes to protect against lightning and keep evil influences away. It was sacred to thunder gods throughout Europe and had a special correspondence with Summer Solstice. In Southern Britain, placing a sprig of mugwort in one's shoes was believed to help the wearer run all day, and the herb was smoked as a remedy against

---

48. David E. Allen and Gabrielle Hatfield, *Medicinal Plants in Folk Tradition: An Ethnobotany of Britain and Ireland* (Portland, OR: Timber Press, 2004), 296.

tiredness and loss of appetite. Mugwort was the first of the nine herbs mentioned in the Nine Herbs charm, a famous poem of enchantment that was included in a tenth-century collection of Anglo-Saxon medical texts, prayers, and remedies:

Keep in mind, Mugwort, what you revealed,
What you established at Regenmelde
You were called Una, the oldest of herbs,
You have power against three and against thirty,
You have power against poison and against infection,
You have power against the loathsome one who roams through
the land.[49]

The complete list of plants included in the Nine Herbs charm are: mugwort, plantain, lamb's cress, fumitory, chamomile, nettle, crab apple, chervil, and fennel.[50]

On the Isle of Man, a British Crown Dependency in the Irish sea that boasts mugwort as its national flower, the herb was traditionally gathered on Midsummer's Eve for protection against witchcraft and would be woven into crowns worn by animals and humans alike to ward off negative influences. Even to this day, people wear a sprig of mugwort (which they call *bollan bane* or "white herb") on Tynwald Day, the national holiday of the Isle of Man. Tynwald Day is marked by many ceremonies and rituals, some of which are believed to have pre-Christian origins, including the open-air proclamation of new laws from the top of a human-made mound.[51]

Today, mugwort is burned, worn, smoked, and ingested as a weak tea in small quantities to bring on prophetic visions and lucid dreams.

49. M. L. Cameron, *Anglo-Saxon Medicine*, (Cambridge, UK: Cambridge University Press, 2006), 144.

50. Ibid., 147.

51. Allen and Hatfield, *Medicinal Plants*, 297.

It is the primary ingredient in dream pillows and can be found bundled into smudge sticks that are burned to clear a space of negative energies and in preparation for divinatory workings.

Mugwort's ability to protect the traveler from harm while also granting them the endurance required to continue on their journey makes it a powerful companion for shadow work. That it dispels evil influences while opening the inner eye is critical in allowing us to see the truth of our shadow with clarity, while also helping us to build inner discernment and trust in our intuitive selves. Mugwort opens the way to the Otherworld and is a powerful place to begin an immersion into experiencing the Avalonian Cycle of Revealing.

Moon 2
THE MOON OF DISTILLATION

Herbal Ally: Yarrow

Botanical Name: *Achillea millefolium*

Welsh Name (s): Milddail, Llysiau Gwaedlif, Llysiau'r Gwaenling, y Milddcil, y Wilffrai

Other Common Names: Milfoil, woundwort, carpenter's weed, nose-bleed, herba militaris, staunchweed, knights' milfoil, sneezewort, soldier's woundwort

---

Yarrow (*Achillea millefolium*) was prized by many ancient cultures as a panacea or heal-all. It is best known for its ability to staunch bleeding and prevent wounds from becoming infected. The first part of its botanical name connects the herb with the Greek hero Achilles; a pupil of the wise centaur Chiron who was deeply knowledgeable of the healing arts, Achillies is said to have used yarrow to heal his warriors on the battlefield. The second part of yarrow's name means "thousand leaves" and describes the many feathery segments that characterize the herb's leaves. Yarrow was once called "nosebleed" because it was sometimes used to stop a nosebleed, while other times it was used to cause nosebleeds as a treatment for headaches; sticking yarrow leaves up the nose of a headache sufferer in order to cause bleeding was thought to relieve sinus pressure.

It is an excellent herbal diaphoretic that encourages therapeutic sweating to assist the body in eliminating toxins and reducing fevers. Yarrow is also a vasodilator that helps to lower blood pressure and has strong anti-bacterial and expectorant properties, making it a powerful ally for treating colds, flus, respiratory infections, as well as infections of the urinary tract. The herb has antispasmodic properties that help both to relive stomach cramps and stimulate digestion. Yarrow is also anti-inflammatory and is thus used in treating rheumatoid arthritis. It is an uplifting herb that can be used in remedies to fight depression. An emmenagogue, yarrow should not be taken internally during pregnancy as it can bring on uterine bleeding.

Folkloric uses of yarrow associate it with divination both in the East as well as the West. Traditionally, a bundle of sixty-four yarrow staves are cast to form the hexagrams used in the Chinese system of *I Ching*. In the British Isles and Ireland, the herb was widely used for love divination: when placed under the pillow, a woman would dream of her future husband; cutting green yarrow stalks could reveal the initials of a future lover; and casting some of the herb into the fire could provoke visions of one's true love. These kinds of yarrow divination were especially potent if performed the night before Beltane or Calan Haf. Brides would carry yarrow in their bouquets as good luck charms, and eating yarrow at the wedding feast was believed to strengthen the bonds of love between the couple.

Famously, yarrow leaves were placed over the eyes to bring about the Sight and to see into the Otherworld. In his *Irish Fairy and Folk Tales*, W. B. Yeats records the use of the *cappeen d'yarrag*, a cap with a sprig of yarrow in it that permits the wearer to fly when the correct charm is uttered. Legend has it that druids used yarrow staves to predict the weather but the exact method is unknown. Yarrow was known to be a protective herb as well. Wearing yarrow flowers or attaching a bundle of the herb onto a baby's crib would ward off any evil magic, and hanging a bunch of yarrow in the home on Midsummer's Eve was believed to protect its residents from illness for an entire year

As an herb of healing and clear sight, yarrow is a powerful ally on our quest for wholeness and authenticity, as it helps us to separate that which is in support of our personal Sovereignty from the illusions of self that originate in the realm of the shadow. It assists in setting and keeping good personal boundaries, as well as shielding the self from external influences. This protective energy is critical as we learn to separate the truth of who we are from the compensatory behaviors we have adapted in response to people and situations in our lives that have caused us stress and trauma. Yarrow's protective nature helps us to see with clarity as we strive to reclaim the truth of who we are from self-definitions that no longer serve us.

Moon 3
The Moon of Transformation

Herbal Ally: Wormwood

Botanical Name: *Artemisia absinthium*

Welsh Name (s): Wermwd Lwyd, Chwerwddail, Chwerwlys

Other Common Names: Green ginger, green fairy, old woman, blood of Hephaistos

---

A famously bitter herb like mugwort, wormwood is in the *Artemisia* family, named in honor of the Greek goddess of the moon. It too thins the border between the worlds, and has a reputation as a psychic stimulant when used magically as an incense or in herbal talismans. Its most well-known claim to fame is as an ingredient in the liquor absinthe, whose green fairy can stimulate poetry or madness, depending on the drinker's state of mind. Wormwood's narcotic actions make it an effective remedy for insomnia, although dosage needs to be precise as it can cause intestinal pain and vomiting if too much is taken at once.[52]

Used as a funerary herb, wormwood was placed in graves as well as burned in funeral pyres in Germanic tradition. It was considered a protective herb and was burned as incense to guard against both witchcraft and evil spirits. Sprigs of wormwood were lain with clothing to keep moths away, and an infusion of the herb was added to ink to keep mice from chewing manuscript pages. Wormwood is said to have aphrodisiac qualities as well; it was used as a component in love charms and spells to attract a mate, and dancers wore wormwood flowers as garlands during Germanic summer solstice fertility rites.

---

52. Allen and Hatfield, *Medicinal Plants*, 300.

Medicinally, it is a nervous tonic and can be helpful in treatment of depression. It is an excellent digestive, appetite stimulant, and is a useful liver tonic. It is an especially popular remedy for issues of digestion and upset stomach in Wales and is perhaps the most widely-used herb in rural areas of Wales, country-wide.[53] Wormwood is named for its ability to rid the system of parasites and worms. Its bitterness made wormwood an excellent brewing herb; it was used in beer making as an alternative to hops. As an oil, it is an excellent topical treatment for rheumatoid arthritis and is an effective insect repellent; that said, wormwood oil should *never* be taken internally. This is an herb requiring a great deal of respect, as it can be poisonous in large doses; be sure you consult a qualified herbalist before taking this plant medicinally. It should never be taken internally while pregnant or breastfeeding as it is a powerful and potentially dangerous abortifacient.

---

53. Allen and Hatfield, *Medicinal Plants*, 300.

Moon 4
THE MOON OF GERMINATION

Herbal Ally: Vervain

Botanical Name: *Verbena officinalis*

Welsh Name (s): Cas Gangythraul, Llysiau'r Hudol, Y Dderwen Fen-digaid, Briw'r March

Other Common Names: Herb of grace, herba sacra, holy wort, druid's weed, enchanter's plant, van van, ferfaen, verbein, verbena, verbinaca, dragon's claw, tears of Isis, Juno's tears, herba veneris, persephonion, demetria, Mercury's moist blood, mosquito plant, peristerium, sagmina, pigeon grass, pigeonwood, frog-foot, simpler's joy, altar plant, wild hyssop

---

Vervain (*Verbena officinalis*) is one of the most sacred Druidic herbs and is believed to have been used in their rites of prophecy and divination. They would gather the plant during the dark of the moon, leaving an offering of honey in the earth to replace what they had taken. Sprinkling an infusion of vervain around the sacred grove before offering sacrifices to the Gods both purified the space and protected it from evil spirits and negative magic. In the fourteenth-century Welsh poem "Cadeir Taliesin" ("The Chair of Taliesin") which some scholars have interpreted as representing a bardic initiation rite, vervain is mentioned as one of the herbs brewed in the Cauldron of Inspiration.

In his *Natural History*, the Roman historian Pliny writes of the Celtic uses of vervain:

> The people in the Gallic provinces make use of [vervain] for soothsaying purposes, and for the prediction of future events; but it is the magicians [Druids] more particularly that give utterance to such ridiculous follies in reference to

this plant. Persons, they tell us, if they rub themselves with it will be sure to gain the object of their desires; and they assure us that it keeps away fevers, conciliates friendship, and is a cure for every possible disease; they say, too, that it must be gathered about the rising of the dogstar—but so as not to be shone upon by sun or moon—and that honeycombs and honey must be first presented to the earth by way of expiation. They tell us also that a circle must first be traced around it with iron; after which it must be taken up with the left hand, and raised aloft, care being taken to dry the leaves, stem, and root, separately in the shade. To these statements they add, that if the banqueting couch is sprinkled with water in which it has been steeped, merriment and hilarity will be greatly promoted thereby. As a remedy for the stings of serpents, this plant is bruised in wine.[54]

The Romans also used vervain ceremonially to cleanse their ritual spaces, and called it *herba sacra*, the holy herb; in fact, all of their altar herbs came to be called *verbena*. They even held an annual festival called the Verbenalia to celebrate the plant and its connection to Venus, the goddess of love. It was woven into bridal wreaths in order to sanctify marriages and was used as a powerful aphrodisiac. Vervain was added to the water blacksmiths used to temper their metals, believing it would endow weapons with increased strength and hardness. Similarly, it was believed to rekindle the dying embers of a love that was burning out, fortifying the bonds of love as well as the strength of arousal shared between lovers.

Vervain was also a potent herb of protection. The Physicians of Myddfai recommended that warriors wear sprigs of the plant into battle in order to evade their enemies. Roman messengers wore crowns of

---

54. Pliny, *Natural History* 25, chapter 59.

vervain on their heads during times of war; this was considered a sign of truce which permitted these messengers, called *verbanarii*, "one who bears sacred boughs," to cross into enemy lines unhurt. The plant is considered sacred to the goddess Isis and is said to have sprung up each time one of her tears touched the earth as she gathered the dismembered remains of her husband, Osiris. Christian legend places vervain on Mount Cavalry during the crucifixion of Jesus, and attributes the holiness of the plant to it having been used to staunch the bleeding of Christ's wounds.[55]

A powerful magical herb, it is used to open doorways of the Sight and is a herb of increased creativity, protection, and purification. When vervain leaves were rubbed on a person, it was said to grant any wish and impart good luck. Children who wore vervain were said to be good-natured, well-behaved, and excellent students with a great love of learning.

Vervain has a great many medicinal properties and is considered a cure-all. The herb is thought to have gotten its name from the Celtic *ferfain*, meaning "to cast away stones," a reflection of its use to tonify the bladder and help remove calculi or stones. Vervain reduces fever, brings on detoxifying sweating, tonifies the nervous system, and reduces mental stress and depression. It clarifies the skin, is a useful diuretic, treats gout, assists in respiratory complaints, improves digestion, and is cleansing for the liver. It is an excellent women's herb, as it is a good galactagogue for nursing mothers and a helpful uterine tonic that aids in bringing on menstruation and facilitating contractions during labor; it is not recommended to take vervain during pregnancy because of these actions.

---

55. Anne McIntyre, *Flower Power: Flower Remedies for Healing Body and Soul Through Herbalism, Homeopathy, Aromatherapy, and Flower Essences* (New York: Henry Holt and Company, 1996), 233.

HERBAL ALLIES FOR THE
TIME OF BLODEUWEDD

Moon 5
THE MOON OF EVOCATION

Herbal Ally: Broom

Botanical Name: *Cytisus scoparius*

Welsh Name(s): Banhadlen; Banadle (N. Wales); Banadlen (S. Wales); Banad, Banal, Ysgub Fanadl, Aurfanadl, Melynog-y-waun, Helynog-y-waun

Other Common Names: Scotch broom, common broom, broom tops, Irish tops, banal, besom, basam, bisom, bizzom, browme, brum, breeam, green broom, genista, link, ginster, hagweed

———————————

Broom (*Cytisus scoparius*) is a powerful cleansing herb both energetically and physically. It is traditionally used in the making of besoms, as its name suggests. This common plant has roots that anchor soil thereby preventing erosion (especially on the coastline), and branches that shelter wildlife. It is a protective herb and can be burned to dispel negative influences. Broom was famously used in Brittany as a heraldic device, and the English royal house of Plantagenet took the plant's medieval name, *planta genista*, as their own.[56]

In Wales, broom is considered a magical plant where it is not only used to affect healing and attract love, but also by witches…and against witches with evil intent.[57] Indeed, broom itself seems to have both a light and a dark side. Sometimes the plant is considered unlucky; broom growing on your property was a sign of misfortune unless there were many flowers upon it, in which case it became sign of fertility and abundance.[58] Sweeping one's home with a besom of broom that still has flowers on it was said to bring grave misfortune into the house; however, hanging broom in the house was a protective act to keep evil away. Despite its dualistic nature, it was generally still considered a flower of good fortune and was used to decorate wedding feasts as symbols of abundance.[59] Burning broom flowers as incense affects a cleansing of the space and increases psychic awareness.[60]

Along with blossoms of oak and meadowsweet, broom was one of the three flowers Gwydion and Math used to create Blodeuwedd as a bride for Lleu. Both Welsh literary tradition and present-day vernacular use the flowers of broom as a descriptor for the color yellow, especially when referring to the color of a woman's hair. In parts of Scotland, the peeled white branch of the broom was used as a wand for the corn-sheaf Bride doll made on Imbolc. Broom's narcotic properties were well-known and are immortalized in the ballad "The Broomfield

---

56. Jocelyne Lawton, *Flowers and Fables: A Welsh Herbal* (Bridgend, Wales, UK: Seren Books, 2006), 32.

57. David Hoffmann, *Welsh Herbal Medicine* (Aberteifi, Wales, UK: Abercastle Publications, 1978), 35.

58. Paul Beyerl, *The Master Book of Herbalism* (Blaine, WA: Phoenix Publishing, 1984), 205.

59. Lawton, *Flowers and Fables*, 33.

60. Scott Cunningham, *Cunningham's Encyclopedia of Magical Herbs* (St. Paul, MN: Llewellyn Publications, 1985), 63.

Hill," where the heroine is advised to keep her knight asleep by using broom as a strewing herb.[61] Sheep enjoy eating the pods of the broom plant which causes them to become intoxicated; the effect is short-lived and does not seem to be harmful to the sheep.

Medicinally, broom has been used traditionally to treat complaints of the cardiovascular system and the renal tract, to induce labor, and as an abortifacient; however, caution should be practiced when taking this herb internally and it should *only* be used under professional supervision—there is a danger of poisoning. It is a powerful diuretic whose green tops contain the chemical constituent sparteine, which is known to increase urinary output.[62] Broom has anti-hemmoragic properties, and it was traditionally used to treat cases of excessive menstruation.

An overall useful plant, broom buds were pickled and eaten like capers, and its seeds were prepared as a coffee substitute. Its twigs were gathered and woven together to create baskets. Broom bark was high in tannin and was used to tan leather, while the fiber of its bark could be spun into cloth and was also used to make paper. The plant's leaves also yield a beautiful green dye.[63]

61. Tess Darwin, *The Scots Herbal: The Plant Lore of Scotland* (Edinburgh, Scotland, UK: Mercat Press, 1996), 112.

62. Allen and Hatfield, *Medicinal Plants*, 162.

63. Malcom Stuart, ed., *The Encyclopedia of Herbs and Herbalism* (New York: Grosset & Dunlap, 1979), 260.

Moon 6
THE MOON OF ACTIVATION

Herbal Ally: Meadowsweet

Botanical Name: *Filpendula ulmaria*

Welsh Name(s): Erwain, Brenhines y Weirglodd, Blodau'r Mel, Llysiau'r Forwyn, Chwys Arthur

Other Common Names: Bridewort, queen of the meadow, gravel root, goat's beard, old man's pepper, courtship-and-matrimony, bittersweet, dropwort, my lady's belt, sweet hay, lus chuchulainn, little queen, trumpet weed, steeplebush, meadsweet, mead wort, pride of the meadow, meadow maid, honeysweet, dollor, bridgewort, dollof, lace-makers-herb

---

Also called bridewort, the sweet smelling flowers of the meadowsweet (*Filpendula ulmaria*) are a traditional addition to the bridal bouquet. It was also a common funerary herb, potentially because the sweetness covered up any odors that might be present, or perhaps instead the flowers represented the transition from one life phase to the next. In 2006, archaeologists excavated a Bronze Age round cairn on the crest of Fan Foel, one of the mountain peaks above Llyn y Fan Fach, home of the Lady of the Lake who was the ancestress of the Physicians of Myddfai (See chapter 10 for more information). In it, they found the cremated remains of a child, believed to be under the age of twelve. Pollen samples taken from the site show that bunches of meadowsweet were included in the burial, echoing a pattern exhibited in Bronze Age burials throughout Wales and Scotland.

According to Grieve, Druids held meadowsweet in high regard and counted it as one of their three most sacred herbs along with vervain and water mint. In the Fourth Branch of *Y Mabinogi*, meadowsweet is one of the three flowers used by the magicians Math and Gwydion to create Blodeuwedd to be Lleu's bride. The Irish name for the herb, *Lus Cuchulainn*, means "Belt of Cuchulainn" and refers to the meadowsweet baths used to cure the fevers and soothe the rages of the legendary warrior. In Irish tradition, the flowers are sacred to Áine, Sovereignty goddess of Munster, and it is said that she gave the flower its sweet scent. She was also revered as a fairy queen, which may have some connection to a folk tradition from County Galway: if someone was wasting away as a result of having contact with fairy folk, it was believed that placing meadowsweet flowers under their bed would restore them to health by the next morning. However, this was a dangerous remedy as the flowers put the ill person at risk of falling into a deep sleep from which they would never wake.[64]

Meadowsweet can be used for a type of divination that can help catch a thief: gather some flowers on Midsummer's Eve and place the flowers on some water. If the flowers float on the water, it was a woman who robbed you; if the flowers sink, the thief was a man.

The sweet-smelling plant was a popular herb to strew on the floor of halls and bedrooms, and it was said to instill a sense of gladness and peace. Meadowsweet flowers were a popular ingredient in the making of mead and ale, and it is possible that its name comes from the Anglo-Saxon words *mede* ("mead") or *medo-wort* ("honey herb"); indeed, the flowers are so sweet that it was added to food and drinks as a sweetener.[65] In Yorkshire, the herb was called "courtship and matrimony," believed to be a reflection of the two different scents of the meadowsweet plant: the sweetness of the flower stands in contrast to

---

64. Niall MacCoitir, *Ireland's Wild Plants: Myths, Legends & Folklore* (Cork: The Collins Press, 2015), 85

65. Lawton, *Flowers and Fables*, 134.

the bitter almond-like scent of the leaves, just as a courtship is blissful while a marriage can be bitter.[66]

Medicinally, meadowsweet contains salicylates, the primary component of aspirin, and so has traditional usage for pain relief and the reduction of fevers, but since it contains mucilages, it does so without irritating the stomach like aspirin. It acts as an excellent tonic for the digestive tract, and soothes heartburn, diarrhea, peptic ulcers, and nausea. Meadowsweet is useful for colds and respiratory infections, and it also reduces the pain of rheumatoid arthritis. It is a useful diuretic that helps remove toxins from the body, such as in the case of gout, and it is an overall aid to the kidney and bladder, especially when calculi are present. It is an excellent anti-spasmotic and assists with menstrual cramps. It has long been used medicinally in Wales as it grows there in great abundance.

---

66. MacCoitir, *Ireland's Wild Plants*, 85.

Moon 7
The Moon of Revelation

Herbal Ally: Nettle

Botanical Name: *Urtica dioica*

Welsh Name(s): Ddynhaden, Danadl Poethion

Other Common Names: Stinging nettle, hoary nettle, tall nettle, slender nettle, heg-begs

---

Nettle (*Urtica dioica*) is famous for its sting and is one of the most commonly used herbs in folk medicine. "Three nettles in May keeps all diseases away" is an old English saying, reflecting the plant's medicinal worth. It is a powerful antihistamine and an anti-inflammatory herb, especially as concerns the respiratory system; it is used to treat hay fever, sinusitis, and asthma. Nettles are one of the most nutritious plants known to us: they provide a range of necessary vitamins, minerals, and protein, all in a very bio-available form. Its high iron content assists in the treatment of anemia, and it also has strong anti-hemorrhaging or hemostatic properties. It is said that putting a nettle leaf on the tongue and pressing it to the roof of the mouth will stop a nose bleed.[67]

Considered a powerful cleanser of the blood, nettle tea was taken to clear the skin and tonify the circulatory system. Externally, it was used as a hair wash to stimulate growth and clear up dandruff; this is in alignment with the Doctrine of Signatures, as the nettle plant is covered in fine hairs. Nettle is tonic for the urinary system, acting both as a powerful diuretic and to inhibit nighttime urinary urgency. It removes excess uric acid, thereby relieving gout. It treats fibromyalgia as well as the pain and inflammation of rheumatoid and osteoarthritis. Grieve

---

67. Timothy Coffey, *The History and Folklore of North American Wildflowers* (New York: Houghton Mifflin, 1993), 34.

mentions that the process of *urtication*, which is the act of flogging parts of the body with nettle stalks, was an old way to treat chronic rheumatism and muscular weakness; the same process was also applied to the genital area of men to address impotency. In France, young men were encouraged to roll around in nettle patches before going courting, as a way to stir up their "natural heat" as Galen put it.[68]

Another excellent ally for women's health, nettles is an overall women's reproductive tonic, with the arial portions of the plant a specific for the female system. It is an aid in pregnancy and prevents hemorrhage in childbirth, regulates the menstrual cycle, and treats the symptoms of PMS. The roots of nettle are a specific for prostate issues in men, and it is a sexual tonic for both genders; a popular folk practice was to place nettle leaves in a man's shoes as a form of contraception. It was believed that fevers could be cured by picking nettle by its roots and speaking the name of the ill person and their family. Nettle was counted among the nine sacred herbs in Anglo-Saxon folklore along with plantain, chamomile, mugwort, watercress, chervil, fennel, and crab apple.

The word "nettle" is believed to have come from the Anglo-Saxon word *noedl*, which means "needle." This etymology could reflect the plant's traditional use as a very sturdy textile fiber that was spun and woven into linen. It may also refer to the nettle's stinging properties, which is also alluded to in its botanical name *urtica*, which means "burning." Indeed, the nettle plant is equipped with thousands of stinging hairs that cover the stalk and leaves. Each of these hairs is a hollow spine with a sac-like structure at its base; this sac is filled with a liquid substance comprised of histamines, serotonin, acetylcholine, and formic acid—the latter being the venom fire ants produce when biting in self-defense. When a person or animal brushes up against the stinging nettle, the fragile tips of the hairy shafts break off, which then cause them to act like hypodermic needles that inject the liquid irritant into the skin of the offender.

---

68. McIntyre, *Flower Power*, 229.

This defense mechanism is intended to act as a deterrent to plant eating animals (and likely generations of herbalists and wise women who have gathered the plant for its medicinal qualities).

While the sting of the nettle is very unpleasant, it typically only lasts for about a day unless the affected person has an allergy to the plant; if this is the case, it is crucial to seek medical attention right away as the reactions can be potentially life threatening, especially when respiration becomes affected. However, as a reflection perhaps of the innate intelligence of nature which seeks to maintain balance in its system, where stinging nettles grow, the remedy for its burning almost always grows nearby—the juice of yellow dock (*Rumex crispus*) or another member of the dock family (*Rumex* spp.). Grieve records a charm to that is to be recited slowly as the liquid from the bruised dock leaf is applied to the affected area:

> "*Nettle in, dock out.*
> *Dock rub nettle out!*"

Charm aside, it is good practice to try not not touch the area of a nettle sting for at least ten minutes to allow the irritant chemicals to dry and make the hairs easier to remove without affecting other parts of the skin. Leaving the affected site alone also prevents driving the spiny hairs deeper into the skin; these can be removed later using tape to lift the spines out. Fortunately, when nettles are boiled to be eaten, the heat deactivates its venom so the nutritious plant can be safely enjoyed.

According to folklore, apple trees that have nettle plants growing beneath them produce very large apples that ripen more quickly than other apples. There is something to this belief, as nettles thrive in soil rich in nitrogen. The presence of nettle anywhere is a good indicator of quality soil. In fact, it is nettle's high nitrogen content that makes it an excellent activator of compost.[69]

---

69. Laura C. Martin, *Wildflower Folklore*, 75–76.

Nettle was hung around the house or burned in bonfires to protect the household and crops from lightning.[70] Nettle that was picked on the Summer Solstice was believed to undo a spell reducing milk production when taken from property of the witch who cast the spell and placed under the milking pails of the affected cattle. In Scotland, it was believed that nettles harvested on Halloween night and placed in the bedding of someone you fancied would make them fall in love with you. The positive effect of nettle on both the women's reproductive system and men's virility made it a natural aphrodisiac and a common component in love spells.

70.Lawton, *Flowers and Fables*, 189.

Moon 8

The Moon of Liberation

Herbal Ally: Red Clover

Botanical Name: *Trifolium pratense*

Welsh Name(s): Meillion Coch

Other Common Names: Trefoil, wild clover, shamrock, broad-leaved clover, cowgrass, honeysuckle clover, cleaver grass, cow clover, marl grass, meadow clover, meadow honeysuckle, meadow trefoil, peavine clover, sweet clover, honeystalk

---

In folklore, red clover (*Trifolium pratense*) is said to ward off evil influences and serve as a powerful psychic protector. Its botanical n~ *folium*, means "three leaved," and indeed it has ancient assoc1. ..ɔ with the Celtic love of triplicities, extending into the Christian period where it represented the Holy Trinity. Its common form as a triple-leaved plant underscores the rarity of finding a four-leaf clover, that very famously potent lucky charm. Traditionally, red clover was considered an herb for healing and blessing animals; placing a four-leaf clover in the barn where cows live was said to ward against evil spells and ensure an abundant flow of quality milk.[71]

Pollinated almost exclusively by bumblebees, clover is used to attract wealth and abundance, and is believed to increase fertility. These beliefs are likely related to the plant's medicinal property to regulate the reproductive cycle of women, as well as its ability to enrich the soil where it grows by providing it with nitrogen which in turn creates greater crop yield in the future. Dreaming of clover is said to be an omen of

---

71. Lawton, *Flowers and Fables*, 163.

great prosperity, and the old English maxim "to live in clover" refers to someone who enjoys a life of luxury.

Red clover is said to bestow fairy sight on those who hold it in their hand, permitting one to see between the worlds and gaze upon the spirits and entities which dwell there. It can be used for divinatory purposes as well; a maiden who finds a four-leaf clover and places it in her shoe will marry the first man she sees or someone with the same name.[72] Similarly, if she were to place a four-leaf clover over her door, the first person to pass under it would be the one she marries. If the maiden swallowed the four-leaf clover, she would be fated to marry the first man whose hand she shook.[73] Finally, placing a four-leaf clover under one's pillow is said to induce dreams of one's true love, even if you've not yet met.[74]

In the Welsh tale *Culhwch ac Olwen*, four white clovers were said to spring up from the feet of the maiden Olwen everywhere she walked; indeed her name means "White Track." White clover (*Trifolium repens*) is one of several plants identified as a shamrock in Ireland and has some similar medicinal qualities as red clover, but the red species has stronger medicinal constituents by far. White clover is primarily cultivated today as a grazing plant or ground cover (*repens* means "creeping"), and it also supports honeybees. That clover comes in both red and white varieties is significant from a magical standpoint, as red and white together are the colors associated with the Otherworld. This magical correspondence may be a contributing factor to the herb's association with fairy sight; another could be its traditional medicinal usage as a remedy for ailments of the eyes.

Red clover is a powerful ally for women's health, as it contains phytoestrogens that assist in regulating the reproductive cycle, help relieve

---

72. Lawton, *Flowers and Fables*, 163.

73. Martin, *Wildflower Folklore*, 244.

74. Beyerl, *Master Book of Herbalism*, 243.

issues with menstruation and menopause, and play a role in protecting against breast cancer and osteoporosis. A strong infusion of red clover can be used as a douche to fight vaginal infections and as a wash to soothe the sore nipples of nursing mothers.[75] Pregnant and nursing women should not take red clover, and those who have been diagnosed with breast cancer should discuss use of this herb with their health care practitioner.

It is a lymph and blood cleanser which helps clear the skin, and its antispasmodic properties are useful as a cough remedy. Red clover flowers help to cleanse the system by stimulating the liver and gallbladder, acting as a diuretic and mild laxative, and it has a traditional usage as a blood thinner. It can reduce atherosclerois because it contains beta-sitosterol, which acts to block the absorption of cholesterol, and also has a role in tumor reduction.[76] Red clover has anti-viral and anti-fungal qualities, and an infusion of the flowers was used topically to treat snake bites and was placed in the eyes both to address the formation of cataracts as well as to soothe dry, irritated eyes.[77] It is a nervine and has sedative qualities, so its use helps reduce nervous tension, treat insomnia caused by over-thinking, and ease symptoms of stress such as tension headaches.

Red clover is an herb of cleansing on multiple levels; the flower essence is said to help clear any negativity picked up from others and is especially effective during times of personal or community crisis. It helps us bring our energies to a place of balance and is particularly useful in assisting us in maintaining a solid center of calmness and clarity, regardless of what may be going on around us.[78] An herb of the Sight, red clover acts to increase our self-awareness—an important foundation for undertaking shadow work.

---

75. McIntyre, *Flower Power*, 222.

76. Ibid., 222.

77. Allen and Hatfield, *Medicinal Plants*, 162.

78. McIntyre, *Flower Power*, 222.

HERBAL ALLIES FOR THE
TIME OF RHIANNON

Moon 9
THE MOON OF DEDICATION

Herbal Ally: Burdock

Botanical Name: *Arctium lappa*

Welsh Name(s): Y Cyngaw, Cyngaf Mawr, Ciawg.

Other Common Names: Lappa major, great burdock, beggar's buttons, beggar's lice, love leaves, hurt butt, hurr-burr, burr seeds, happy major, cocklebur, bardana, burdocken, flapper-bags, lappa, gypsy's rhubarb, pig's rhubarb, snake's rhubarb, lappa, fox's clote, thorny burr, cockle buttons, philanthropium, personata, happy major, clot-bur

---

Burdock (*Arctium lappa*) was renowned in folk belief as a powerful charm against evil and misfortune, especially when gathered at Midsummer; its association with Thor for Germanic peoples caused it to be hung in households to protect against lightning strikes. Hanging burdock in the house guarded it against negative influences, and wearing the dried roots was considered to be a charm of protection.[79] Eating raw burdock stems was believed to increase lustfulness, and one of

---

79. Cunningham, *Encyclopedia of Magical Herbs*, 64.

the plant's common names was "love leaves," a fact reflected in its use in love potions.[80]

In Scotland, an area of Edinburgh called South Queensferry celebrates Burry Man's Day on the second Friday in August. This folk practice of unknown antiquity consists of a man chosen from the community who would take on the role of the Burry Man, spending the day walking around the town in a heavy costume comprised of patches made from burdock burrs that had been harvested and dried the week before. Additionally, burrs were placed in sensitive areas of the Burry Man's crotch and underarms, further complicating his walk. Wearing a face mask and holding two flower-bedecked poles to support his arms, he would shuffle around the town for nine hours beginning at 9 a.m., and would be given whiskey to drink through a straw as he walked the seven miles through town.

Although this practice is only attested to have existed from the early nineteenth century onwards, locals believe this tradition is much older, dating back to Pagan times, even though they are unsure of its ultimate purpose. Some believe the Burry Man's walk was intended to confer blessings of abundance on the fishermen and the coming harvest, while others theorize the practice to be the remnants of a scapegoating ritual. In the latter case, the burrs of the costume worn by the suffering man were thought to pick up negative energies as he walked through the town; and when he was clear and away, his costume was burned and all of the negative influences it had attracted were burned with it.[81]

Medicinally, burdock is an excellent liver cleanser and tonifier; as such, it works to bring the endocrine system back into balance and is very helpful in treating skin disorders such as acne, psoriasis, boils, and eczema. Burdock's ability to stimulate the gall bladder, liver, thyroid, and the adrenal cortex permits the body to metabolize fats and pro-

---

80. Martin, *Wildflower Folklore*, 17.
81. Darwin, *Scots Herbal*, 75–76.

teins more effectively.[82] It is tonic to the kidneys and a good diuretic. Burdock has been used for treating diabetes and hypoglycemia, and it has both anti-fungal and antibiotic qualities. It is a bitter herb, which helps to stimulate digestion. Burdock helps reduce the inflammation of rheumatoid arthritis and can be used to treat symptoms of gout when applied externally. The plant appears to have some anticancer properties, and its leaves have been used externally to reduce tumors. Burdock is an excellent stimulator of the lymphatic system, so its activating energy is contraindicated during pregnancy as it might stimulate the uterus.[83]

About burdock, the seventeenth-century English herbalist Nicholas Culpeper wrote:

"Venus challengeth this herb for her own; and by its seed or leaf, you may draw the womb which way you please, either upward by applying it to the crown of the head, in case it falls out, or downward in fits of the mother, by applying it to the soles of the feet; or, if you would stay it in its place, apply it to the navel, and that is likewise a good way to stay the child in it…"[84]

The plant boasts burrs that attach to clothing and the fur of animals, helping to scatter its seeds over wide areas of land. In accordance with the Doctrine of Signatures, the burdock pods were eaten to help improve memory, as it was believed they could help things stick in your brain.[85]

82. Matthew Wood, *The Earthwise Herbal: A Complete Guide to Old World Medicinal Plants* (Berkeley, CA: North Atlantic Books, 2008), 203.

83. Angela Paine, *The Healing Power of Celtic Plants: Their History, Their Use, and the Scientific Evidence That They Work* (Winchester, UK: O Books, 2006), 59.

84. Nicholas Culpeper, *Culpeper's Complete Herbal* (London: Richard Evans, 1816), 29.

85. Martin, *Wildflower Folklore*, 17.

Moon 10
The Moon of Consummation

Herbal Ally: Dandelion

Botanical Name: *Taraxacum officinalis*

Welsh Name(s): Dant y Llew, Clais, Dail Clais

Other Common Names: Lion's tooth, blowball, cankerwort, piss-a-bed, priest's crown, swine snout, wild endive

---

Dandelion (*Taraxacum officinale*) is a cheery yellow flower associated with the life-giving energies of the sun. Its name comes from the French "tooth of the lion," an animal with strong solar associations. Traditionally, it was woven in the bridal bouquet to grant luck to the new couple. In the Victorian language of flowers, dandelion represents love and flirtation but also faithfulness to one's mate; the latter characteristic is related to how tenaciously enduring this ubiquitous "weed"—in truth, a highly nutritious and helpful medicinal plant—really is. Dandelions scatter many seeds and propagate new plants abundantly and quickly, and their roots run very deep, a protective measure that gives them some drought resistance and keeps them safe from animals, brush fires…and lawnmowers.[86]

Called a rustic oracle, dandelion is prized as a divinatory tool; blowing upon the fluffy seed head could determine if your lover was thinking about you or how many children you would have. Blowing on the seeds is also a powerful way to send one's wishes out into the Universe, and it was believed that you could send a message to your beloved by whispering it to the puffball of the seed heads before sending them on their way with your breath. A dandelion gone to seed is an effective ba-

---

86. McIntyre, *Flower Power*, 217.

rometer for weather, as it closes its head when rain is imminent; it has also gained renown as a sort of country clock, believed to open up its head at 5:00 a.m. and close it again at 8:00 p.m.

Rubbing dandelion all over one's body was believed to be a magical charm that would see you welcomed everywhere you went and would also make all of your wishes come true.[87] The flower is said to bring good luck, and it can assist in bringing positive and psychic dreams. In Wales, it is believed that dandelions gathered on Midsummer's Eve and placed over the windows and doors of the house will protect against the magic of dark witches, perhaps because the flowers are thought to hold the light and blessings of the sun.[88]

One of the Gaelic names for the plant is *an bearnan Brighde* ("the notched plant of Bridget"), and perhaps its association with the goddess/saint of fire and healing is a reflection of dandelion's reputation as a helpful medicine and association with the sun.[89] An excellent liver and blood cleanser, dandelion is bursting with vitamins and minerals, and is prized around the world for its medicinal and nutritional value. It tonifies the organs of the digestive and urinary systems, stimulates the flow of bile and the production of red blood cells, and assists in correcting issues arising from the build up of toxins in the blood, especially those which cause inflammation such as gout, rheumatoid arthritis, and jaundice. It assists in the control of cholesterol, helps normalize blood sugar issues, and is effective in removing gallstones and reducing the inflammation of the gallbladder.[90]

Culpeper writes of dandelion:

"It is under the dominion of Jupiter. It is of an opening and cleansing quality, and therefore very effectual for the obstructions of the liver,

---

87. McIntyre, *Flower Power*, 217.

88. Lawton, *Flowers and Fables*, 63.

89. Darwin, *Scots Herbal*, 82.

90. Hoffmann, *Welsh Herbal Medicine*, 45.

gall and spleen, and the diseases that arise from them, as the jaundice, and hypochondriac; it openeth the passages of the urine both in young and old; powerfully cleanseth imposthumes and inward ulcers in the urinary passages, and by its drying and temperate quality doth afterwards heal them …"[91]

Dandelion is an especially potent ally for women's health: it helps tonify the entire reproductive system, reduces PMS symptoms, supports pregnancy, and promotes the production of milk. Scientific research has praised dandelion for its antioxidant properties and its potential value in inhibiting the growth of cancer cells. In addition to its medicinal uses, dandelion greens are eaten in salads and soups, its roots are roasted and brewed into a coffee-like drink, and its flowers make a beautiful summer wine.

---

91. Culpeper, *Complete Herbal*, 62.

Moon 11

THE MOON OF PURIFICATION

Herbal Ally: Wild thyme

Botanical Name: *Thymus serpyllum*

Welsh Name(s): Gryw, Grywlys, Gruwlys Gwyllt Mwyaf, Teim

Other Common Names: Mother of thyme, lus an righ ("the king's plant")

Thyme (*Thymus serpyllum*) has been used in ancient times as a cleansing herb and was burned to clear spaces and purify the altars of the Greeks and Romans. It also had funerary uses—the plant was placed in coffins and used as incense to help the departed make their way into the Otherworld. Wild thyme's aromatic properties are thought to lift depression and to bring courage; medieval warriors would carry the herb sewn into tokens they would carry with them into battle. Indeed, the Greek word *thumus* means "strength," although an alternative etymology for the plant's botanical name sees *thymus* as deriving from *thumos*, from the Greek word meaning "smoke" or "fumigant." This latter etymology may refer to thyme's ancient use as an incense of purification.[92] Certainly it is this cleansing and clearing attribute which is related to the belief that thyme could to prevent nightmares, and that hanging it in the home repels evil influences and brings good luck.

Sometimes called "Mother of Thyme," this herb has a special affinity for the uterus, having both a strengthening and energizing effect. In the middle ages, it was used to treat infections of the female reproductive system and was considered a menstrual regulator. Thyme can be a useful emmenagogue and as such should not be used during pregnancy. Its

---

92. McIntyre, *Flower Power*, 204.

energizing properties helped build thyme's reputation as an aphrodisiac as well.

Medicinally, wild thyme is especially useful in addressing issues of the respiratory system; it fights both bacterial and viral infections such as bronchitis and pneumonia, and it is particularly useful for treating whooping cough and sore throat. It has a powerful calming effect on the nervous system, reducing anxiety, releasing nervous exhaustion, and alleviating disturbed sleep. In Scotland, sprigs of thyme were put under pillows, or an infusion of the herb was taken before bed in order to prevent nightmares.[93] Of it, Culpeper wrote:

"Mother of Thyme is under Venus. It is excellent in nervous disorders. A strong infusion of it, drank in the manner of tea, is pleasant, and a very effectual remedy for headaches, giddiness, and other disorders of that kind; and it is a certain remedy for that troublesome complaint, the night-mare."[94]

Wild thyme is an excellent topical antiseptic, although care must be taken as the oil can burn the skin when used full strength. As a tincture or infusion, thyme can be used internally to rid the system of parasites. It stimulates digestion, and helps to alleviate flatulence, cramps, and heartburn. Thyme takes action on the correspondingly named thymus gland; it stimulates immunity, and tonifies the adrenal cortex.[95]

As a flower essence, wild thyme can help ease stress and relieve insomnia, helping the heart and mind to heal from trauma and shadow issues that arise from deep in the unconscious. It increases energy, stamina, and concentration, and is especially helpful in helping with seasonal transitions and processing the passage of time.[96]

---

93. Mary Beith, *Healing Threads: Traditional Medicines of the Highlands and Islands* (Edinburgh: Polygon, 1995), 246.

94. Culpeper,*Complete Herbal*, 184.

95. Wood, *Earthwise Herbal*, 484.

96. MacIntyre, *Flower Power*, 216.

Moon 12
The Moon of Reconciliation

Herbal Ally: Motherwort

Botanical Name: *Leonurus cardiaca*

Welsh Name(s): Llysiau'r Fam, Mamoglys, Mamlys

Other Common Names: Lion tail, of the heart, cowthwort, lion's ear, throw-wort, heartwort

---

Motherwort (*Leonurus cardiaca*) was known as "she-vervain" on the Isle of Man, where it was venerated as a "gender twin" to the sacred herb vervain; as such, it was associated with the sacred feminine and was revered as an herb of inner wisdom and healing. It is a protective herb, especially for mothers and children, and has traditionally been used in fertility charms. Burning motherwort is said to gladden the heart, and hanging it around the home will keep evil influences away. It is an herb that can impart a sense of purpose where there has been none, and generally fosters a sense of self-trust and optimism, even in the face of hard work and challenges to come.[97]

As suggested by its name, motherwort is an herbal ally for women's health. It is generally tonifying for the reproductive system, stimulates menstruation especially when it is delayed due to anxiety, assists with the symptoms of PMS, and is useful in childbirth in that it stimulates uterine contractions and helps to expel the placenta. It also works to relieve hot flashes and heart palpitations associated with menopause. Motherwort addresses anxiety, especially when caused by hormonal fluctuation, and is a wonderful remedy to help relieve nervous tension, over-emotionality, and excessive churning of the mind.

---

97. Beyerl, *Master Book of Herbalism*, 235.

The herbalist Culpeper thought highly of motherwort, saying: "Venus owns the herb, and it is under Leo. There is no better herb to take melancholy vapours from the heart, to strengthen it, and make a merry, cheerful, blithe soul than this herb … Besides, it makes women joyful mothers of children, and settles their wombs as they should be, therefore we call it Motherwort. It is held to be of much use for the trembling of the heart, and faintings and swoonings; from whence it took the name Cardiaca."[98]

It is traditionally used as a heart tonic, a practice reflected by the Doctrine of Signatures in the way the flowers present in a rhythmic fashion along the stem of the plant which is suggestive of the pulse or a heartbeat.[99] Motherwort has diuretic properties, is helpful in reducing fevers, and helps regulate cholesterol. It is a vasodilator and an antispasmodic, and other traditional uses of motherwort include treating issues of the respiratory system, such as bronchitis and asthma. It can be used in cases of hyperthyroidism to bring the metabolic rate back into balance. It is contraindicated while taking heart medications and generally during pregnancy,[100] although some herbalists say it can be taken safely during this time and is especially helpful in easing maternal anxiety.[101]

---

98. Culpeper, *Complete Herbal*, 99.

99. Wood, *Earthwise Herbal*, 318.

100. Paine, *Celtic Plants*, 162.

101. Wood, *Earthwise Herbal*, 318.

HERBAL ALLY FOR THE
TIME OF BRANWEN

Moon 13
THE MOON OF REFLECTION

Herbal Ally: Woad

Botanical Name: *Isatis tinctoria*

Welsh Name(s): Glaslys, Lliwlys, y Glas, y Glaiarlys, Melsugn, Mel y Cwn, Melengu, y Weddlys, Llysiau'r Lliw Melyn, Gweddlys

Other Common Names: Dyer's weed, glastum, asp of Jerusalem

———————

Woad (*Isatis tinctoria*) is probably best known as the dye that British Celtic warriors used to paint their skin before running naked into battle. Indeed, there are many classical references to "woad-blue Britain" although the type and purpose of the ornament differs from one author to the next. In perhaps the most famous extant account, which dates to the first century BCE, Julius Caesar wrote:

> *All the Britons dye their bodies with woad (vitrum), which produces a blue color, and this gives them a more terrifying appearance in battle.*[102]

———————

102. Caesar, *De Bello Gallico* V, xiv.

Similarly, in his 1st century work, *Naturalis Historia*, Pliny writes:

"There is a plant in Gaul, similar to the plantago in appearance, and known there by the name of 'glastum': with it both matrons and girls among the people of Britain are in tile habit of staining the body all over, when taking part in the performance of certain sacred rites; rivaling hereby tile swarthy hue of the Ethiopians, they go in a state of nature."[103]

In contrast, instead of the Britons covering their bodies completely in the blue dye, the second century CE Greek historian Herodian wrote:

"They also tattoo their bodies with various patterns and pictures of all sorts of animals. Hence the reason why they do not wear clothes, so as not to cover the pictures on their bodies."[104]

Several writers also allude to the use of woad as part of a scarification process,[105] while others mention the Celts as having their bodies "marked with iron"[106]; it is unknown if the iron is that which colors the skin or if the authors are referring to iron needles used to place the images there.

While we cannot be completely sure of the purpose, or the process (or processes) that the Celts used to paint their bodies, the properties of woad make it a good choice for the most commonly recorded uses. Woad is a styptic as well as being antibacterial, therefore, not only can it staunch bleeding, but it also helps prevent wounds from becoming infected. These are clearly desirable properties for when one enters battle, especially when naked, as well as for use in tattoos or scarification.

Pliny suggests a magico-religious purpose to these ornaments, and certainly one can imagine a warrior getting tattooed using a sacred

---

103. Pliny, *Naturalis Historia* 22, ii.

104. Herodian, III, xiv, 7.

105. Solinus, *Collectanea Rerum Memorabiliam* 22, 12.

106. Claudian II, *Poem on Stilicho's Consulship* II.247.

herb with an animal that will give her strength, or an entire war band being consecrated in ritual with a protective ointment with the power to make them less vulnerable to harm. Today, woad is used to assist in recalling past lives, and some believe it had been used in ancient shape-changing rituals.

Traditionally, woad was only used externally; the herb is too poisonous and astringent to be taken internally. In addition to the properties already mentioned, it can reduce inflammation and repel insects, and it was made into an ointment for ulcers. Today's medicine has found that it shows great promise as an anti-cancer drug, especially for treating breast cancer.

Far greater than its use as a medicine, however, was woad's ability to produce a color-fast blue dye. As far back as the La Tène period (the early Celtic culture of Switzerland in the fifth century BCE) are pieces of archaeological evidence that show woad's use as a textile dye. Woad was an incredibly important dye plant in Europe before indigo from India started to become more readily available in the 1700s, and cultivation of the herb peaked to become an important industry in England in the sixteenth century.[107] Interestingly, the soil and climate of Somerset in England was especially conducive to growing large quantities of woad; the cities of Glastonbury, Bath, and Wells became centers for its cultivation and production—and a production it was, as there were many phases of the process necessary to prepare woads dye from the plant.[108]

Traditionally, the blue dye was obtained using the following process: The leaves of the woad plant would be gathered and then "... crushed by horse-drawn rollers. The pulp obtained is then hand kneaded into

107. V. Zech-Matterne and L. Leconte, "New archaeobotanical finds of isatis tinctoria L. (woad) from iron age gaul and a discussion of the importance of woad in ancient time", *Vegetation History and Archaeobotany*, 19(2), 2010: 137–142.

108. Jamieson B. Hurry, *The Woad Plant and its Dye* (London: Oxford University Press, 1930).

round masses of about four inches in diameter and afterwards taken to the drying ranges, where the balls, as they are called, are dried. When the drying process has been completed, the lumps are again rolled and the powdered mass is taken to the couching house, where it is allowed to ferment for about nine weeks. The dark clay-like residue is then packed in wooden barrels and sent to the dyer."[109]

From the perspective of the Avalonian Tradition, there are some interesting connections between woad and Glastonbury, the small town in southern England and potential real-world location for Ynys Afallon. A possible etymology for the name Glastonbury derives from *glaston*, the Celtic word for woad; Glastonbury would therefore mean "the place where woad grows." In Welsh, *glas* means "blue," while the English word "woad" derives from the Saxon *waad*.[110]

An early name for Glastonbury in Welsh was *Ynys Wintrin*, which most people translate as meaning "Island of Glass." This appears to be a folk etymology, however, based on the erroneous assumption that the *glas* in Glastonbury literally referred to glass, rather than woad. The Latin word for woad is *vitrum*, which is also one of their words for "glass".[111] There is some debate around what the contemporary classical accounts meant when they used the word *vitrum* in association with Britain, with some scholars arguing that they did actually mean glass; however, Bostock and Riley posit that the word "glass" arose from the blue tint that characterized the substance.[112]

109. Hurry, *The Woad Plant*, 277.

110. Frank D. Reno, *The Historic King Arthur: Authenticating the Celtic Hero of Post-Roman Britain*, (Jefferson, NC: McFarland & Co Inc, 1997), 222.

111. W. J. Keith, *John Cowper Powys's A Glastonbury Romance: A Reader's Companion–Updated and Expanded Edition*, 2010, 24.

112. John Bostock and H. T. Riley, trans., *The Natural History of Pliny* (London: H. G. Bohn, 1855–1857).

HERBAL ALLY FOR THE
TIME OF ARIANRHOD

The Moon of Cycle

Herbal Ally: Queen Anne's lace

Botanical Name: *Daucus carota*

Welsh Name(s): Meddyglyn, Moron Gwylltion, Moron Y Meysydd, Moronen Goch, Moronen Y Maes, Nyth Aderyn

Other Common Names: Wild carrot, bee's nest, bird's nest, crow's nest, bishop's lace, devil's plague, fool's parsley, lace flower, mother die, philtron, lady's lace, fairy lace, keck, kecksie, hedge parsley, rabbit meat, rantipole, herbe a dinde, yarkuki

---

Queen Anne's lace (*Daucus carota*), or wild carrot, is a powerful women's ally; it is an emmenagogue which helps increase menstrual flow, eases painful menstruation, and its seeds can be used as a form of natural contraception. It has diuretic properties and remedies many complaints of the urinary system, including kidney stones and cystitis. Wild carrot helps with indigestion, constipation, and flatulence. Its use is contraindicated in pregnancy. Recent studies have shown that essential oils made from Queen Anne's lace are a powerful anti-fungal and show promise in eliminating overgrowths of candida from the system.[113]

Queen Anne's lace is believed to be the wild progenitor of the cultivated or domesticated carrot that most of us are familiar with. The roots of the wild carrot are edible but not as tasty as those of domesticated carrots; conversely, domesticated carrot plants have similar medicinal qualities as Queen Anne's lace but are much less effective as their wild cousins. In the British Isles is another plant with the common name of Queen Anne's lace, but it's a completely different species whose botanical name is *Anthriscus sylvestris*.

The herb gets its name from the frilly appearance of the umbrella-like spray of white flowers that comprise its arial parts. The characteristic single purple floret in the center of the spray looks like a drop of blood that results from the pricking of one's finger during the process of tatting lace. It is believed that this purple floret helps to attract pollinators to the flowers, and in folk medicine these purple florets were believed to treat epilepsy. It is said to be named for either the first or last queen of the English House of Stuart, both of whom were named Anne; but some sources believe the plant is named for St. Anne, mother of the Virgin Mary.

There are several plants that resemble Queen Anne's lace that are dangerously poisonous, so care must be taken when wildcrafting this herb. One of these is hemlock (*Conium maculatum*), a poisonous herb that famously ended the life of Socrates; when consumed, hemlock causes respiratory paralysis that leads to death. Another similar-looking herb is giant hogweed (*Heracleum mantegazzianum*). This invasive plant can cause a dangerous reaction when its sap comes in contact

---

113. Jorge M. Alves-Silva, Mónica Zuzarte, Maria José Gonçalves, et al., "New Claims for Wild Carrot (Daucus carota subsp. carota) Essential Oil," Evidence-Based Complementary and Alternative Medicine, vol. 2016, Article ID 9045196, 10 pages, 2016. https://doi.org/10.1155/2016/9045196.

with skin that is subsequently exposed to sunlight; a serious burning rash develops, causing painful blisters that result in scarring. Getting giant hogweed sap in the eye can cause temporary or even permanent blindness. To positively identify Queen Anne's lace, look for the purple flower at the center of the spray of small white flowers that make up the basket or umbel. Unlike hemlock or hogweed, Queen Anne's lace has a hairy stem whose leaves smell like carrots; the other two plants have a very unpleasant odor. Hogweed's stem has distinctive purple streaks and blotches, and the plant can grow to be over seven feet tall if left undisturbed; Queen Anne's lace, on the other hand, typically only grows to be one to three feet tall. Above all, the best course of action if you aren't sure of a plant's identity is to consult a guide—a person or a book—and don't leave it to chance!

One of the most powerful uses of Queen Anne's lace is as an herbal contraceptive; its recommendation for this usage in the West goes at least as far back as the writing of Hippocrates in the fifth or fourth century BCE. In his excellent book, *Eve's Herbs: A History of Contraception and Abortion*, John Riddle has this to say about Queen Anne's lace:

> Its seeds, harvested in the fall, are a strong contraceptive if taken orally immediately after coitus. Extracts of its seeds have been tested on [small mammals]. In mice given the seeds (doses of 80–120 mg) on the forth to sixth days of pregnancy, the pregnancies were terminated. The action is such that the implantation process is disrupted and a fertilized ovum either will not be implanted or, if…implanted for only a short period, will be released. In other experiments…, the seeds were found to inhibit implantation and ovarian growth and to disrupt the estrous cycle.[114]

114. John M. Riddle, *Eve's Herbs: A History of Contraception and Abortion in the West* (Cambridge, MA: Harvard University Press, 1997), 50.

Riddle goes on to say that the herb also appears to disrupt progesterone production.

When mentioned at all, most ancient and medieval herbal treatises simply refer to Queen Anne's lace as an emmenagogue, a typical euphemism for an abortifacient. However, like many anti-fertility herbs or abortifacients, the qualities of Queen Anne's lace appear to have been passed along through oral tradition among women, as evidenced by its widespread usage all over the world by women throughout time who even in the present day ingest or chew these seeds in an effort to control their fertility. If you are seeking to use Queen Anne's lace as a natural "morning after" contraceptive, please do so with an *abundance* of caution; be sure to research herbal protocols fully, be conscientious with tracking your menstrual cycle, and—with the understanding that no form of contraception is 100 percent effective—avoid using it as your sole method for preventing pregnancy. Herbalist Robin Rose Bennet has developed protocol for the use of Queen Anne's lace as a natural form of contraception, and has conducted several controlled studies exploring its efficacy in preventing pregnancy, the outcomes of which are discussed on her website.[115]

Interestingly, for all of its pregnancy deterring qualities, the ancient Greeks believed Queen Anne's lace to be an aphrodisiac that acted to increase arousal in men and fertility in women. Carrots in general have an association with inciting lust because of their color and shape. The plant is considered invasive in some areas because it produces so many seeds that it can take over an area in no time; sometimes this is a nuisance if it chokes out other plants in the garden, but as a plant that loves meadows and hedgerows, and grows wildly in ditches along roads, their beautiful white and lacy heads bring welcome ornament to otherwise dull places.

---

115. https://www.robinrosebennett.com/resources/wild-carrot-
    exploration-summary-august-2011.

Queen Anne's lace has a reputation as a flower that takes care of itself. In wet weather, the area of the stem a few inches below the flowers becomes flexible enough to allow the head of the flower to bend and face downward, thus protecting its pollen from being washed away by the rain; interestingly, in older plants that have already lost their pollen, the flowers remain upright and do not bend even in the heaviest of rain.[116]

Queen Anne's lace is an herb of Sovereignty. There is no doubt that one of the ways that patriarchy controls women is through the control of their fertility; Queen Anne's lace helps women take that power back. She is an herb that supports letting go of emotional attachments, things from our past, as well as outcomes for our future. She assists us in seeing the truth of our self-destructive patterns; these are often the result (or cause) of long standing shadow issues that keep us bound up in fear and reactive to situations that feel even remotely like ones that were a source of pain in the past.

---

116. Martin, *Wildflower Folklore*, 122.

Conclusion

THE GREAT WORK

THE CYCLE OF THE LUNAR dance reveals the ring of pearls that crowns a night-dark vessel. It is the Cauldron of the Chief of Annwn, sovereign of the Otherworld, and it will not boil the food of a coward. When consciously tended with intention, however, a seeker may use its power to accomplish the Great Work.

In the personal Otherworld of the Unconscious within each of us, this potent vessel of transformation awaits. Like Arthur, we must undertake a journey to reclaim this powerful artifact, but it that is only the beginning of the process. What this vessel of intention yields depends wholly upon what we bring to it; like countless before us, we are called to take a close look at the circumstances and content of our inner and outer lives, and for each component we must ask ourselves the Grail question: Whom does this serve? If the answer is anything but service to our authentic sovereignty, we have found where work must be done.

One way to engage in this revelatory process is by following the pearlescent pathway laid out to us in myth. Like Ceridwen, we must set the cauldron to boil, activating it by kindling our inner hearth fire through our focused and directed will. A year's worth of healing herbs are placed within this vessel: each one a resonance of the lessons found in the stories of the goddesses of Avalon, each one a Green Ally to help us reflect these lessons onto the stories of our own lives.

Each moon is a mirror, each pearl a key to our own unfolding. We work to distill the darkness of our shadow so that we may liberate the bright drops of our wisdom. We work to catalyze our growth so that we may drink deeply of our sovereign nature.

The Great Work is to seek and fully embody the recognition of the truth of our ultimate union and connection with the Divine. We may accomplish it through the rarification of the Self until consciousness of our wholeness is obtained and our sovereign potential is realized. This path of personal alchemy both accompanies and is supported by the process of shadow integration. We must seek out outmoded and unconscious reactionary defense strategies so that we may repattern them into deliberate responses that are centered in clarity and personal sovereignty. Our goal as evolving beings is to live in the now as consciously as possible without being limited by pain from the past or fear of the future. When we center ourselves in the flow of nature and work with it rather than against it, we are able to harness the powerful tides of these cyclic forces to clear, cleanse, and empower ourselves to actualize the person we were each born to be.

Healed. Holy. Whole.

Appendix

THE LUNAR KEYS
OF AVALON—
A TEACHING SONG

CRAFTING POETIC MNEMONICS AND SETTING them to music is a bardic technique that assists in the memorization of lore and collectives of information. In this spirit, here is a teaching song to help seekers remember the names, associated herbs, and energetics for each Lunar Key of the Avalonian Cycle of Revealing in order. The lyrics are set to a reclaimed traditional folk tune from the British Isles perhaps best known as the melody to "In the Month of January."

The Lunar Keys:
A Teaching Song

Tune: Traditional
Lyrics by Jhenah Telyndru
Arrangement by Ariana Telyndru

Full Lyrics:

THE LUNAR KEYS: A TEACHING SONG
To the Tune of "In the Month of January" (traditional)

Capo 3

Verse 1—*Time of Ceridwen*
In the Moon of Initiation
Bitter Mugwort shows the way.
And in the Moon of Distillation
For Yarrow's healing we pray.
In the Moon of Transformation
Wormwood's second sight is found.
And the Moon of Germination
Earns us holy Vervain's crown.

Verse 2—*Time of Blodeuwedd*
Though the Moon of Evocation
Broom's cleansing can be gained.
And in the Moon of Activation
Meadowsweet soothes a spirit's pain.
And the Moon of Revelation
Suffers Nettle's strengthening sting.
In the Moon of Liberation
Clover's balancing powers we sing .

Verse 3—*Time of Rhiannon*

In the Moon of Dedication
Burdock shields us from all harm.
And the Moon of Consummation
Dandelion is Sovereignty's arm.
In the Moon of Purification
Thyme sanctifies the soul.
In the Moon of Reconciliation
Motherwort's heart is whole.

Verse Four—*Branwen and Arianrhod*

In the Moon of Reflection
Woad shifts the mortal form.
In the Moon of Cycle, Queen Anne's lace
Guides us through the inner storm.
These lunar pearls 'round Annwn's cauldron
Guide us as we go.
Down sovereign pathways of the heart
To reveal our Priestess soul.

BIBLIOGRAPHY

Bianchi, U., and L. Jones, ed. "Twins: An Overview" in *Encyclopedia of Religion*. 2nd ed., vol. 14. Detroit: Macmillan Reference, 2005.

Bostock, John, and H. T. Riley, trans. *The Natural History of Pliny*. London: H. G. Bohn ,1855-1857.

Brewer, J. S., ed. *Giraldi Cambrensis Opera, scilicet, Speculum Ecclesiae*. Rolls Series, no. 21, vol. 4. London: Her Majesty's Stationery Office, 1873.

Bromwich, Rachel, ed. and trans. *Trioedd Ynys Prydein: The Welsh Triads*. Cardiff: University of Wales Press, 2006.

Bror wich, Rachel, and D. Simon Evans, trans. *Culhwch and Olwen: An Edition and Study of the Oldest Arthurian Tale*. Cardiff: University of Wales Press, 1992.

Bugge, John. "Fertility Myth and Female Sovereignty in 'The Weddynge of Sir Gawen and Dame Ragnell'" in *The Chaucer Review*, Vol. 39, No. 2, 2004.

Caesar. *The Gallic War*. Translated by Carolyn Hammond. Oxford, UK: Oxford University Press, 1996.

Cameron, M. L. *Anglo-Saxon Medicine*. Cambridge, UK: Cambridge University Press, 2006.

Cartwright, Jane. *Feminine Sanctity and Spirituality in Medieval Wales.* Cardiff: University of Wales Press, 2008.

Chadwick, Nora K. *The Celts.* Harmondsworth: Penguin, 1970.

Claudian. "Poem on Stilicho's Courtship," *II*. Translated by Maurice Platnauer. London: William Heinemann, 1922. Retrieved from: http://www.gutenberg.org/files/51444/51444-h/51444-h .htm#STILICHIO_II.

Cross, T. P., editor, and C. H. Slover, translator. *The Boyhood Deeds of Finn mac Cumhaill.* New York: Henry Holt & Co., 1936.

Davies, Sioned. *The Four Branches of the Mabinogi.* Llandysul, Wales, UK: Gomer Press, 1993.

Davies, Sioned, trans. *The Mabinogion.* New York: Oxford University Press, 2007.

De la Villemarqué, Viscount Théodore Hersart, trans. *Popular Songs of Brittany: Barzaz-Breiz.* Paris, 1846.

Eliade, Mircea. *A History of Religious Ideas, Vol. 2: From Gautama Buddha to the Triumph of Christianity.* Translated by Willard R. Trask. Chicago: University of Chicago Press, 1982.

Ellis, T. P. "Legal references, terms and conceptions in the Mabinogion" in *Y Cymmrodor* volume 39, 1928.

Ford, Patrick K. *The Celtic Poets: Songs and Tales from Early Ireland and Wales.* Belmont, MA: Ford and Bailie Publishers, 1999.

Ford, Patrick K., trans. *The Mabinogi and Other Medieval Welsh Tales.* Berkeley, CA: University of California Press, 1977.

Geoffrey of Monmouth. *Historia regum Britannie* (*History of the Kings of Britain*). Translated and updated by Aaron Thompson and J. A. Giles. (originally published 1136). London: [n.p.], 1848.

Gerald of Wales and John William Sutton, trans. "The Tomb of King Arthur" from *The Camelot Project.* 2001. d.lib.rochester.edu/camelot/text/gerald-of-wales-arthurs-tomb.

Green, Miranda. *The Gods of the Celts.* Phoenix Mill: Sutton Publishing Ltd., 2004.

———. "Vessels of Death: Sacred Cauldrons in Archaeology and Myth" at https://www.cambridge.org/core.

Green, Miranda, and Malcom Todd, ed. "Gallo-British Deities and Their Shrines" in *A Companion to Roman Britain.* Oxford, UK: Blackwell Publishing, 2004.

Gruffydd, W.J. *Folklore and Myth in the Mabinogion.* Cardiff: University of Wales Press, 1958.

———. *Math vab Mathonwy: An Inquiry into the Origins a Development of the Fourth Branch of the Mabinogi, with the Text and a Translation.* Cardiff: University of Wales Press, 1928.

———. *Rhiannon: Inquiry into the First and Third Branches of the Mabinogion.* Cardiff: University of Wales Press, 1953.

Guest, Lady Charlotte, trans. *The Mabinogion.* London: Bernard Quaritch, 1877.

Gwyndaf, Robin. *Welsh Folk Tales.* Cardiff: National Museums and Galleries of Wales, 1999.

Hahn, Thomas, ed. "The Wedding of Sir Gawen and Dame Ragnelle" in *Sir Gawen: Eleven Romances and Tales.* Kalamazoo, MI: Medieval Institute Publications, 1995. http://d.lib.rochester.edu/teams/text/hahn-sir-gawain-wedding-of-sir-gawain-and-dame-ragnelle.

Hamp, E. P. "Imbolc, óimelc" in *Studia Celtica*, 14, 106, 1979.

———. "Mabinogi and Archaism" in *Celtica* 23, 1999.

Haycock, Marged, ed. and trans. *Legendary Poems from the Book of Taliesin*. Aberystwyth, Wales, UK: CMCS, 2015.

Herodian of Antioch. *History of the Roman Empire*. Translated by Edward C. Echols. Berkeley and Los Angeles: University of California Press, 1961. Retrieved from: http://www.tertullian.org/fathers/herodian_03_book3.htm.

Jackson, Kenneth. *The International Popular Tale in Early Welsh Tradition*. Cardiff: University of Wales Press, 1961.

Jenkins, Dafydd, and Morfydd E. Owen, eds. *The Welsh Law of Women: Studies Presented to Professor Daniel A. Binchy on His Eightieth Birthday*. Cardiff: University of Wales Press, 1980.

Jones, Thomas Gwynn. *Welsh Folklore and Folk-Custom* (London: Methuen & Co., Ltd., 1930).

Keith, W. J. *John Cowper Powys's A Glastonbury Romance: A Reader's Companion—Updated and Expanded Edition*, 2010. http://www.powys-lannion.net/Powys/Keith/Gcompanion.pdf.

Koch, J. T. "Matronae" in *Celtic Culture: A Historical Encyclopedia*.

Lawrence, Elizabeth A. *Hunting the Wren: Transformation of Bird to Symbol*. Knoxville: University of Tennessee Press, 1997.

The Laws of Hywel Dda. *The Cambro-Briton* vol. 2, no. 21. May 1821.

Mac Cana, Proinsias. *Celtic Mythology*. London: Hamilin Publishing Group, 1970.

———. *The Mabinogi*. Cardiff: University of Wales Press, 1992.

MacKillop, J. "Efnysien" in *A Dictionary of Celtic Mythology*. London: Oxford University Press, 2004.

McKenna, C. "The Theme of Sovereignty in *Pwyll*" in C. W. Sullivan, ed., *The Mabinogi: A Book of Essays*. New York: Garland Publishing, 1996.

Markale, Jean. *Women of the Celts*. Rochester, VT: Inner Traditions, 1986.

Miles-Watson, Jonathan. *Welsh Mythology: A Neo-Structuralist Approach*. Amherst, NY: Cambria Press, 2009.

Nitze, William A. "The Sister's Son and the Conte del Graal" in *Modern Philology* vol. 9, no. 3, 1912.

Northrup, Christine. *Women's Bodies, Women's Wisdom: Creating Physical and Emotional Health and Healing*. New York: Bantam, 2010.

Owen, Morfydd. *Meddygon Myddfai: A Preliminary Survey of Some Medieval Medical Writing in Welsh*, in *Studia Celtica*; 1975.

Parker, Will. *The Four Branches of the Mabinogi*. Oregon House, CA: Bardic Press, 2005.

"Phases of the Moon and Percent of the Moon Illuminated." http://aa.usno.navy.mil/faq/docs/moon_phases.php.

Pliny the Elder. *The Natural History*. Translated by John Bostock and H. T. Riley. London: Henry G. Bohn, 1855. Retrieved from: http://data.perseus.org/citations/urn:cts:latinLit:phi0978.phi001.perseus-eng1:25.59.

Rees, Alwyn. "The Divine Hero in Celtic Hagiology," in *Folklore*, vol. 47, no. 1, 1936.

Rees, Alwyn, and Brinley Rees. *Celtic Heritage: Ancient Tradition in Ireland and Wales*. London: Thames and Hudson, 1961

Reno, Frank D. *The Historic King Arthur: Authenticating the Celtic Hero of Post-Roman Britain*. Jefferson, NC: McFarland & Co Inc., 1997.

Ross, Anne. *Folklore of Wales*. Stroud, UK: Tempus Publishing, 2001.

―――. *Pagan Celtic Britain*. Chicago: Academy Chicago Publishers, 1996.

Sessele, Erica J. "Exploring the Limitations of the Sovereignty Goddess through the Role of Rhiannon" in *Proceedings of the Harvard Celtic Colloquium* Vol. 14, 1994.

Sheehan, Sarah. "Matrilineal Subjects: Ambiguity, Bodies, and Metamorphosis in the Fourth Branch of the "Mabinogi," in *Signs*, 34 (2), 2009.

Siewers, Alfred K. "Writing an Icon of the Land: the Mabinogi as a Mystagogy of Landscape" in *Journal of the Medieval Academy of Ireland*. Peritia 19, 2005.

Sikes, Wirt. *British Goblins: Welsh Folk-lore, Fairy Mythology, Legends and Traditions*. London: Willian Clowes and Sons, 1880.

Skene, William F. *The Four Ancient Books of Wales*. Edinburgh: Edmonston and Douglas, 1868. http://www.sacred-texts.com/neu/celt/fab/fab000.htm.

Solinus. *Collectanea Rerum Memorabiliam*. Translated by Arthur Golding. London: Thomas Hacket, 1587. Retrieved from: http://name.umdl.umich.edu/A12581.0001.001.

Telyndru, Jhenah. *Avalon Within: A Sacred Journey of Myth, Mystery, and Inner Wisdom*. Woodbury, MN: Llewellyn Publications, 2010.

―――. *Rhiannon: Divine Queen of the Celtic Britons*. Alresford, Hampshire, UK: Moon Books, 2018.

Thomas, Gwyn. *Dafydd ap Gwilym: His Poems*. Cardiff: University of Wales Press, 2001.

Thompson, Stith. *Motif-index of folk-literature: a classification of narrative elements in folktales, ballads, myths, fables, medieval romances, exempla, fabliaux, jest-books, and local legends*. Bloomington, IN: Indiana University Press, 1955-1958. Via: www.ruthenia.ru/folklore/thompson/.

Valente, Roberta Louise. "Gwydion and Arianrhod: Crossing the Boarders of Gender in Math" in *Bulletin of the Board of Celtic Studies* 35, 1988.

———. "Merched Y Mabinogi: Women and the Thematic Structure of the Four Branches" (unpublished) PhD thesis, Cornell University, 1986.

Waddell, John. *Archaeology and Celtic Myth*. Dublin: Four Courts Press, 2014.

Warner, George F., ed. *Giraldi Cambrensis Opera, Vol. VIII, De Principis Instructione Liber*. Rolls Series, vol. 8, no. 21. London: Her Majesty's Stationery Office, 1891.

Wentersdorf, Karl. "The Folkloric Symbolism of the Wren" in *The Journal of American Folklore* vol. 90, no. 358, 1977.

Winward, Fiona. "The Women in the Four Branches" in *Cambrian Medieval Studies* 34, 1997.

"The Wisdom of the Cymry" in *The Cambro-Briton*, Vol. 3, No. 26, 1822.

Herbalism

Allen, David E., and Gabrielle Hatfield. *Medicinal Plants in Folk Tradition: An Ethnobotany of Britain and Ireland.* Portland, OR:Timber Press, 2004.

Beith, Mary *Healing Threads: Traditional Medicines of the Highlands and Islands.* Edinburgh, UK: Polygon, 1995.

Beryl, Paul. *The Master Book of Herbalism.*Washington: Phoenix Publishing Co., 1984.

Coffey, Timothy. *The History and Folklore of North American Wildflowers.* New York: Houghton Mifflin Company, 1993.

Culpeper, Nicholas. *Culpeper's Complete Herbal.* London: Richard Evans, 1816.

Cunningham, Scott. *Cunningham's Encyclopedia of Magical Herbs.* St. Paul, MN: Llewellyn Publications, 1985.

Darwin, Tess. *The Scots Herbal: The Plant Lore of Scotland.* Edinburgh: Mercat Press, 1996.

Davies, Hugh, Welsh Botanology: *A Systematic Catalogue of the Native Plants of the Isle of Anglesey in Latin, English and Welsh with the Habitats of the Rarer Species, and a Few Observations.* London: W. Merchant, 1813.

Green, James. *The Herbal Medicine-Maker's Handbook: A Home Manual.* Berkeley, CA: Crossing Press, 2000.

Grieve, Margaret. *A Modern Herbal: The Medicinal, Culinary, Cosmetic and Economic Properties, Cultivation, and Folk-Lore of Herbs, Grasses, Fungi, Shrubs & Trees with Their Modern Scientific Uses.* Mineola, NY: Dover Publications, 1971.

Hoffmann, David. *Welsh Herbal Medicine.* Aberteifi, Wales, UK: Abercastle Publications, 1978.

Hurry, Jamieson B. *The Woad Plant and its Dye*. London: Oxford University Press, 1930.

Landsberg, Sylvia. *The Medieval Garden*. Toronto: University of Toronto Press, 2003.

Lawton, Jocelyne. *Flowers and Fables: A Welsh Herbal*. Bridgend, Wales, UK: Seren Books, 2006.

Locke, Tony. *Tales of the Irish Hedgerows*. Dublin: The History Press, 2017.

MacCoitir, Niall. *Ireland's Wild Plants: Myths, Legends & Folklore*. Cork, IE: The Collins Press, 2015.

Martin, Laura C. *Wildflower Folklore*. Charlotte, NC: East Woods Press, 1984.

McIntyre, Anne. *Flower Power: Flower Remedies for Healing Body and Soul Through Herbalism, Homeopathy, Aromatherapy, and Flower Essences*. New York: Henry Holt and Company, 1996.

Mercatante, Anthony S. *The Magic Garden: The Myth and Folklore of Flowers, Plants, Trees and Herbs*. New York: Harper & Row, 1976.

Paine, Angela. *The Healing Power of Celtic Plants: Their History, Their Use, and the Scientific Evidence That They Work*. Winchester, UK: O Books, 2006.

Rätsch, Christian, and Claudia Müller-Ebeling. *The Encyclopedia of Aphrodisiacs: Psychoactive Substances for Use in Sexual Practices*. Randolph, VT: Park Street Press, 2013.

Riddle, John M. *Eve's Herbs: A History of Contraception and Abortion in the West*. Cambridge, MA: Harvard University Press, 1997.

Roth, H. "Vervain Herb from Alchemy Works" via *Alchemy Works*, 2012. http://www.alchemy-works.com/herb_vervain.html

Stuart, Malcom, ed. *The Encyclopedia of Herbs and Herbalism*. New York: Grosset & Dunlap, 1979.

Watts, D. C. *Dictionary of Plant Lore*. London, UK: Elsevier, 2007.

Williams, John, and John Pughe, trans. *The Physicians of Myddvai; Meddygon Myddfai; or the medical practice of the celebrated Rhiwallon and his sons, of Myddvai, in Caermarthenshire, physicians to Rhys Gryg, Lord of Dynevor and Ystrad Towy, about the middle of the thirteenth century; From ancient Mss. in the libraries of Jesus College, Oxford, Llanover, and Tonn; with an English translation; and the legend of the Lady of Llyn y Van*. Llandovery, Wales, UK: [n. p.], 1861.

"The Woad Plant and Its Dye: A Review" in *Scottish Geographical Magazine*, 47:5, 1931.

Wood, Matthew. *The Earthwise Herbal: A Complete Guide to Old World Medicinal Plants*. Berkeley, CA: North Atlantic Books, 2008.

Zech-Matterne, Veronique, and Luc Leconte. "New archaeobotanical finds of Isatis tinctoria L. (woad) from iron age gaul and a discussion of the importance of woad in ancient time" in *Vegetation History and Archaeobotany*. 19 (2), 2010.

INDEX

Pwyll, 49, 50, 194, 206, 208, 210, 212–214, 216, 217, 222, 223, 225–227, 231, 242, 243, 246

Queen Anne's Lace, 46, 51, 101, 105, 287, 303–305, 367–371, 378

Red Clover, 46, 49, 101, 189, 197, 198, 349–351

Rhiannon, 6, 47, 49, 50, 55–57, 62, 63, 65, 66, 68–70, 72, 126, 134, 142, 152, 170, 176, 178, 184, 187, 196, 205–211, 213–217, 219, 221–227, 229, 231–233, 235, 237–239, 241–248, 250, 251, 254, 258, 263, 268, 274, 290, 293, 303, 353, 378

Rigantona, 205, 246, 268

Sacred Marriage, 16, 177, 193, 206, 209, 257

Second Branch, 50, 176, 205, 207, 236, 257, 258, 264, 267, 271

Shadow, 1, 14, 15, 17–19, 21–23, 26, 27, 31, 32, 37, 38, 57, 64, 80, 81, 85, 89, 93, 99, 119–121, 124, 129, 131, 132, 137, 138, 147, 161, 165, 167, 183, 189, 213, 223, 253, 254, 259, 264, 265, 272, 280, 291, 296, 297, 300, 323, 324, 330, 332, 351, 360, 371, 374

Shadow Work, 17, 18, 32, 121, 132, 291, 330, 351

Sisterhood of Avalon, 20

Sovereign Moon, 22, 34, 35, 39, 57

Sovereignty, 14, 15, 17, 19, 23, 27, 39, 41, 47, 61, 81, 82, 84, 89, 98, 102, 112, 119, 121, 125, 134, 142, 145, 151, 161, 164, 167, 170, 176–178, 186, 189, 193–196, 205, 206, 209, 211, 213, 214, 216, 217, 223, 227, 234, 235, 237, 241, 244, 248, 252, 257, 264, 265, 267–269, 271, 274, 280, 284, 285, 290–294, 297, 300, 302, 309, 310, 323–325, 332, 343, 371, 373, 374, 378

Sovereignty Goddess, 164, 195, 205, 206, 209, 285, 343

The Spoils of Annwn, 25

Station of Confrontation, 21, 22, 53, 57, 62, 64, 67, 126, 135, 143, 145–147, 151, 152, 171, 179, 187, 197, 218, 228, 238, 249, 275, 300, 303